The Tweakmen Start with S

What you really need to know about looking after your skin

Alice Hart-Davis

ACCLAIM FOR ALICE'S WORK

'Alice would always be my go-to resource for anything skincare related. Her knowledge spans from the teenage years through to the more mature skin. As a journalist and author, she has written about and trialled virtually everything on the market, and her in-depth knowledge is legendary.'

> – **Millie Kendall MBE**, CEO of the British Beauty Council

'As far as beauty is concerned, Alice is the expert's expert, someone who knows more about the industry than it does about itself.'

> – **Dylan Jones**, Editor-in-Chief of GQ

'AHD is my absolute go-to for anything relating to procedures and the skin. There is nothing she does not know.

'Her integrity and passion for our industry, paired with her journalistic excellence and tenacity, are exactly what is needed at a time when science and facts are routinely being ignored for marketing and spin. I am so very grateful that she continues to share her vast wealth of knowledge with us all.

'I trust her implicitly.'

> – **Caroline Hirons**, facialist, skincare- and beauty-industry expert

'Alice is a fountain of knowledge when it comes to skincare.'

> – **Trinny Woodall**, founder of Trinny London

'Alice is truly a bible of everything skin – from topical to supplement to treatment – she's the credible source on it all. Not only that, but she is one of the kindest humans in our industry.'

> – **Nicola Kilner**, co-founder and CEO of Deciem

The Tweakments Guide:
Start with Skincare

ACCLAIM FOR ALICE'S WORK

'Alice is a fearless, future-forging beauty journalist, who covers the world of aesthetics and cosmetics with equal parts expertise and accessibility.'

   – **Marcia Kilgore**, founder of beautypie.com

'Alice is one of the leading and most trusted voices in skincare.'

   – **Liz Earle MBE**, author, presenter, and entrepreneur
   in beauty and wellbeing.

'I've known Alice all my beauty life for 20 years, and she is a well-respected and loved beauty journalist. Her expertise and deep knowledge is a shining example to us all. She is a leading authority in the industry when it comes to tweakments and skincare, and the fact she looks even more glam and fresh now than when I first met her 20 years ago says it all!'

   – **Dr Ateh Jewel**, award-winning journalist

'If I ever want to know anything about cosmetic procedures, aesthetic practitioners or state of the art tweakments, I turn directly to Alice Hart-Davis. I believe there is no one with such a breadth of knowledge in this highly specialised area of beauty – truly, there is no question on lasers, injections, or peels that she can't answer. Alice's passion, boundless curiosity, and commitment to best practice make her the leading consumer voice in a sector that desperately needs her clear sightedness and journalistic vigour.'

   – **Sali Hughes**, beauty journalist, host, author, and
   broadcaster

'Alice is one of my most trusted sources of independent information about skincare; importantly, she also has a solid comprehension of the science.'

   – **Sarah Stacey**, joint editor of beautybible.com

ACCLAIM FOR ALICE'S WORK

'Alice is a proper grown-up investigative expert with years and layers of experience and knowledge. She tries everything so the rest of us don't have to! So she's perfectly poised to share with readers what works, what doesn't – and who you can trust your face and body to.'

　– **Jo Fairley**, entrepreneur, author, co-founder of
　　Green & Black and joint editor of beautybible.com

'If anyone knows the science behind skincare, and how products work with the body, it's Alice. I am continually impressed and inspired by the amount of effort and time that goes into her research, her knowledge on the skin is impressive!'

　– **Nausheen Qureshi**, biochemist and founder of
　　Elequra

'I have worked with Alice Hart-Davis on many occasions over many years and her ability to combine a razor-sharp knowledge of skincare with journalistic communication skills is something to admire. Her expertise speaks for itself, an award-winning beauty journalist and author with a sustained and excellent track record. Alice has this great ability to engage with everyone, while at the same time, she does not let anyone get away with "blagging it".'

　– **Professor Mark Birch-Machin**, Professor in
　　Molecular Dermatology and Director of Business
　　Development (Faculty of Medical Sciences),
　　Newcastle University

ABOUT THE AUTHOR

Alice Hart-Davis is an award-winning beauty journalist and author. She has been writing about skincare for 20 years, and has tried out countless products in order to assess and review them.

She has travelled widely in pursuit of skincare news, from European laboratories to shop launches in Shanghai and dermatologists' conventions in the USA, interviewing experts and brand creators along the way, in order to try to keep up to date with the fast-moving world of skincare technology.

Alice has won awards for her articles on skincare and the science behind it, though none of these gives her quite the same buzz as hearing that a product she has suggested to someone has changed their life by improving their skin, which in turn has made them feel much better about themselves.

She lives in London, and keeps a magnifying glass on her desk and beside every basin, in order to be able to read the INCI lists on the back of products – the small print that tells you which ingredients the product contains.

Editor and Typesetter: Guy Hart-Davis

Research Assistant: Tilly Rigg

Cover Image: John Godwin, johngodwin.co.uk

Cover Design: Alex Nicholas

Jenni Woodhead, gaiadesignstudio.co.uk

Published in 2020 by Tweakments Guide Limited

1st Edition Printing: August 2020

ISBN 978-1-9993596-2-1 (paperback)
ISBN 978-1-9993596-3-8 (ebook)

Printed on responsibly sourced paper

DISCLAIMER

This book is intended for reference and information only. The author is not a medical practitioner. The information given here is based on the author's experience and is for your consideration. It is not intended as medical advice on which you can rely. Any reliance placed by you on the information in the book is done by you at your own risk. If you suspect that you have a medical problem, you should seek professional medical help.

DISCLOSURES

I have been writing about skincare for 20 years. During this time, I have been sent press samples of innumerable different skincare products in all price brackets and been given many different facial treatments, none of which I have paid for, in order that I could write about the products and understand better how they work.

Also, over the years, I have taken press trips with, or worked as a consultant for, or on projects with, many companies that produce these products, including, in alphabetical order, Boots UK (WBA), Deciem, Dior, Estée Lauder, Johnson & Johnson, L'Oréal, Procter & Gamble, and Unilever.

This has helped to give me a unique, in-depth understanding of the field. Does this make me biased towards certain brands, or products? I really don't think so. All the opinions in the book are my own, except, obviously, for the quoted views of industry experts, which are in their own words.

I have not been paid for recommendations of the products mentioned in this book.

There's a shop on my website selling some of the products and devices which I truly rate. Often, these are products that I have been recommending – in my journalism and on social media – for years. If you're not sure about my objectivity, take a look at the consumer reviews on the product pages.

ACKNOWLEDGEMENTS: A FEW 'THANK YOU'S

Firstly, huge thanks to all the skincare experts, dermatologists, facialists, and other aestheticians who have talked me through the ins and outs of skincare over the past 20 years, and done their best to educate me. Also, to the brands and their long-suffering PRs who have sent me their products and dealt with my endless queries, always on the tightest of deadlines.

Next, massive thanks to my brother Guy Hart-Davis, one of the most patient, skilled and tactful copy-editors you could ever find. He has the knack of nicking out idiocies and straightening jumbled thoughts in the kindest possible way ('I've had a go at unpacking the next sentence...'), and having survived the rigours of editing *The Tweakments Guide* has bravely opted to dig deep into the world of skincare for this volume, and has taken the book the whole way through from raw copy to print-ready files.

Also, grateful thanks to the experts who read my early drafts and who have advised me on technical points; to my assistant and right hand Tilly Rigg, without whose tireless work all aspects of The Tweakments Guide would fail to function; and to my daughter Beth Hindhaugh for her patient, painstaking work on the glossary and index.

And particular thanks to my husband Matthew Hindhaugh, who for 20 years has put up with a bathroom stuffed with a ridiculous number of products, and who has learned (after a couple of incidents involving my finding an experimental scoop had been taken out of the latest pot of wonder-cream with a large finger) to demand a special safe zone for his own, limited selection of basic skincare (not even joking; he's allergic to many products).

DEDICATION

This book is for my friends Divya and Sally, who are avid users of skincare and always keen to hear my recommendations, yet tend to look a bit baffled when I start explaining why they might want this product for that concern.

I suspect they're not the only ones overwhelmed by the sheer variety of skincare products and confused about which ones might help them most.

I thought if I put it all down in a book, I might be able to explain it all a bit better and more logically; and they – and everyone else – could read it, digest it, and make up their own minds about what their skin might need.

CONTENTS AT A GLANCE

TABLE OF CONTENTS

INTRODUCTION

Our skin is our protective canopy against the world. It's the biggest organ in our body; and whether you're looking at it from the point of view of function, comfort, or durability, you'll benefit from keeping your skin in good health.

Because that's what skincare is about. Aside from keeping our faces looking good for longer, which is what makes most of us pay attention to our skin, skincare is all about fixing problematic issues with the skin, and bringing it into better health, so that it works well, and looks glowing and healthy.

Once it's healthy, we can nudge it with stimulating ingredients, to coax it towards looking better and fresher.

We tend to think of our skin as it is at the moment. 'My skin is so dry,' we'll say, or 'My skin is so temperamental.' But just because that's how your skin has become, because of your genes and your lifestyle and the products you've been using or not-using, it doesn't mean you can't shift it into a happier state by using effective products that suit it.

And as to whether it's worth paying good money on skincare products, I'd offer that old truism that you wear your skin every day. Your face is what people notice when they meet you. We are hard-wired by evolution to be able to assess other people's age and health by the state of their skin, and whether it's smooth, clear and fresh-looking, or whether it's wrinkled and spotted with pigmentation, or roughened by time and the weather.

We often spend a lot of time and effort on our clothes, our hair, and our make-up, in order to present ourselves as we'd like to be seen.

It's worth spending some time, effort, and money on your skin, too.

WHO THIS BOOK IS FOR AND WHY I WROTE IT

20 years ago, my boss called me over to her desk on a London newspaper, and tapped the luxurious, tissue-filled presentation bag at her feet with a designer-shod toe. 'D'you want it?' she asked. 'I've got one already.'

'It,' was a jar of Crème de la Mer, launching that week, and already creating a sensation for its £115 price tag – as well as its supposed rejuvenating powers. 'Wow, yes!' I said keenly, and made off with the bag before she could change her mind.

It's hard to describe how unbelievably excited I was to have my hands on that product. I'd been delving into the fast-developing field of anti-ageing skincare since I joined the *Evening Standard's* features team. The paper carried little in the way of beauty and skincare writing – which was left to glossy magazines – but I'd taken it on myself to cover this area along with the health pages, just in case I got the chance to write about the extraordinary world of high-tech skincare, by which I was mesmerised.

Could these new products possibly do what they claimed, and actively improve the look and feel of the skin, and reduce wrinkles and pigmentation? I took every opportunity to quiz the brands and the developers behind the products, and the dermatologists and skincare scientists who would regularly bring me back down to earth by pointing out where a cream's claims were dubious – or ludicrous.

But to cut a long story short, I began to learn what worked, and which products could provide actual proof – preferably in the form of proper clinical trials – that they did what they claimed. I've tried an enormous number of products over the years, and written about them for magazines and newspapers. I've won awards for my writing interpreting skincare science and attempting to explain it to readers. It's an area that continues to fascinate me as the technology behind the ingredients becomes ever more focussed, and complex. Ingredients that turn the blue light from the devices from something that harms the skin into something that boosts collagen? They're on the way. Personalised products created to treat your skin's needs? They're here already, and they don't cost the earth. Serums loaded with ingredients that make up for the deficiencies in your skin's DNA? They're here too, and though the current versions aren't as exciting as they sound, they will surely be what we all use in the future. If we have the funds.

And as for Crème de la Mer? Many of the brand's newer products are super high-tech and work a treat, but that original cream didn't do the trick for me. On my combination skin, it slid about and provoked breakouts, as it's a heavy cream based largely on mineral oil and petrolatum (yes, petroleum jelly, like Vaseline; and mineral oil, such as baby oil). Not such a miracle, though I still have friends that swear by it. Most people have a naturally dry skin type, so the mineral oil content helps this by preventing water loss from the skin and keeping it feeling smoother and softer. That's why so many women – especially mature women, whose skin has become drier with the loss of sex hormones with age – fell in love with this product.

So what products should you use on your face? What is worth trying? What reliably gives results? Where do you start with all this, and how do you put together a skincare regime?

A great deal of skincare coverage – in the media, and on social media – is dedicated to the latest discoveries, new miracle products, and trends in product use. Much of it is marketing-led. These new products and trends are entertaining, maybe even thought-provoking, but they are the bells and whistles of the skincare world. They distract our attention from the fundamentals of skincare – the need to keep our skin, our barrier between our insides and the outside world, clean, protected and in good shape.

This book is for anyone – young or old, male or female – who is confused about what they should be putting on their face, when there is so much overwhelming choice, and so much conflicting advice about which products to use.

WHAT WILL THIS BOOK TEACH YOU?

This book tells you what you need to know to look after your skin effectively. The book consists of three parts:

- Part One explains what you need to understand about modern skincare to get the most benefit from it.

- Part Two teaches you the seven crucial rules for looking after your skin. It also tells you about the best skincare products I've discovered at low, medium, and high price points.

- Part Three shows you how to put these rules into a workable daily skincare routine, which can be as simple or as complex, as cheap or as expensive, as you like. In Part Three, you'll also find answers to the 12 biggest questions about skincare concerns – from wrinkles to melasma, and from rosacea to rough skin, taking in large pores, acne, and the menopause along the way.

WHERE SHOULD YOU START?

Start wherever you want, really. Part One is background, scene-setting, explaining some of the key issues at play in the skincare arena, and what I think about them, and why.

But maybe you'd prefer to get into the more practical part? If so, just dive straight into Part Two, which tells you the key rules about caring for your skin.

Or perhaps you would like to cut to the chase, and move straight to Part Three, where I set out some suggestions for skincare 'recipes' – how to put together a skincare routine to suit your particular skincare requirements.

Obviously, I think it should be read from the start (well, I would, wouldn't I?) but I appreciate that you may not feel the same. See what works for you.

And I know I've set the skincare part down as 'rules'. But as we all know, rules are there to be broken. I just think you should know what they are before you start bending and breaking them to suit yourself.

PART ONE

18 Home Truths About Skincare

Skincare is fundamental to keeping our faces looking good, and hence to how we feel about ourselves. It's an intrinsic part of grooming, of self-care. The skin, as I'm sure you'll have read before, is the largest organ in our bodies. It's our biggest natural defence organ against the outside world. It's a living thing. It needs constant, careful nurturing.

Before we get into the detail of which products do what and how to use them, there are a number of things you need to know about skin and skincare.

1. WHAT SKINCARE CAN DO (AND WHAT IT CAN'T)

So many people still think that skincare is 'hope in a jar'. It certainly used to be. Today, depending on what you choose, skincare can be powerful stuff.

Here's what skincare can do:

- Soften wrinkles
- Increase the hydration of the skin
- Reduce water loss from the skin to the air
- Firm and strengthen skin from the inside out
- Lighten pigmentation
- Improve skin radiance
- Clear blemishes and breakouts
- Smooth out rough dry patches
- Tone down the flush of rosacea
- Coax the fabric of your skin into better health.
- Make you look fresher and more rested

And here's what skincare can't do:

- Lift the skin
- Plump the skin more than a few micrometres
- Change the contours of your face
- Change your skin overnight

WHAT IS A SKINCARE PRODUCT?

A skincare product is a cosmetic cream – or lotion, liquid, or paste – that can be used 'topically' (in other words, applied to the skin) to improve the skin's condition and appearance.

Skincare products are classed as cosmetic in the UK, so by law they should have only a cosmetic effect on the skin. Anything that has a far-reaching physiological effect on the skin should be classed as a medicine. There's more on this in the section '8. You Need to Use Skincare Like Medicine' on page 7.

---

2. IT'S ALL A MATTER OF OPINION

The key thing you need to know upfront is that most of what you hear about skincare is a matter of opinion, rather than fact. Should you wear sunscreen all year round? Should you exfoliate before you cleanse, or vice versa? Should you use a special eye cream or not? Should you worry about how 'natural' a product is?

This book is giving you my opinion on all these issues, and many more: my considered opinion, formed from 20 years of hearing it from all angles from facialists, formulators, dermatologists, skin doctors, cosmetic scientists, biochemists, aestheticians… but still, just my opinion.

With this book, I'm trying to give you enough knowledge that you can make up your own mind about what matters most to you for your skin, form your own opinions, and put together a plan to enhance your skin.

3. SKINCARE DOESN'T HAVE TO BE EXPENSIVE TO BE EFFECTIVE

How much do you have to spend on skincare? That's entirely up to you. It really is. What you need to think about is how many products you plan to use, and what budget you have for each of these.

Do you want one day product and one night product, and that's it? Or have you the time and energy, as well as the cash, for a full suite of cleansers, acid toners, serums, and masks?

It makes more sense, for example, to buy a cheaper cleanser – which is going straight down the drain – and splash out on a well-proven face-repairing serum, than vice versa. There are plenty of decent products at bargain prices which will do a good job for you if you use them persistently, as directed. In which case, I hear you thinking, why on earth spend more?

4. BUT EXPENSIVE PRODUCTS ARE OFTEN BETTER THAN CHEAPER ONES

Are expensive products better? The short answer? Sometimes. But not necessarily. I don't mean that to be unhelpful, but that's a really difficult question to answer, and here are some of the reasons why it's hard to answer, and why expensive products may or may not be better.

We assume that more expensive products must be, or at least ought to be, better than cheaper one. People love luxury skincare, and sales of it have consistently been booming.

But the past decade has also seen the arrival of a number of 'single-ingredient' brands such as The Ordinary, Garden of Wisdom, and The Inkey List that knock the established paradigm for six by offering products focussed on key skincare ingredients such as hydrating hyaluronic acid, or skin-repairing retinol, for a tenner or less.

Are these products cheap rubbish? Not at all. They're a good place to start if, say, you want to see what a particular ingredient that skincare bloggers are raving about might do for your complexion. So why buy anything else? Well, you need more than one ingredient for the everyday health of your skin. These products can help with short-term issues with skin, but it's like hearing kale is the latest superfood and deciding to make kale the only vegetable you eat. It's not exactly bad for you, but it would be of greater benefit for your skin's health to have support from a variety of other ingredients.

Then you need to consider other factors, from the quality and complexity of the ingredients all the way through to the product packaging. The following sections discuss these factors.

Quality of the Ingredients

More expensive products may well contain more expensive ingredients. It's not dissimilar to finding ingredients for cooking, or composing perfume. Some of us are happy with a mass-market version of the ingredient which will give the right taste or smell and basically do the job; others will spend a lot of time and money seeking out the finest, most carefully sourced version of the ingredient which, to them, produces an entirely different result.

Complexity of the Ingredients

Some ingredients are straightforward, widely available, and cheap. Others are high-tech and their patents are closely guarded. Guess which costs more?

Quality of the Formulation

I'm often told that the formulations of cheaper products aren't that sophisticated. This may well be true, but it's hard to judge unless you are a cosmetic formulator. Will you get good results just from popping a layer of plain hyaluronic acid on your skin? Or would your skin derive more benefit from this ingredient if it came in combination with others? Usually, it's the latter.

Marketing and Advertising Costs

The marketing campaign. The poster and magazine and TV advertising. The celebs that feature in said advertising. Taking influencers and press around the world for a launch. (I once attended a launch in a chateau outside Paris where 15,000 long-stemmed roses had been flown in for the event, along with a global selection of big-name influencers.) It all costs a huge amount of money, and that will be reflected in the price of the product.

Packaging

That beautiful packaging. The bottle cap that shuts with a beautifully engineered, soft magnetic click. It doesn't come cheap. Some people are happy to pay for this, and feel it adds to the whole experience of using the skincare.

Economies of Scale

The whole equation is then further confused by the fact that larger companies clearly have economies of scale – if they're buying in-gredients, and packaging, by the tonne rather than the ounce, the production costs of each product will be less than if it is being made in small batches.

So if you're looking at a product with a clever new formulation engineered by a cosmetic scientist with a reputation for exciting skincare – it is likely to cost a lot, but it could well be worth it.

5. HOW MANY PRODUCTS YOU USE IS UP TO YOU

You don't have to become a complete skin geek to improve your skin, nor do you have to spend hours in the bathroom. As with how much you spend, how much you should bother about your skin is completely up to you. I'm not going to come after you if you don't cleanse twice a day. You could use one product a day; you could use 10 products. But the key point is, if you're trying to make a change in your skin, you need to be doing something different to what you've been doing before. And that implies a degree of being bothered to do at least something – maybe something more than you were doing before.

6. CONSISTENCY IS KEY

Your skin needs looking after on a daily basis. It's also key that you're reasonably consistent with what you do with your skin. A lot of skin advisers are keen on using an analogy to exercise. You wouldn't just go to the gym once a week and expect to get fit, they say. It's the same with your skin. You can't just deep-cleanse once a week and slap on a mask and hope that will do the trick. You need to give your skin regular, daily attention.

Though, as with exercise, you don't want to overdo it with skincare. Throwing too many different products at your skin may well result in flare-ups or break-outs, and if you've been using a lot of stuff, it will be hard to pinpoint what it was that pushed your skin to the point where it reacted.

Like many of my colleagues, I've had episodes of 'beauty-editor skin' after testing too many products in too short a space of time, to the point where my skin has gone haywire. Then, the only hope is to rein the regime right back and wait for everything to calm down.

7. HOW SOON WILL IT WORK?

Another common issue with skincare products is expecting them to work miracles within minutes. Ok, some of them appear to do exactly that, but that is more common with cosmetics, which may be full of clever light-diffusing particles that make your skin appear very different the moment you apply them.

With skincare, it's different. Some products do produce an immediate effect. Hydrating serums, for instance, which are absorbed into your skin and stuff the outer layers full of moisture, can give an immediate plumping effect. It's only fractional, this effect, seeing as how your skin is so thin, but it's enough to soften the appearance of wrinkles.

Moisturisers or serums that contain light-reflecting particles will make skin look instantly more radiant, but that's because they're having a cosmetic effect and bouncing back the light from the skin's surface.

If those moisturisers have a few silicones among their ingredients, they can make the skin look dramatically better at once. How? Those silicones can fill the tiny crevasses in the skin; the moisturiser adds some plumping hydration; and hey presto, your skin looks a whole lot smoother – but again, the effect is temporary.

Acids that gently resurface the skin can have a swift effect. Glycolic-acid lotions or creams that are left on overnight can show a small improvement by the next morning, though their real benefits – of improving skin radiance by clearing dead cells from the skin's surface, and of improving hydration – will come with consistent use.

But the way that skincare can create genuine change in the skin is a slower process. It takes weeks for new skin cells, which are formed deep down in the dermis, the lower layers of the skin, to work their way to the surface. In young skin, this process takes four weeks; but cell turnover slows down as you get older, so it will take more like six weeks if you are in your fifties. This means that any product which is claiming to change your skin by stimulating the growth of collagen will need time to work its magic, for its ingredients to take effect on the skin and, slowly, change the appearance of the skin, from the bottom up. So don't dismiss the latest wonder-cream that you have invested in just because you're not seeing any difference after a week or two. You need to be patient, and use it like medicine for at least two months, before you decide whether it is working or not.

Having said that, skincare companies are well aware that we're not generally very patient, and that if we don't see results, and soon, we'll be off to try another product. The canniest skincare brands take time to develop products which give an immediate, visible (albeit cosmetic) result to keep us happy while the key ingredients in the product continue its real work at a slower pace in the deeper layers of the skin.

8. YOU NEED TO USE SKINCARE LIKE MEDICINE

Many people are reluctant to believe that skincare will really change their skin. On the one hand, that is precisely what they want the stuff to do – why they keenly peruse the beauty pages and read up about the latest wonder cream. But on the other hand, there is a strong undercurrent in their mind that says, 'I don't suppose it will work for me'.

This may be a peculiarly British attitude, which persists in thinking that skincare is still 'hope in a jar', even when so many millions of pounds have been spent on clinical trials that can demonstrate very real results in improving the look and texture of ageing skin.

But the key to getting the best out of your skincare – particularly out of skincare products that are making some kind of promise to change your skin, and which have been shown by clinical trials to have produced this kind of effect on other people – is to take it seriously and to use it like medicine. If you are given a course of antibiotics to clear up an infection, you take them every day, as directed. You don't decide to skip them one night or not pack them when you go away for the weekend. In the same way, you need to use skincare as directed. Twice a day, without fail, or whatever it says on the packaging. That way, you stand a chance of seeing the results that the product claims to make.

You also need to bear in mind that it will take three or four weeks, or longer if you are older, of consistent use for a product to show results. That's because your skin cells are constantly renewing themselves, and new cells rise up through the epidermis towards the surface as the cells on the skin's outer surface die and are sloughed off. This cycle takes around four weeks if you are in your thirties, and slows down with age.

9. EMOTIONAL FACTORS INFLUENCE OUR SKINCARE CHOICES

Emotional factors? I'm talking about the feel and smell and image of a product. Actually, how a product feels on your skin is really important. If it glides on, spreads evenly, is well absorbed and leaves a smooth, comfortable-feeling surface, that's major. If it's hard to spread and makes the skin sticky, it's a complete turn-off.

The smell of a product is really important, too. On the one hand, a product's smell has nothing whatsoever to do with its efficacy, but for many people, an appealing smell is a big selling point. It absolutely shouldn't be, given that fragrance is the ingredient most likely to provoke a reaction in skin that is sensitive to it, but there you go.

Then there is the intangible factor of what you think the product or the brand says about you. Again, that shouldn't be a thing, but it absolutely is. Lots of women have told me that they'd never use one brand or another, because it was 'my mother's cream', or 'my granny's one'. Fair enough – if your granny was using the products, time and cosmetic formulations will have moved on. But it does a disservice to brands like Olay which have a long heritage, yet now boast cosmetic technology that's world-class.

10. TEN-STEP REGIMES VS ALL-IN-ONE CREAMS

If you're into skincare, you'll have heard of – or maybe even tried – the complicated, multi-step skincare routines popularised by Korean beauty influencers. The sort where you, say, double-cleanse, exfoliate, use an acid toner, then a prepping essence, then an antioxidant serum, then a hydrating serum, then a barrier-boosting moisturiser, then a sunscreen, then a spray sunscreen powder just for good measure (and if that all sounds like double-Dutch, don't worry, Part Two will explain it all).

Yes, there are benefits to using all these products – but all at once? To my mind, it's far too much, and unnecessary.

What seems much more alluring, particularly these days when we're all time-poor and busy being busy, is the idea of an all-in-one wonder cream which is the only thing you need to use. I'll mention a few of these in due course, too.

A wonder cream is a nice idea, but I feel you need to do a bit more than that. There's a happy medium somewhere in the middle. As I'll try to make clear all through this book, there are some things to do with skincare which I feel are non-negotiable – such as cleansing, and wearing sun-protection – but everything else is up to you.

11. SKINCARE REALLY CAN CHANGE YOUR SKIN

Skincare can be really effective. How effective? Well, ideally, the company behind the product will have conducted enough tests on the product to give us some idea. What sort of tests? And what sort of proof can these offer?

Studies Have Shown...

In 2006, Boots introduced a new product in its No7 range, the Protect & Perfect Beauty Serum. The product didn't garner much interest immediately. It was ahead of its time; few people understood what a 'serum' was, or why they should use it. But in early 2007, the serum featured in a BBC Horizon programme which flagged up the (extraordinary, back then) fact that No7 had conducted decent clinical trials on the product which had been 'shown scientifically to repair photo-aged skin and improve the fine wrinkles associated with photo-ageing.' In short, it reversed the signs of ageing created in the skin by sun damage, and genuinely did exactly what it claimed.

The product, which had been earmarked to be discontinued because it wasn't selling well, sold out within hours and remains a bestseller.

Ever since then, skincare companies have been scrambling to 'prove' how well their products work. How do they do this? With a trial of some sort. But not all trials are equal.

Clinical Trials vs Consumer Trials

Clinical trials are research studies carried out to discover whether a particular product or ingredient is effective.

Proper clinical trials should be:

- **Placebo-controlled.** Half the people in the trial are given a placebo instead of the real thing.
- **Double blind.** Neither the scientists conducting the study nor the participants know who is getting the actual product and who is getting the placebo.
- **Randomised.** People are randomly assigned to the two groups.
- **Independent.** Conducted by an independent laboratory.

- **Conducted on a finished product, not an ingredient**. Even if an ingredient has impressive clinical results, will it work its magic when mixed in with other ingredients? You won't know unless the finished formula is tested.
- **Closely supervised, and the results carefully measured.** It's almost too obvious to say, but being meticulous with the details and the data in a trial is crucial.

The longer the trial continues for, and the more people are involved in it, the better from the point of view of the resulting data. If a trial proves that a product shows measurable results in a lot of people – well, that's gold dust when it comes to selling the product.

Is a successful clinical trial real proof that a product works? Yes, though the real test is whether this well-proven product can replicate its results on your skin. Not everyone responds the same way to products, or ingredients; and even within impressive clinical trials, there will be participants who simply didn't get any measurable result from the product.

Why Don't All Brands Put Their Products Through Clinical Trials?

Because clinical trials are expensive. Nowhere near as expensive as the pharmaceutical trials a new drug product has to go through; but a double-blind, randomized, placebo-controlled trial will set a brand back upwards of £20,000; and the more complex the trial is, and the longer it goes on for, the more expensive it becomes, so they're beyond the range of smaller companies.

Consumer trials, by contrast, cost relatively little. It only costs a few thousand pounds to conduct a self-assessment survey among 20 or 40 women, after which a brand can legally claim that, for example, '90 per cent of women who tried this product felt their skin was more radiant'. That claim can go on the packaging, and looks impressive, but it doesn't carry the weight of a proper clinical trial – and this distinction may not be so obvious to those of us who haven't had the difference between these types of trials pointed out to us.

Trials like this aren't useless. The participants will have been asked to answer questions – possibly, leading questions – about how they viewed their results. If 90 per cent of them felt their skin radiance was improved, well, that's great. But unless you know more about those participants, it may not mean very much. For example, did those women have dull skin that had failed to respond to other types of skincare? If so, that improved radiance would be quite a claim. Or was this the first moisturiser that they had ever used consistently? If so, it wouldn't be surprising that their skin looked better afterwards.

Ingredient Testing vs Product Testing

New skincare products are often promoted with impressive claims, though when you read the small print, the claim rests on the fact that an ingredient they contain has been shown to work in clinical trials. That's all fine and dandy, but it doesn't necessarily follow that, once mixed into the product formula, that result will hold true.

What's more helpful is when a company has put the finished product through trials (preferably clinical trials, as above). Then you know there's a chance that you might get the same results if you use the product with dedication.

In Vitro Testing vs In Vivo Testing

Then there's the question of how the ingredient, or the product, has been tested. *In vitro* is Latin for 'in glass', ie the test has been conducted in a lab, in a test tube or petri dish. If it works, great – but will it work on your skin?

In vivo, by contrast, means 'in real life' – the product has been tested on a living organism, in this case, someone's skin. If that gives decent results, that's better news.

12. THE FACTORS THAT MAKE SKINCARE MORE EFFECTIVE

Creating effective skincare is what every formulator is trying to do, whether that is with a simple moisturiser to keep the skin feeling comfortable; or a high-tech serum intending to rev up the skin's idling repair mechanisms into overdrive, and strengthen the skin; or hydrate it; or minimise pigmentation...

BEWARE OF MEANINGLESS TERMS ON PACKAGING

While we're on the subject of testing, can I just bring your attention to a couple of really meaningless terms that get inscribed on skincare packaging as if they were holy writ?

'Dermatologically tested' sounds great. It implies that the product has met some specific standard, demanded by dermatologists, before it can be unleashed on the market. But the term means little, as there is no standardised test that dermatologists must put products through. It only means that a dermatologist was in charge of the testing phase. It doesn't even mean that the product passed any particular test, like not causing irritation. It just means the product was tested.

'Ophthalmologically tested' is similar. This term means that an ophthalmologist – an eye specialist – reviewed the test that the manufacturer uses to assess whether the product could irritate the eyes. The product will have been tested to ensure that it can be tolerated in the eye area, but the term doesn't mean that the product is particularly gentle.

What makes the difference is whether the product contains decent quality ingredients, at sufficient levels of concentration to give a result, in a formula that gets them where they need to go.

Where do the ingredients need to get to? That depends:

- A moisturiser only needs to sit on top of skin and hold moisture inside the skin. Similarly, a sunscreen needs to sit on the skin and protect it from UV light.
- Exfoliating acid products also work on the skin's surface, to loosen the bonds that are tethering dead skin cells in place.
- Hydrating serums need to wiggle in a bit deeper, to plump up the top layers of the skin from the inside.
- But serums that work on pigmentation, or that stimulate collagen production in the skin, need to actually penetrate the skin in order to go to work on the lower layers.

What the Skin Can Absorb

There's a lot of talk on the internet about how the skin absorbs all the products placed on it, and that 'harmful chemicals' in skincare will be absorbed by the body and 'get into' the bloodstream. These websites will quote the fact that if you rub garlic onto the soles of your feet, you can taste garlic in your mouth within the hour. Or cite the popular use of stick-on patches that deliver nicotine or HRT (hormone replacement therapy) into the skin.

Those last two things are absolutely true. Garlic and the contents of nicotine patches can penetrate the skin and can be absorbed into the bloodstream – but they're exceptions. The skin is there as a barrier, to defend what's inside our bodies from the external environment, and it's a pretty good barrier. It is an impermeable membrane that makes us waterproof, so we can swim and bathe and be out in the rain without melting or swelling up like a sponge. Our skin keeps out dirt and viruses and bacteria. It's not keen to let stuff through. It really doesn't absorb very much.

The Trend for Miniaturised Ingredients

The fact that the skin is such an effective barrier is a challenge for cosmetic formulators, who have to devise delivery mechanisms that will ease their precious ingredients through the stratum corneum – the top layer of dead cells that sits on top of the skin – and into the lower layers of the epidermis, where they are needed, and where they can go to work.

One approach that had seemed promising for this was the way that nanotechnology could miniaturise the molecules of skincare ingredients, so that they could slip through minute gaps in the skin barrier, and thus reach their targets. 10 years ago, there was a huge buzz around in the skincare around nanotechnology, and larger skincare companies were filing multiple nanotech patents. Recently, though, we haven't been hearing so much about nanotechnology.

The problem with miniaturised ingredients is that they would be no good to the skin if they slipped off into the bloodstream, so they need to be large enough to travel into the skin but no further.

Nanoparticles are also helpful for sunscreen ingredients such as titanium dioxide and zinc oxide, which produce a white formula that can look chalky on the skin. When miniaturised, they give a clearer product with a better cosmetic finish.

Scientists have raised questions over whether nanoparticles of sunscreen are safe. Although the latest view of organisations such Australia's Cancer Council (cancer.org.au) is that nanoparticles in sunscreens don't post a risk, many companies don't want nano materials in their products while these questions remain unanswered.

The Case for Cosmeceuticals

What's a cosmeceutical? It's a skincare product that's halfway between cosmetic, available-over-the-counter skincare, and a pharmaceutical, prescription product. Or that's the idea. There's no precise, or legal, definition of 'cosmeceutical', but they're usually the sort of brands you will find in cosmetic clinics rather than in department stores, such as NeoStrata, Medik8, SkinCeuticals, iS Clinical, Alpha H, Elequra, Skinbetter Science, Paula's Choice, and ZO Skincare. You'll find I mention cosmeceuticals a good deal in this book, as they're the type of products I think are the most effective.

Is It Skincare or Is It Medicine?

How potent and effective can skincare get before it has to be classed as medicine? That's a good question.

Many non-pharmaceutical products have plenty of proof – in the form of clinical trials – that they work. But by law a cosmetic product should make only a cosmetic change to the skin. If it makes a physiological change to the skin – ie it actually changes the skin in some way, which is very much what most active skincare is aiming to do – then, technically, shouldn't it be classified as medicine?

The short answer is – no, as long as the product isn't making a medicinal claim. That applies even if the product is claiming to improve wrinkles. As far as the Medicines and Healthcare Products Regulatory Agency (MHRA) is concerned, wrinkles are not an adverse medical condition, so claims to reduce their appearance, or to increase the elasticity of skin, fall under cosmetic regulation.

If you want to read a longer piece I've written about this topic, follow this link to the GQ website: gq-magazine.co.uk/article/best-mens-skincare-moisurisers-serums-that-give-results.

How Skincare Affects the Way Our Skin Genes Behave

There are about 2,000 genes related to the way our skin ages. The study of genes and the way they function is called *genomics* – and Procter & Gamble, the pharmaceutical company behind brands such as Olay, has been studying skin genomics for over a decade.

'The genes you are born with won't change through your life,' explains Dr Frauke Neuser, Senior Director of Scientific Communications at Procter & Gamble, 'but what will change is how dynamic those 2,000 genes are. We know the group of genes that is important to make you look young. The next step is to overlay this with the active ingredients we have in our database and work out which skincare ingredients can affect gene expression.'

Even skincare products in this area are not classed as medicines. That's because, even if they are improving the expression of certain genes – for example, switching back on the ones that make collagen – the products are not making medicinal claims.

13. NATURAL, ORGANIC, VEGAN, 'CLEAN'

Natural beauty sounds like a lovely idea. Organic beauty, too. We all have a romantic notion that natural things are good for us – and often they are – and we like to extend that to skincare. If we want to eat natural, unadulterated foods, preferably organic, why wouldn't we want to use 'natural', unadulterated products that are 'kind' to our skin?

I've put those inverted commas because – reality check – when it comes to skincare, it's not that simple. There's no agreed definition of what 'natural' means in skincare. Many brilliant natural-beauty brands (eg Weleda, Green People, Dr Hauschka) have clear standards and follow them scrupulously; but in marketing terms, it's quite possible to slap the word 'natural' on a product if there is just one natural ingredient in it – say, lavender oil.

Organic skincare is more precise. In order to meet the standards for organic certification, a product has to be made from organically farmed ingredients. You can read more about this on the Soil Association website, www.soilassociation.org.

As for vegan skincare, there's no legal definition of precisely what makes a vegan beauty product; but vegans will have a pretty clear idea of the types of ingredient that they want to avoid, ie anything that is animal-derived. So no beeswax and no collagen (which all comes from animal sources); but – perhaps less obviously – no retinol, which is usually derived from animal sources. Other ingredients, such as hyaluronic acid and glycerin (which is every-where), can be either animal-derived or plant-derived; you'll need to check which.

Then there's the point made by cosmetic scientists, that skincare products made with natural or vegan ingredients won't be as efficacious as those containing synthetic active ingredients. Why? Because plants have cell walls made from cellulose, which don't get broken down by the enzymes on the skin, so a plant cell won't really deliver its nutritious ingredients quite so well.

And I'm not against any of these – each to their own, and all that – but the clean beauty movement really winds me up.

Why 'Clean Beauty' Drives Me Mad

Clean beauty? If you haven't heard of it, it's the beauty equivalent of 'clean eating'; and in the same way, it demonises a great many good beauty brands and products and ingredients by implying they're not as 'clean' as they should be.

Clean beauty is one of the biggest skincare movements just now and, if you ask me, one of the most maddening. It has grabbed the moral high ground on dubious reasoning – and it somehow man-ages to imply that all other skincare is, by contrast, 'dirty'. Not a good word.

Why I find the concept of clean beauty particularly irritating is that it manages to wrap all the standard arguments in this area into one big virtuous package: the supposed supremacy of natural skin-care; the hackneyed 'natural' vs 'chemical' ingredients issue (see the section 'Making Sense of the "Natural" vs "Chemical" Debate' on page 18 for more on this); scaremongering about the need to avoid 'nasties' (a generic term for ingredients that clean beauty fans deem to be bad or, worse, 'toxic'); and give longstanding, well-accredited ingredients – such as parabens, mineral oil, and sulphates – a real bashing along the way. Clean beauty does all this by using emotional arguments and banking on people's lack of understanding of science to create a sense of alarm and worry, that by using products that aren't 'clean', people are actively harming their skin and their bodies.

Oh, and clean beauty usually grabs a part of cruelty-free beauty and 'free from' tagging for good measure.

An added annoyance for those of us in the beauty industry is that the sweeping popularity of this movement is dragging cosmetic formulations back decades by chasing older, more 'natural' ingredients and ignoring the extraordinary new ones that cosmetic science is conjuring up just now.

Also, they're just wrong, if you ask me. Why do I say that? Here goes.

Natural Doesn't Mean 'Better'

I'm not 'anti-natural'. I'm really not. I just feel it needs saying that not everything 'natural' is 'better' for the skin. Also, I object to the way that people who are passionate about the supposed benefits of natural products argue their case by appealing to people's emotions rather than by using scientifically based facts. Even an emotionally-driven, non-scientific person like me can see that that doesn't make sense.

Making Sense of the 'Natural' vs 'Chemical' Debate

I have put the words 'natural' and 'chemical' in inverted commas because in scientific terms, every substance in the world, including every substance used in making skincare and cosmetics, has a chemical formula, whether it's water or beeswax or a new kind of high-performance anti-wrinkle neuropeptide. Using the word 'chemical' as a stick to beat much of modern skincare with is the sort of thing that drives cosmetic scientists mad.

Ten years ago, the Royal Society for Chemistry announced that it would pay a £1million bounty to the first person who could show them a chemical-free skincare product. Of course, their money is quite safe as no such thing exists; they were doing this to make a point, and the offer still stands.

'The challenge has been set because research by the UK's cosmetic and toiletries industry reveals 52% of women and 37% of men actively seek out chemical-free products, demonstrating the deep-seated public confusion about the role and application of chemicals in daily life,' said the RSC's press release at the time, adding that the popular perception of chemicals was 'something harmful to be avoided, a view shared by 84% of consumers who feel at some level concerned about the health impact of the chemicals in their everyday products'.

You might say that's nit-picking, but I think it's a point worth making. And, semantics aside, you may well prefer skincare products based on natural ingredients. What I'd ask is, 'Why?'

An answer I often get when I ask this is that people want to avoid 'harsh chemicals'. That sounds fair enough – but seriously, what are these 'harsh chemicals'? Every formulation for every skin-care product that goes on sale, from kitchen-table concoctions to mass-market brands, is subject to EU cosmetic regulations, specifically to ensure that it contains nothing harmful. No one puts lead in cosmetics, as was the popular practice in the 16th century. The main purpose of those regulations is to ensure 'human safety'.

WHAT HAPPENS TO COSMETIC REGULATIONS IN THE UK IF THERE IS NO FREE TRADE AGREEMENT AT THE END OF THE BREXIT TRANSITION PERIOD?

Here's what the website of the Cosmetic, Toiletry and Perfumery Association (CTPA) says:

If the UK leaves the EU single market without a Free Trade Agreement at the end of the implementation period, trade between both parties will operate under WTO (World Trade Organisation) Rules. The UK will have a standalone regulatory framework, but the spirit of the legislation will remain, providing safe and effective products that consumers can use safely with confidence.

When pressed on what these 'harsh chemicals' are, naturals-fans will name categories of ingredients such as parabens, which are used as preservatives; sulphates, which are foaming ingredients; and mineral-oil derivatives. (I'll get onto the ins and outs of these below.) 'They're dangerous,' they'll say. 'I've read so much about it online. You really shouldn't use these things.'

Ah yes, online. I hope we are all a little more aware now of how easy it is to get into an echo chamber of views online, which applies as much to skincare as to politics. Once you're in there, it becomes harder to believe that so many people could be wrong… Yet those types of ingredients mentioned above are all absolutely safe to use on the skin. Also, it's worth noting that many of these feared ingredients are natural derivatives. Parabens are found in coffee and blueberries; sulphates such as sodium lauryl sulphate can be derived from coconut oil or palm oil.

For sure, lots of natural ingredients are great for the skin, but natural ingredients aren't without issues. Any kind of fragrance can be irritating to the skin, and that includes essential oils. Any ingredient derived from lemon or other citrus fruit sensitises the skin to sunlight. But as with most things in life, there are few blanket rules of good and bad here; and as with many modern beliefs about skincare, things get taken out of context and blown out of proportion.

Lavender oil has a long-standing popular reputation for helping repair burns and heal wounds. Yet if you search online for 'lavender oil causes cell death', you will find a number of references to stand this up, including the studies showing that lavender oil is indeed toxic to skin cells. But this experiment was done 'in vitro', in a lab, and exposed cells directly to lavender oil. In real life, skin cells live among other tiny structures in a swamp of cellular fluid in the dermal matrix of the skin, and are protected from the world by the stratum corneum, the outer layers of the epidermis, so you'd never get that oil directly onto a skin cell, even through wounded skin. So using lavender oil on pulse points to calm you down (a very real effect; I'd strongly advise you not to do this when driving) or to heal a burn is not going to kill your skin cells. Honestly.

I could go on.

Years ago, I chaired a debate at the Royal Society of Chemistry on behalf of the Society for Cosmetic Scientists (SCS). The debate was about Cosmetics, Chemicals and the Truth, and we waded through either side of these issues until the panel and the audience were both feeling exhausted. One moment of clarity for me came when a younger member of SCS stood up to speak. 'Look,' she said, 'I'm a cosmetic formulator. I just want to put forward the idea that there is no right or wrong; what there is, is just options and choices. So, for any given brief, I can choose natural or synthetic chemicals. You have got to look at the performance of the product you are trying to achieve, the price point that you are retailing it at, and also the aesthetics. With that in mind, you come up with a formulation involving a cocktail of chemicals which will be a mix of both natural and synthetic.'

A choice – that's what it comes down to. I don't want to start sounding as if I'm a 'chemicals-only' sort of person – I'm really not – but I do find it tiresome that many people, particularly the fans of 'natural' beauty products, seem to assure that big beauty companies are in some way out to get them, and to ruin their skin, by selling products containing dangerous ingredients, which simply isn't the case.

14. 'NASTIES' AND 'TOXIC' INGREDIENTS

To recap what I said above, there are no toxic ingredients in skincare. There really aren't. I really object to the word 'nasties', too, which is used vaguely to demonise a whole host of cosmetic ingredients. So why do so many people think that many common ingredients are such a problem? Let's take a look at the key ingredients, or ingredient groups, that people think are problematic.

What's Wrong with Parabens?

If you've heard of parabens, the chances are that you won't like the sound of the word. They're bad, aren't they? So many skincare products proudly proclaim that they are free from parabens. Surely, parabens must be bad?

In a word – no, there's nothing wrong with parabens. They've been unfairly demonised through a combination of bad science, media hype, and popular hysteria.

WHAT ARE PARABENS?

Parabens are commonly used preservatives, which are good at doing their job – preventing the growth of mould, fungi, and bacteria in cosmetic products – without irritating the skin.

Parabens are derived from para-hydroxybenzoic acid (PHBA), which is found in foods like blueberries and onions, so our bodies are used to dealing with the stuff. The parabens in cosmetics are not naturally derived, because it's cheaper to make them in the lab than to extract them from blueberries, but they are 'nature-identical', which means they have the same chemical formula, so our bodies convert them to PHBA and dispense with them.

WHAT ARE PARABENS CALLED, AND WHAT DO THEY DO?

What are parabens called on the packaging label? Parabens have names such as methylparaben, ethylparaben, butylparaben, propylparaben, isopropylparaben, and isobutylparaben. 20 years ago, you would find such parabens in most cosmetic products that had water in the formulations, as preservatives to prevent contamination.

WHAT DO PEOPLE THINK IS WRONG WITH PARABENS?

But a research study published in 2004, which found parabens in breast cancer tissue, changed all that. Could the parabens have found their way into the tumours from the beauty products these women might have used? Was common skincare causing cancer? I remember reading the headline at my desk at the *Evening Standard* and, like most other women who read it, feeling complete horror – were we killing ourselves in the pursuit of beauty? The media seized on the story, and it shot around the world, raising more questions than it answered. Were parabens dangerous? How had they got into the breast tumours? Had they caused the tumours? Was it deodorant that was to blame?

My alarm soon turned to bafflement, because when I turned to my expert contacts for information – the toxicologists, the skincare formulators, industry experts – it appeared that the story had got ahead of the facts. The study, it turned out, was fundamentally flawed. It didn't compare the breast tumour tissue to healthy tissue, and what went unreported was the fact that concentrations of parabens were also found on the control slides, the blank slides with no breast tissue on them. Could that have been because all the slides used in the experiment had been cleaned, before use, with a solution containing parabens? In which case, were the parabens in the original tumour slides actually just on the slides, and not in the tumours at all?

Discrediting the study made absolutely no difference to the ongoing storm in the cosmetics industry and the consumer hysteria around the potential dangers of parabens. Companies hustled to remove parabens from their products and find alternative preservatives. However natural the natural lobby would like their products to be, the products need preservatives, or else they'll develop (entirely natural, but unpleasant) mould and become unusable.

And so parabens became the bad guys. There's a lot on the internet about their 'oestrogenic potential' – the ability of parabens to mimic the effects of oestrogen in the body. Yes, that sounds really damning. But cosmetic scientists and toxicologists beg to differ, pointing out that the oestrogenic potential of parabens is vanishingly small – thousands of times less than oestrogenic substances in food such as chickpeas and linseeds. You'd need a dose of butylparaben 25,000 times higher than what is used in a cosmetic, to see this effect.

There have been many further studies on parabens and breast cancer, but none of these has found any link between the two. The parabens-are-bad lobby persists, citing the 'cosmetic cocktail' effect, suggesting that a small effect may become more of a problem if a person uses many paraben-containing products in a day. Cosmetic formulators and scientists dismiss the cocktail theory, and I'm totally with them. Most skincare products and their ingredients sit on the surface of the skin. It's a struggle to get them into the skin tissue where they're needed. They don't simply slip down through the layers, get absorbed into the bloodstream, and start creating havoc.

The European Scientific Committee on Consumer Safety considers parabens to be safe. So does the American FDA. But that isn't going to stop the rumour-mill or put the parabens-genie back in its bottle. The misinformation has spread widely, and the natural-and-clean beauty movements have perpetuated online concerns around parabens. Making this worse, most of us don't understand science well enough to argue effectively against the misinformation and distortions. As a result, people have decided that parabens are a bad thing, and see 'free from parabens' as a clear benefit when it's stated on packaging. As a journalist, I find editors have little interest in stories along the lines of 'old-style preservatives not as bad as they've been made out to be'.

Many skincare companies have told me privately that they don't have a problem with parabens, but the companies can't include parabens in their formulations because consumers fear them so strongly. This topic isn't going to go away, but honestly, there's nothing wrong with parabens.

One last thought: Parabens are widely used in the food industry as preservatives. I suspect an awful lot of people who fear parabens in skincare don't know they're eating them…

> The race to remove parabens from cosmetics created further problems, as one of the first preservatives called into play was methylisothiazolinone (MI), which works well enough as a preservative but also provokes contact allergy in many people. Dermatology centres, such as the Leeds Centre of Dermatology and the St John Institute of Dermatology at Guy's Hospital in London, reported rates of contact allergy due to MI and its close cousin MCI rising sharply around 2011/2012 to around 10 per cent. In the past, preservatives which had this effect were banned by the EU, but MI/MCI is still around.

What's Wrong with Mineral Oil?

Another ingredient condemned by natural beauty fans is mineral oil, one of the longest-standing, cheapest and most commonly used cosmetic ingredients.

WHAT IS MINERAL OIL?

Mineral oil is a by-product of the process that makes petrol, so it's not remotely 'green' or environmentally friendly – but is it actually bad for the skin, as people think? No, it's not.

WHAT DOES MINERAL OIL DO?

Mineral oil makes a really effective moisturiser because it is so 'occlusive', which means it sits on the surface of the skin and holds in moisture.

Many people love using Johnson's Baby Oil on damp skin after a shower, to 'seal in' moisture; many others love Bio-Oil for softening the skin. These are both made from mineral oil.

Petroleum jelly, another by-product of petrol manufacture, which most of us know as Vaseline, works well to keep lips soft (again, by sealing in moisture).

So mineral oil has its uses. But it has been demonised over recent years by the popular and vocal natural-skincare community, to the extent that most people think they should avoid it because it is somehow 'bad'. It really isn't.

WHAT DO PEOPLE THINK IS WRONG WITH MINERAL OIL?

Here's what people think is wrong with mineral oil:

- **It 'clogs' the skin.** Mineral oil is very effective at keeping moisture in the skin – hence the longstanding practice of using oil on damp skin after a shower, to 'seal in' moisture.

- **It blocks pores and causes spots.** Well, technically, highly-refined mineral oil is non-comedogenic (which means it does not contain ingredients that are known to block pores), because its large molecules are too big to stuff themselves into the openings of pores. But because it is so effective at sealing over the skin, if your skin is buzzing with acne bacteria and has pores that are already threatening to block because of hormonal imbalances, mineral oil is not a helpful thing to spread all over it. So no, just don't use mineral-oil products if you're prone to spots.

- **It 'suffocates' the skin and stops it from 'breathing'.**
  The skin doesn't have a respiratory system; it doesn't 'breathe', so covering your skin in oil won't stop it breathing (and no, Jill Masterson, the character in the Bond film *Goldfinger*, who died from 'skin suffocation' after being painted with gold paint – that couldn't happen IRL). But, as I've said, mineral oil makes a very effective barrier, so it can help stop water escaping from the skin, which keeps skin better moisturised.

- **It is thought to be cancer-causing.** Some components of industrial-grade mineral oil have been found to be carcinogenic, but these components are not found in cosmetic-grade mineral oil. Other concerns include the suggestion – no more than a suggestion at the moment – that mineral-oil hydrocarbons may 'contaminate' the body, possibly by being absorbed through the skin, though we also absorb these pollutants from food and from the air.

So depending on your views about skincare and its origins, you may want to avoid mineral oil.

Do I put mineral oil on my skin? Yes, but not often, just because I am always trying out new products, and most newer products don't contain it.

Mineral oil may not be a modern or eco-friendly choice for skincare, but it is not evil incarnate. I know a couple of cosmetic doctors who apply it at night on top of their expensive skin-renewing and hydrating night serums, specifically in order to keep moisture in the skin, even around the eyes. And yes, I do still reach for the Vaseline as a lip-smoother or Vaseline Intensive Care lotion as a body moisturiser from time to time.

What's Wrong with Sulphates?

Another widely used ingredient that draws widespread vilification is sulphates.

WHAT ARE SULPHATES?

Sulphates are a group of ingredients that help products to foam up and produce lather. Sulphates are detergents – effective de-greasing agents – so you will find them in body washes, bubble baths, and foaming face washes, as well as shampoos and toothpastes.

WHAT DO PEOPLE THINK IS WRONG WITH SULPHATES?

Sulphates can irritate the skin. Also, depending on their concentration, many people feel sulphates can wash rather more natural oils out of the skin than is good for it. And 'detergent' sounds a bit blunt for a product you'd be using on your face, doesn't it?

The main types of sulphates that come in for criticism are:

- **Sodium Lauryl Sulphate (SLS)**. This is an effective lather-producing ingredient; it's also cheap, so it's widely used. But SLS is also a well-known skin irritant. In fact it is irritating enough to be used as a control in tests for skin irritancy of other substances. This is what has led to its bad reputation. How could we deliberately put an ingredient – or as many would phrase it, a 'chemical', which makes it sound even worse – into products that everyone uses? The simple answer is because almost every product SLS is used in is a wash-off, and most people aren't sensitive enough to SLS for it to be a problem in products that are only in contact with the skin for a short stretch of time as a shampoo or a face-wash. But if you *are* sensitive to SLS, then it's one to avoid. And whatever the scaremongering websites may say, SLS is not carcinogenic.

- **Sodium Laureth Sulphate (SLES)**. This is a close cousin of SLS, but not as cheap and a bit less irritating to the skin. But then both these sulphates have the potential to irritate the skin, as does any other ingredient ending in -sulphate which is used to replace SLS and SLES. Sulphate-replacement ingredients like cocomidopropyl betane, which is usually just used as a lather-booster, don't have the same ability to produce lather on their own.

The bottom line? Sulphates are only a problem if you are sensitive to them – in which case, look for products with alternative foaming ingredients; and bear in mind that foam is the most effective way of transporting dirt away from the skin.

What's Wrong with Silicones?

Silicones are another hapless group of ingredients that has fallen foul of popular opinion.

WHAT ARE SILICONES?

Silicones are ingredients derived from sand which are used in skincare and make-up to give a silky, velvety feel to products, to help them spread, and to help moisturise the skin. Silicones are used in haircare to smooth the hair and protect it from heat styling and humidity.

What are silicones called on the packaging? The one you see most often is dimethicone, which is a silicon polymer. Other ingredients whose names end in -cone, such as methicone and phenyl trimethicone, are also silicones, as are ingredients ending -siloxane (such as cyclopentasiloxane).

WHAT DO PEOPLE THINK IS WRONG WITH SILICONES?

People's objections to silicones are much the same as with mineral oil products. Silicones are thought to smother and block the skin and to provoke breakouts of acne, to prevent active ingredients getting to the skin, and to be hard to remove.

Do silicones deserve this bad reputation? No. Because they spread well and form a smooth covering on the surface of the skin, they're good at helping hold moisture in the skin – they're often recommended for helping scars heal, for this reason – but they're still permeable to gas and moisture, which means that they're not forming a watertight seal on your skin. They don't block pores, so they are 'non-comedogenic'.

Silicones don't stop active ingredients getting into the skin. They themselves will stay on the surface of the skin, but active ingredients within a formulation that contains silicones will find their way downwards into the skin through them. In make-up products, silicones can help kick back the light, to blur the look of wrinkles, which is always helpful for a dull complexion.

The bottom line: there is nothing wrong with silicones. They won't hurt your skin, nor cause spots, nor damage your hair, nor harm the environment, for that matter. But if you find they don't suit you, then of course, look for alternatives.

If you don't like any of the above ingredients, fair enough. It's entirely your choice. I just wanted to point out that they're not quite such bad guys as they are usually made out to be.

15. SUSTAINABILITY MATTERS

In the beauty world, as in other areas of life, sustainability has become a huge issue, and not before time.

Over the past decade, beauty consumers have woken up to the fact that sustainability is a genuine need rather than an add-on choice, and the younger generation is particularly keen on brands that emphasise their sustainability credentials.

And many of us are starting to shop with our consciences. That's certainly how it looks to the skincare-industry bosses.

'We are seeing a real movement, rapidly gathering momentum, where shoppers are no longer prepared to accept products that may have a harmful impact to the environment,' says Victoria Young, general manager for Europe of global skincare brand Yes to Skincare. 'According to Euromonitor, 54 per cent of shoppers think that they can make a difference to the world with their purchases.'

Then there is the issue of sustainability among the residues of personal care products.

'It isn't just about how ingredients are sourced,' adds biochemist Nausheen Qureshi, 'it is how they are washed off in our sinks, not dealt with by waste water treatment plants, and swept into our oceans. They must be sustainable in how they are broken down, too. The formulations themselves must be sustainable.'

If you're concerned about sustainability, keep the following points in mind when evaluating a company or a product:
- How are they minimising their packaging?
- Is the packaging recyclable?
- How are they reducing their carbon footprint?

- How much energy is involved in the manufacture of their products?
- How much water is needed for production?
- Are the formulations sustainable?
- How do the ingredients break down when washed off?
- Do they use plastic? Are those plastics recyclable?
- How much waste do they create?
- Can they trace the origins of their ingredients?
- Are the human rights of their employees protected?
- Are their actions transparent to customers?
- Do they seek to have a 'net positive' effect – putting more back into society, the environment, and the global economy than they take out?

16. OTHER PACKAGING CLAIMS AND WHAT THEY MEAN

In this section, I discuss three other claims you may find on product packaging – that the product calls itself 'anti-ageing', that the product has not been tested on animals, or that it is free from specific ingredients.

Which Products Can Call Themselves 'Anti-Ageing'?

When you see the words 'anti-ageing' on skincare and other beauty products, look further, to see how and why the product claims to work its magic. Some claims are more valid than others.

Most of what we think of as the signs of ageing in the skin – age spots, rough texture, the breakdown of collagen – are due to the damaging effects of ultraviolet light, which add up over time. Sunscreen protects the skin from UV light. So any product containing sunscreen can claim to protect against the signs of ageing. That's a reasonable claim.

With random beauty drinks, the claims are more tenuous. Here's an example. Beauty drink X contains vitamin C. Vitamin C in the diet is proven to contribute to the generation of collagen in the skin (it's a permitted health claim, according to EU regulations). So that beauty drink, which may well be flavoured water with added vitamin C, can say 'proven to maintain the beauty of skin'. But if you look at the small print, the drink contains 40mg of vitamin C, less than the amount you might hope to get from a small glass of orange juice. Pop a standard vitamin-C supplement, and you will get 500mg of the stuff, around half of which will be absorbed by the body (doses of ascorbic 200mg or under are well-absorbed; larger doses much less so). If you take a liposomal form of vitamin C, around 98% of the vitamin C will be absorbed (see the section 'Vitamin C Supplements' on page 165 for more about liposomal vitamin C). Yet we don't tend to call vitamin C supplements 'anti-ageing'.

If you really want to improve your skin by supplementing vitamin C in your diet, I'd suggest you do it with a liposomal vitamin C, rather than a random beauty drink.

Animal Testing: 'Not Tested on Animals'

Pretty much everyone hates the idea of testing cosmetic products on animals. It shouldn't be done, particularly now that there are many other scientifically accepted ways of testing cosmetics for safety and irritancy.

But here's the thing. Animal testing has been banned in the UK since 1997. That's over 20 years. So the fact that 'cruelty free' is often touted as a 'benefit' on many skincare brands really puzzles me. 'We don't test on animals,' says the brand. Great news. Because neither does anyone else who sells products in the UK or the EU – so it's a claim any company in those markets could make.

Yes, there have been loopholes. The 1997 ban was on testing finished cosmetic products, but 2013 saw a European ban on the testing of any individual cosmetic ingredients that were used in products sold in the EU.

But what about China? That is a problem, because China requires all imported cosmetic products to be tested on animals. So companies that sell their products in China currently have to agree to, and pay for, animal testing on any product sold there. However, there is real hope that this is about to change. Last year (2019), the

Chinese government announced its intention to lift the requirement on animal testing for imported cosmetic products in 2020, so we wait to see. Meanwhile, some smaller British manufacturers are involved in a pilot scheme that works around the current animal testing requirements by importing their own ingredients and manufacturing their products locally in China – because domestically produced cosmetics are not required to undergo animal testing.

But it's sad that this is still an issue when there are an increasing number of options for testing products for safety, efficacy, and irritancy without resorting to cruel and outdated animal tests. There are types of lab-produced skin such as Episkin (owned by L'Oréal) and EpiDerm (owned by MatTek), which can be used, and which are available to cosmetics companies worldwide.

(So why does L'Oréal get so much grief from the anti–animal testing brigade? Because it has continued to sell its products in China…)

'Free From'

'Free from' claims are a bit of a minefield. They sound appealing, but they can be manipulative. If a product claims that it is 'free from preservatives', it needs to be able to prove that it doesn't contain any ingredients shown to have a protective effect against micro-organisms. That's fair enough, isn't it?

These claims are fine where they're helping inform decision making, which is one of the common criteria for justification of claims, as laid out in EC Cosmetic Products Regulation. Saying a product is 'free from animal-derived ingredients' helps vegetarians decide whether it is appropriate for them.

The trouble comes if the claims make us, as consumers, feel that products with 'free from' claims are better or safer than ones that don't have these claims – which isn't true, since, as above, all cosmetic products have to be safe for use, by law.

Then there's the aspect of fairness, another of those common criteria. 'Free from' shouldn't be used to imply a denigrating message, based on a negative perception about a group of ingredients which are judged safe by that same Cosmetic Products Regulation. Is it fair to say 'free from' about parabens, for example, when this denigrates the entire group of parabens?

Nor should 'free from' be used in a dishonest way, by referring to ingredients that aren't typically used in a particular type of product. You wouldn't find 'free from preservatives' found on a bottle of fragrance, just because the product contains so much alcohol that it doesn't need any other preservatives. You can read more about this issue on the website of the Cosmetics Toiletry and Perfumery Association, www.ctpa.org.uk. Meanwhile, when you see a product that claims to be 'free from' something, take a closer look to decide whether it's a helpful claim or a manipulative one.

17. KNOW YOUR SKIN TYPE

One of the first questions that anyone selling you skincare will ask is, 'What's your skin type?' And the options for describing our skin are usually laid out as Dry, Normal, Oily, or Combination. Which is useful up to a point, but these really only address skin oiliness or otherwise.

What else could we add in? Let's start with these options:

- **Dehydrated.** Your skin looks and feels dry, however much product you pile on.
- **Reactive/sensitive.** Your skin is likely to kick off, with no warning, if you use products it doesn't like.
- **Stressed.** Your skin is dull, prone to flushing.
- **Acne-prone.** Your skin may break out in spots when you use the wrong products.
- **Fatigued.** Your skin is dull and lacking radiance. It looks like it needs a holiday.
- **Erratic.** Your skin is fine some days, but not others.
- **Balanced.** (You lucky person… you lucky, lucky person!)

Not sure about your skin type? It's straightforward to assess how oily your skin is. Cleanse your skin, and then leave it alone for an hour; then press pieces of thin tissue (a normal tissue pulled in half) to your face and see if the tissue picks up any oil. If the tissue comes away with any oily patches on your forehead, nose and chin, then you have combination skin. If there's oil all over, then clearly your complexion is oily. If there's no oil, it's on the normal-to-dry end of the scale (normal, if your skin feels just fine without moisturiser; dry if it feels a bit tight or rough).

Talking of normal, relatively few of us have 'normal' skin. Perhaps 'well-balanced' skin is what we should be aiming at. Experts say that around 70 per cent of us have combination skin. That's not just a marketing conceit, designed to get us to buy more stuff, but a reflection of the fact that there are more oil glands on the forehead, nose, and chin than there are on the cheeks or the neck. It's also worth knowing that just because your skin is oily, or sensitive, at the moment, it doesn't mean you're stuck like that for life. Your skin may have a tendency to be like that, but using the right products will help steer it back into a better balance.

18. UNDERSTAND AND USE THE INCI LIST

How do you know what's in a product? You read the small print on the back, which tells you all the ingredients.

The list of all the ingredients that a cosmetic product contains is known as the INCI list, which stands for International Nomenclature for Cosmetic Ingredients. It's the one printed in such small letters that I've got into the habit of keeping a magnifying glass beside the bathroom sink as well as on my desk.

What the INCI List Will Tell You

The INCI list shows the ingredients in the formula, using the names that are internationally recognised by the scientific community. Ingredients are listed by weight, starting with the largest, in descending order, until you get down to one per cent, after which the remaining ingredients can be listed in any order.

How do you know when you're getting to the less-than-one-per-cent tail end? Scan the list for an ingredient called phenoxyethanol, which is a common and widely used preservative. This can by law only be used at a maximum of 1% in cosmetic formulations. So anything that is listed after phenoxyethanol is only present in tiny quantities.

If a key ingredient in a product is present at less than one per cent – is that a problem? You might expect if an ingredient is being talked about as being vital to the effectiveness of the product, that there would be more that one per cent of it in the formula. But it depends on the ingredient. Hyaluronic acid, for example, is always present in serums at less than 1%, because that is the optimal amount.

If you are allergic to specific ingredients, scan the INCI list for them. Ingredients known to be allergens have to be listed, by law.

What the INCI List Won't Tell You

The INCI list tells you which ingredients a product contains, but it won't tell you the following:

- **How the ingredients were sourced.** The INCI list doesn't give an ingredient's source – for example, whether it is derived from plants, derived from animals, or made in a lab.
- **The quality of the ingredients.** As with most substances, you can get cheap versions of cosmetic ingredients as well as expensive, carefully sourced ones.
- **Exactly which fragrance ingredients are in there.** Manufacturers are allowed to list all the fragrance ingredients as 'parfum' (although, as above, potential allergens will be listed). If you're sensitive to some fragrance ingredients, or to fragrance in general – and fragrance is the ingredient most likely to set off skin sensitivities and allergies – you'll want to keep an eye out for that.

> To find out more about an ingredient, look it up in the EU Cosmetic Ingredients Database (ec.europa.eu/growth/sectors/cosmetics/cosing_nn).

PART TWO

THE SEVEN RULES OF SKINCARE

Seven rules sounds awfully formulaic. And rigid. I don't mean it to come across like that. These steps are the building blocks of caring for your skin, and I'm listing out all of them to give you a picture of what full-spectrum skincare can look like.

Do you have to do all this? Of course not. Or not all at once. But you need to know why each of the steps is important, and which are non-negotiable and which are optional, then you can make your own decisions about what will suit you, and the type of products to use.

What are my skincare seven?

- **Rule One: Cleanse (and Tone).** Keep your skin clean.
- **Rule Two: Exfoliate.** Clear the surface of debris.
- **Rule Three: Treat.** Use treatment products to address what's bothering you.
- **Rule Four: Moisturise.** Hydrate, for better skin health
- **Rule Five: Protect.** Keep ultraviolet light and environmental damage at bay.
- **Rule Six: Support.** Improve your lifestyle to benefit your skin.
- **Rule Seven: Indulge.** Pamper your skin to enhance it further.

PRODUCT SUGGESTIONS

Wherever I've mentioned products to try, I've suggested several different ones, at varying price points. Some of the products are from widely available brands that you may be familiar with already; others are from specialist brands, which you may not know.

I was going to call this second bunch 'cosmeceutical' brands, though that word isn't ideal. Why not? The word is a mashup of 'cosmetic' and 'pharmaceutical', and there is no specific definition of what a 'cosmeceutical' skincare product is. Brands in this area focus on creating effective skincare using well-tested ingredients; they tend to sell through skin-care clinics rather than through high-street retail outlets, and rarely market themselves directly to the public, which is why you may not have heard of them. Most of these brands can be bought online, but some can only be bought after consultation with a skincare advisor.

I don't want to call the two groups 'normal' and 'cosmeceutical', as that implies that the 'normal' lot aren't great products, which they most certainly are. So I've ended up separating them into 'well-known brands' and 'specialist brands'.

So for most product types, you'll find two lists: first, a list of products from well-known brands; and second, a list of products from specialist brands. Each list is sorted by price, so the least expensive item appears first.

RULE ONE: CLEANSE YOUR SKIN

Cleansing is the starting point of skincare. Whatever else you are planning on doing with your face – whether you are getting ready for the day, putting on makeup, lining up an evening of at-home pampering, or winding down for the night – you need to get your face clean before you start.

There are many different ways to cleanse, and many different products to do it with. But before I get onto that, here are a few whys and wherefores.

Why Bother with Cleansing When My Face Doesn't Look Dirty?

I hate to say it, but it's probably dirtier than it looks. Sweat, dirt, bacteria, and sebum (the natural oil produced by the sebaceous glands in the skin) build up on your face during the day; if you live in a city, your face will be picking up particles of pollution, too. And that's without make-up.

So, getting your face properly clean, every day, is the corner-stone of good skincare and will help your skin look better. Apart from basic hygiene, regular cleansing helps skin function properly, doing its job of facing the world and protecting what's underneath.

You can wash, you can use oil and a flannel, you can use a fashionable cleansing balm and a muslin cloth, you can use lotion and cotton wool, you can use the latest micellar cleansing water – as long as you do it.

What Cleansing Does

When cleansing your face, you're trying to remove whatever has built up on it during the course of the day, or overnight. Even if your face doesn't seem dirty, it still needs cleansing. Besides, if you have invested in special skincare products, stop and think. You wouldn't dream of putting those onto dirty skin, would you? They don't work by magic – they need to be absorbed into the skin – and that won't happen if you simply plonk them on top of a cocktail of old skin oil and general dirt. Clean your skin carefully, and any products you use will stand a better chance of being properly absorbed and of doing their job.

Don't Over-Cleanse

What you're aiming at is for your skin to be clean but not overclean, if that makes sense. You don't want to try to get your skin 'squeaky-clean'. That might sound like a good idea, and it's great if you're trying to strip dirt from a car windshield, but much as we dislike the idea of having a face that is in any way oily, the sebum that our skin secretes is its natural moisturiser.

If you wash your face until it feels squeaky-clean, it does more harm than good, because it upsets the skin barrier. Why? Because skin that has had every scrap of oil removed from it will try to rebalance itself by producing more oil to get things back to normal. If your skin is oily, the last thing you want is more oil. If your skin is dry, and not good at producing enough sebum in the first place, it won't manage to compensate for over-cleansing and will become even drier. So don't overdo the cleansing.

When to Cleanse Your Skin

Cleanse your skin morning and evening. If you cleanse thoroughly in the evening, you might be tempted to get away with a quick splash of water in the morning. But stop for a moment to think how you have been lying in bed for many hours, during which time your body has sweated out around a pint of water, and the oil glands on your face have been producing oil on your nose, chin, and forehead. Given this, you can see the sense in using your cleansing products before you jump in the shower.

One suggestion about evening cleansing. Don't wait until bedtime, by which time you're wishing you were already in bed and can barely be bothered. Cleanse your face when you get back home from work; or, if you are at home all day, use cleansing your face as a way to mark the transition between daytime and the evening. Get it done then, before you run out of energy or collapse in front of the television.

What to Use for Cleansing Your Skin

Use whatever you like – or whatever you like most, because if you like it, the chances are that you will go on using it. In this section, I'll tell you about the different types of cleansers that you could use, their pros and cons, and which types of skin they suit best.

OIL AND OIL-BASED CLEANSERS

GOOD FOR: DRY SKIN, MATURE SKIN

Despite a growing trend for oily cleansers, most of us are still reluctant to put oils onto our skin. 'Who wants oily skin?' is the first thought that goes through our heads when the word *oil* is mentioned. Yet oils make brilliant cleansers and also remove make-up, sunscreen, and waterproof mascara effectively.

Oils work by loosening and lifting away dirt and make-up from the skin surface. Oils bind to the skin's natural oils, so they can lift away excess oil without scouring off every last bit – and by leaving a fine protective layer on the skin, they help skin to stay moisturised. Massage them into your skin, emulsify them by adding some water, then continue adding water to rinse them away.

I've said above that cleansing oils are great for drier, or older skin, but really they are good for most skin types. If you have oily skin, you may instinctively shy away from cleansing oils, but they won't make your skin oilier.

'Emulsify' means to mix together two ingredients that wouldn't usually combine, like oil and water. In skincare products, this is done by including ingredients called emulsifiers in the formulations. Cleansing oils contain emulsifiers so that when they are mixed with water, they turn into a milky liquid – an emulsion – which is easy to rinse or wipe away. That's why a cleansing oil comes cleanly off your face, whereas if you rub, say, olive oil over your face, plain water won't remove it.

I prefer to follow an oil or an oil-based cleanser with a wash-off cleanser to remove that fine protective layer. I do this because I'm always using 'active' skincare products, and I don't want a layer of oil getting in the way of their absorption. But you might prefer to leave that tiny smidge of residue alone.

Here are three of my favourite oil and oil-based cleansers from well-known brands:

- **Simple Cleansing Oil**, £6.99, boots.com. Good and straightforward, does the job.
- **DHC Deep Cleansing Oil**, £12.50, dhcuk.co.uk. Terrific cleansing oil which I particularly like because it rinses off so cleanly.
- **Votary Rose Geranium and Apricot Cleansing Oil**, £45, votary.co.uk. The classic cleanser from this much-loved brand.

Here are three of my favourite oil and oil-based cleansers from specialist brands:

- **Skincity Pre-Cleansing Oil Stick**, £8, skincity.co.uk. Super-handy little stick of solid oil which melts as you wipe it over the face. Massage it in to lift dirt and make-up off the skin, then add water to emulsify the whole mixture and rinse it away. If you're double-cleansing, follow with something that reaches deeper into the skin.

- **Paula's Choice Perfect Cleansing Oil**, £22, paulaschoice.co.uk. Another conditioning, oil-based cleanser that will shift sunscreen, makeup, and everyday grime, and which can be used as a pre-cleanse or a full cleanse, as you prefer.

- **Medik8 Lipid Balance Cleansing Oil**, £27, thetweakmentsguide.com. Massage this into your skin and it will remove everything, including waterproof mascara, and rinse cleanly away without upsetting or drying out your skin. Good for all skin types, even oily skin, as oil is good at removing excess oil from the skin.

BALMS

GOOD FOR: DRY SKIN, MATURE SKIN, DELICATE SKIN

Balms are like solid oils. Massaging them into the skin loosens up the dirt and debris on the skin, and adding water turns them into a milky liquid which can be rinsed away, or removed with a cloth – a muslin or a flannel – that has been dipped in water and wrung out.

As with cleansing oils, I prefer to follow heavier balm cleansers with a cleanser that will remove the oily residue.

These are my favourite balms:

- **Body Shop Camomile Sumptuous Cleansing Butter**, £11, thebodyshop.com/en-gb/. Thick and smooth, but easy enough to massage in, and comes off cleanly with a flannel.

- **Caroline Hirons Pixi Double Cleanse**, £24,
  pixibeauty.co.uk. The single tub contains a solid cleansing oil
  on one side (which melts on the skin, to dissolve makeup, oil,
  sunscreen, etc). Clean this off – Caroline, the skincare guru
  who created this product with Pixi, would like you to use a
  wrung-out flannel – and then go again with the cream
  cleanser on the other side of the tub to complete your double-
  cleanse.

- **Elemis Pro-Collagen Cleansing Balm**, £44, elemis.com.
  Fabulous thick, oily balm which melts as you massage it into
  the skin and removes everything in its path. I usually prefer
  fragrance-free products, but this smells so wonderful I'd buy it
  for the citrus-and-eucalyptus smell alone.

I don't have any recommendations for cleansing balms from
specialist brands

CREAM CLEANSERS AND HOT CLOTH CLEANSERS

GOOD FOR: MOST SKIN TYPES, ESPECIALLY DRY, SENSITIVE, OR MATURE SKIN

Classic cream cleansers work for any skin type, and are kind to
drier and older skins. They're less oily than balms, but work in a
similar way. You work them into dry or damp skin and massage so
that they lift away make-up and grime, then wipe them away with
a wrung-out flannel. You could rinse them off, but a cloth is more
thorough and gives a light exfoliation at the same time.

These are three of my favourite cream cleansers and hot cloth
cleansers from well-known brands:

- **The Ordinary Squalane Cleanser**, £5.50,
  theordinary.deciem.com. A thick balmy cream that is both
  gentle and effective at removing dirt and make-up without
  stripping the skin. What's not to like?

- **Liz Earle Cleanse & Polish Hot Cloth Cleanser**, £17, uk.lizearle.com. A classic of a cleansing cream which you massage on, then wipe off with a muslin or flannel that you have dunked in hot water and squeezed out. This perennial favourite suits oily skins as well as dry ones and has spawned dozens of imitators. The flannel, I hope I hardly need to add, needs to go into a hot wash after a couple of uses, so you will need a stack of them.

- **Aurelia Miracle Cleanser**, £42, aureliaskincare.com. Not a miracle, but a really lovely and hard-working cleanser, with an aromatic fragrance of chamomile and eucalyptus and added probiotics which just about justifies its price-tag.

These are two of my favourite creamy cleansers from specialist brands:

- **Medik8 Cream Cleanse**, £18, medik8.com. Lovely. Gentle. Creamy. Not fragrance free, but it feels sumptuous and does a great job.

- **Priori Gentle Cleanser LCA FX110**, £29, thetweakmentsguide.com. A light, balm-type cleanser which is thorough yet gentle on the skin barrier. The 'LCA' complex adds extra moisturisation.

EXTRA-GENTLE CLEANSERS

GOOD FOR: VERY SENSITIVE SKIN AND REACTIVE SKIN

If your skin is feeling sensitive and irritable, these cleansers will treat it very gently. If you've reached the point where even water is making your skin react, one of them can just be wiped away, without rinsing.

These are three of my favourite super-gentle cleansers from well-known brands:

- **CeraVe Hydrating Cleanser**, £9.50, boots.com. This rinse-off cleanser will gently remove make-up, oil, and grime without disrupting the skin barrier or irritating the skin.

- **Avene Extremely Gentle Cleansing Lotion**, £9.50, boots.com. If your skin is feeling so sensitive that even water will stress it out, this is a super-gentle lotion which can be patted over the skin then wiped off without rinsing.

- **La Roche-Posay Toleriane Dermo Cleanser Sensitive Skin**, £12.50, boots.com. A lovely gentle cleanser that won't aggravate reactive, sensitive skin.

These are two of my favourite super-gentle cleansers from specialist brands:

- **Paula's Choice Calm Nourishing Cream Cleanser**, £20, paulaschoice.co.uk. Milky and soothing, this is good for any stressed, sensitive skin.

- **Priori Gentle Cleanser LCA FX110**, £29, thetweakmentsguide.com. A light, balm-type cleanser which is thorough yet gentle on the skin barrier. The 'LCA' complex adds extra moisturisation.

RINSE-OFF FACIAL CLEANSERS

GOOD FOR: CLEANSING IN THE SHOWER

If you prefer to wash rather than wipe off your cleanser, here are some suggestions of cleaners with different textures for doing just that. And if you're using them in the shower, keep the temperature down, as hot water stresses and dries out the skin.

Here are three of my favourite rinse-off cleansers from well-known brands:

- **Caudalie Vinopure Purifying Gel Cleanser**, £16, uk.caudalie.com. A lightweight gel cleanser that's good for oilier skin as it has a touch of natural salicylic acid in it.

- **Dr Sam's Flawless Cleanser**, £16, drsambunting.com. This 'jelly'-type cleanser suits all skin types yet is thorough enough to shift make-up.

- **Lixir Electrogel Cleanser**, £25, cultbeauty.co.uk. A luxurious-feeling cream containing an 'electrogel' ingredient with a negative electrical charge. Why? Because this means it can latch on to positively charged particles such as pollution, free radicals, and heavy metals, and whisk them away.

These are two of my favourite rinseable cleansers from specialist brands:

- **Medik8 Cream Cleanse**, £18, medik8.com. Lovely. Gentle. Creamy. Not fragrance free, but it feels sumptuous and does a great job.

- **Priori Gentle Cleanser LCA FX110**, £29, thetweakmentsguide.com. A light, balm-type cleanser which is thorough yet gentle on the skin barrier. The 'LCA' complex adds extra moisturisation.

FACIAL WASHES WITH ADDED ACIDS

GOOD FOR: OILY SKIN, CONGESTED SKIN, OR DULL SKIN THAT NEEDS GENTLE EXFOLIATION

Alpha Hydroxy Acids (AHAs) such as glycolic acid or the gentler lactic and mandelic acids exfoliate the skin by dissolving the bonds that tether old, dead skin cells to the surface, so they provide a chemical form of exfoliation. So does the Beta Hydroxy Acid, salicylic acid. Why use an acid-infused facial wash, when you could use a leave-on acid toner to exfoliate your skin more effectively? Because you might not want to use an acid toner every day, and a wash-off cleanser delivers a small but useful dose of exfoliation.

These are three of my favourite acid-based facial washes from well-known brands:

- **CeraVe SA Smoothing Cleanser,** £12, boots.com. Great, straightforward cleanser with salicylic acid to help decongest oily skin.

- **Vichy Normaderm Phytosolution Purifying Cleansing Gel,** £13, vichy.co.uk. Added actives in this wash-off gel include salicylic acid and zinc gluconate, to help normalise oily skin.

- **Kate Somerville ExfoliKate Cleanser Foaming Daily Wash,** £16, katesomerville.co.uk. With glycolic and lactic acids, this cleanser manages to shift make-up and excess oil without overly drying the skin.

These are three of my favourite acid-based facial washes from specialist brands:

- **Medik8 Surface Radiance Cleanse,** £18, medik8.com. This product used to be called PoreCleanse gel, because that's what its combination of salicylic, lactic, and mandelic acids is particularly good for. But this product is not just about deep-cleansing and exfoliating; it also contains glycerin to condition the skin.

- **NeoStrata Foaming Glycolic Wash,** £27.50, thetweakmentsguide.com. A foaming face wash with 18% glycolic acid sounds terrifying, but this is fantastic. It's carefully formulated, a delight to use, and works a treat.

- **Dr Levy 3 Deep Cell Renewal Micro-Resurfacing Cleanser**, £39, cultbeauty.co.uk. This isn't just a cleanser with glycolic acid. If you leave it on for five minutes, like a mask, it gives a deeper glycolic exfoliation. This cleanser also contains smooth rice microbeads that help polish your skin as you massage it in and then rinse it off.

MICELLAR WATER

GOOD FOR: A QUICK CLEANSE, OR REMOVING MAKE-UP

Micellar waters have become hugely popular as quick cleansers in the past decade. How do they work? The liquid contains 'micelles', which are composed of a bunch of molecules with hydrophilic (water-loving) heads and hydrophobic (water-hating) tails. Stick with me on this. So these micelles float in a watery solution, with their water-loving heads on the outside and their oil-loving, water-hating tails tucked inside. When you rub them on the skin, the micelles break apart, and the oil-compatible tails grab onto the oil and dirt on your skin, and lift them away. So wiping your face over with a micellar water on cotton wool will definitely cleanse it.

Micellar waters look like an easy cleansing hack – and they are. But they leave a layer of surfactants – detergent-based cleansing ingredients which may be irritating to the skin – on the surface. Most of these surfactants are mild enough to be tolerated, but if your skin is irritable or sensitive, it makes sense to rinse them away with water. Just in case.

These are two of my favourite micellar waters from well-known brands:

- **Bioderma Sensibio H20 Micellar Water**, £10.80, boots.com. A classic, bestselling micellar water which will show you why this type of product is so popular. It clears off make-up and grime, and leaves skin feeling instantly more comfortable.

- **La Roche-Posay Make-Up Remover Micellar Water Gel**, £13, laroche-posay.co.uk. If you dislike the idea of leaving the residue of micellar water on your skin, here's a gel that works on the same principles, but which you rinse off.

I don't have any recommendations for micellar waters from specialist brands.

FACE WIPES

I know wipes are hugely popular, but here's the thing: *Face wipes are not proper cleansing*. To be sure, face wipes are fine if you're stuck in a field camping; any other time, they are better than nothing but they are a last resort. Rather than really get rid of the dirt, face wipes shift it around the surface of your skin.

Wipes are also an environmental menace because most aren't biodegradable. So no, I'm not recommending any. If you must use wipes, look for some that are biodegradable, and be thoughtful as to how you dispose of them. And rinse your face afterwards, if you have the chance.

THE MAGIC CLEANSING CLOTH

Magic cleansing cloths sound too good to be true. These cloths are made from a special type of microfibre and usually have one slightly fluffy side and one super-smooth side. All you do is wet them, then work them gently over your face to remove everything on it, up to and including a full face of make-up.

Do these cloths work? Yes, absolutely; and like the microfibre cloths you might use for eco-friendly household cleaning, all you have to do is chuck them in the washing machine, and they come up smiling. Are they a good way to clean your face? Yes, not bad at all. Though I'd still like to follow them with a dose of cleansing cream, or a glycolic cleanser, just for the sake of it.

> Can you just use household-cleaning microfibre cloths instead? I wouldn't, because they're not so smooth and not so gentle on your face.

Here are two cleansing cloths which I love:

- **Face Halo,** £7 each at boots.com or about £18 for 3 at amazon.co.uk. Dampen these excellent little towelling-type cleansing pads, and they'll take off all make-up that comes their way. They get filthy, but wash off well with soap and water. You might want to invest in the three-pack from Amazon, because they need regular visits to the washing machine for a deep cleanse.

- **The Make-up Eraser Cloth,** £17, makeuperaser.co.uk. This works just like a microfibre cleaning cloth – well, it *is* a type of microfibre cleaning cloth – to remove all make-up and dirt from your face using nothing more than water. It works a treat, and just needs regular inclusion in a hot wash to keep it fresh.

SOAP

I wouldn't use soap – not normal soap, nor black soap, nor silver soap. All soap tends to strip oil from the skin, upset the skin barrier, and leave it feeling dry and tight. African black soap, which is handmade and includes a good deal of ash (which gives the soap its colour), is abrasive as well as drying. Silver soap contains a compound of silver and silica – derived from sand – and claims to 'suffocate' bacteria on the skin. It's still drying. Please. There are so many other products you could choose. Just get a cleanser that's specifically designed to be used on your face.

HOW TO USE YOUR CHOSEN CLEANSER

Once you've chosen your cleanser, use it like this:

- Massage it gently but firmly into your skin with small circular motions (for a description of a brief face massage, see the section 'Add Face Massage' on page 50). Remove with a flannel squeezed out in warm water, or rinse off, as you prefer.

- Ideally, do this morning and evening. But if you're only going to do it once, or your skin is super-sensitive, then do it in the evening.

- Use it every day.

Having said all that, of course the world won't come to an end if you slip up and tumble into bed without taking off your make-up one night. Some very well-known dermatologists, who you would expect to be sticklers for scrupulous skincare, admit to doing just that, though they usually excuse themselves by saying that they were wearing mineral make-up, which is actively good for the skin, so it doesn't matter. But leaving your make-up on overnight is not a good habit to get into. Not least because it will quickly ruin all your pillowcases…

HOW TO MAKE CLEANSING EVEN MORE EFFECTIVE

With skincare, as in so much else in life, it's not just a question of what you use as how you use it. Yes, there are ways of making the products you are using work harder. Here are some things you could try.

Add Face Massage

Adding face massage gives time for the cleanser to bind with whatever it is removing from your skin. Massage also improves circulation in the tiny blood vessels in the skin and improves lymph drainage, which is taking away cell debris and reduces puffiness in the face. We all hold tension in our faces, and gentle, persistent massage knocks that tension right out of the muscles, which makes the massage a soothing and effective treat.

HOW TO DO AN EASY FACE MASSAGE

Here's how to do an easy face massage:

- Apply your chosen cleanser liberally. You want something with a bit of 'slip' to it, so I find a balm, an oil, a melting gel or a thick cream is best. Work the cleanser into the skin using small circular motions.

- Start in the middle of your forehead and work outwards above your eyebrows, using the pads of your fingers.

- Start again at your nose, working outwards across your cheeks and circling gently around your eyes.

- Start again at your chin, and work outwards across your lower cheeks, pinching along your jawline.

Massage your neck, too:

- Sweep cleanser gently along the sides of your neck and under the chin.

- Sweep the backs of your fingers out along your jawline from your chin to your ears.

- Flip your palms down so that you have your index finger in front of your ear and your middle finger behind your ear.

- Swoop your hand, with straight fingers, down and up behind your ear.

- Sweep each hand down the sides of your neck to your collar bones.

As I mentioned above, doing this not only works the cleanser into your skin, dislodging dirt, sweat, bacteria, sunscreen and makeup, but improves the circulation in the skin, knocks tension out of all the little muscles in the face, and boosts lymphatic drainage, too, so it helps stop the face from looking puffy. It only takes a minute.

Try Double-Cleansing

Double-cleansing is what they do in salons. It's all the rage with skincare specialists. What it comes down to is being extra thorough, and cleansing twice.

Here are five ideas for double-cleansing:

- Use the same product for both cleanses, in the way that you would shampoo twice to get your hair properly clean. The first one removes the surface grime, the second one gets deeper into the skin.

> Don't do two applications of foaming cleanser – that will leave even an oily skin too dry for comfort.

- Use a balm to get rid of makeup, then a wash-off gel cleanser to remove any oil residue.
- Use a cleansing oil to pull away surface grime, then massage in a cleansing cream and take it off with a damp flannel or muslin.
- Use a micellar water to shift the most obvious dirt and make-up, then use a wash-off cream cleanser to go that bit deeper.
- Use a microfibre cleansing cloth and follow with a cleansing cream or a glycolic wash-off cleanser.

Use a Cleansing Brush

One of the big beauty hits of the past 10 years has been cleansing brushes.

If you are using skincare products with active ingredients such as vitamin C, retinol or other retinoids, or alpha hydroxy acids, they will all work that much better if they can actually get into your skin. A lot depends on the formulation of the products, but it also helps if their path is not impeded by the sort of everyday accumulation of dead cells that sit on the surface of our skin, cluttering up the complexion.

You don't have to exfoliate like a maniac to get rid of these dead cells, just do a slightly deeper cleanse than usual, and a powered brush can be helpful for that. The best-known cleansing brush has been the Clarisonic, which used a 'sonic' action to bounce dirt out of the pores. I'm using the past tense because, as this book went to print, most of the brand's products have been discontinued, but the Mia Prima brush (£89 at currentbody.com) and the Mia Smart brush (£185, thetweakmentsguide.com) are still available. They're thorough but quite strong, so I'd advise using them just once or twice a week.

I prefer the vibrating Foreo Luna Mini 2 brush (£99, thetweakmentsguide.com), which has soft silicone 'bristles' that don't harbour bacteria and never wear out. It buzzes its way through a 'sonic' cleaning routine with any cleanser you like, and removes make-up, dirt, oil, etc effectively and with absolutely minimal irritation. Each recharge of the device seems to last for weeks, too.

If you like the idea of an exfoliating beauty brush but don't want to invest that sort of money in it, there are others which are less sophisticated and less expensive but will still give your face an enhanced cleanse.

- **No7 Radiant Results Revitalising Sonic Action Cleansing Brush**, £30, boots.com. A battery-powered brush which is not that sturdy, but it makes a decent job of deep-cleansing the skin.

- **Nurse Jamie Exfoliband Silicone Loofah**, £14, cultbeauty.co.uk. This looks like a slice of purple honeycomb; it's made from flexible silicone and, used to massage your cleanser around your face, will shift dead skin cells for a smoother finish.

Whichever brush you choose, they will all help to leave your skin cleaner, and make the products you use work harder. Which makes sense if you are spending money on serums of the sort you'll find further on in this section.

Use an Exfoliating Cleanser

Use a cleanser that includes glycolic acid (see the section 'Facial Washes' on page 46 for some of my favourites), which deep-cleanses the pores and exfoliates the skin, leaving the skin clearer and more receptive to what you put on it.

A FEW WORDS ABOUT TONER

If you've taken any interest in looking after your skin, I'm sure you'll have heard the decades-old mantra that any skincare regime should consist of three steps: 'cleanse, tone, moisturise'.

Toning sounds good, as if it were 'toning' up the skin. But all that most toners are doing, once you have soaked a cotton-wool pad with the stuff, is wiping off any extra bits of cleanser that you haven't already removed from your face.

Old-style 'clarifying' toners often contained alcohol which removed any scrap of grease and dirt from the skin even more dramatically than a foaming face-wash. These toners were harsh and dried the skin out, so they did more harm than good.

You won't find many alcohol-based toners these days, and I have tended to ignore toners on the grounds that they are a waste of time (although, if you feel your routine isn't complete without toner, you do what feels right).

That said, two new categories of product have emerged in the past few years which you could call 'toners with benefits'. Read on to learn about these.

Toners with Benefits

These new 'toners with benefits' are toners with added extras such as exfoliating acids – or hydrating, antioxidant, or anti-bacterial ingredients – and essences, all of which are designed to be used after cleansing. They are worth a try if you are curious about them. What is different about these products is that they deliver positive benefits to the skin rather drying it out.

Acid Toners

Acid toners contain a dose of skin-boosting acids, which help the skin to be better hydrated, more radiant, or more even in tone. The acid is usually an alpha hydroxy acid, such as lactic acid, malic acid, or glycolic acid.

The acid in the toner dissolves the bonds that hold old, dead skin cells onto the skin's surface. This means they gently exfoliate the outer layer of the skin, which makes the skin look smoother and more radiant. Lactic acid and malic acid have larger molecules, so they are gentler; glycolic molecules are smaller, so will wiggle more deeply into the skin and give a more noticeable effect. With regular use, acid toners will brighten the skin, improve hydration, and tone down pigmentation.

To use an acid toner, apply it to cotton wool and wipe over your face after cleansing. Start by using the product a couple of times a week.

These are my favourite acid toners from widely available brands:

- **Nip+Fab Salicylic Acid Tonic**, £14.95, nipandfab.com. Salicylic acid, the beta hydroxy acid, can work its way into blocked pores and help clear them out, so this is a good choice for spot-prone skin.

- **Pixi Glow Tonic**, £18, pixibeauty.co.uk. With a decent (5%) dose of glycolic acid, a quick wipe-over with this will help to gently exfoliate the skin and improve its ability to hold moisture, too.

These are my favourite acid toners from specialist brands:

- **Paula's Choice Skin Perfecting 2% BHA Liquid Exfoliant**, £28, thetweakmentsguide.com. BHA stands for beta hydroxy acid, ie salicylic acid (it's the only BHA there is). Why I love this product is that it will deliver not just a surface exfoliation of the skin, but will delve deep into pores that are threatening to block up and clear them out, as BHA can dissolve the oil that is blocking said pores. It's anti-inflammatory, too. If you think it 2% might be too strong for your skin, there's a 1% version of the same product that you could start with, at paulaschoice.co.uk.

- **Alpha H Clear Skin Tonic**, £34, thetweakmentsguide.com. Another terrific exfoliating skin tonic with 2% BHA – ie salicylic acid – which is great for congested skin. Like alpha hydroxy acids, BHA has a hydrating effect on the skin, and this product has botanical extracts – chamomile, arnica, thyme, and cucumber – which help enhance the anti-inflammatory effects of salicylic acid.

- **SkinCeuticals Blemish + Age Toner**, £36, skinceuticals.co.uk. With three exfoliating acids (glycolic, salicylic, and LHA – Beta Lipohydroxy Acid, a variant of beta hydroxy acid), this will effectively exfoliate, purge pores, and calm inflammation in the skin.

Hydrating, Antioxidant, and Antibacterial Toners

Toners can deliver many benefits, from hydrating the skin to quelling bacteria. This list could run on, but I've kept it short just to give you an idea of the variety of products you could find.

Here are my favourite toners from widely available brands:

- **Avene Gentle Toner**, £11.50, boots.com. It's gentle, it's hydrating, and it's enhanced with antioxidants to help ward off environmental damage, and anti-inflammatory ingredients, plus natural silica which helps to strengthen the skin barrier.

- **Gallinee Face Vinegar**, £23, gallinee.com. 'Vinegar' might sound a bit sharp for the face, but this is a soothing toner. It includes a prebiotic ingredient to support the 'good' bacteria on your skin.

- **By Terry Hydra-Toner**, £42, cultbeauty.co.uk. Lovely, sophisticated toner with an organic hydrating complex which delivers extra moisture to the skin while leaving the skin feeling lovely and fresh.

Here are two favourite toners from specialist brands:

- **Clinisept**, £15, thetweakmentsguide.com. This isn't really a toner, but it's an extraordinary product, so it's a great one to know. It's a spray of hypochlorous solution which is antibacterial, anti-microbial, and anti-viral, and gentle on the skin. It's massively helpful for acne sufferers (and good for skin that has had acne). Spritz it onto the skin after cleansing, leave it for 15 seconds to do its work, then carry on with the rest of your skincare, and see what it can do for you.

- **Medik8 Daily Refresh Balancing Toner**, £15, medik8.com. Hydrating, anti-inflammatory and soothing, with glycerin, niacinamide, and allantoin, to get your skincare routine off to a good start.

Essences

You'd be forgiven for mistaking essences – which are watery in texture and come in large bottles – for toners, but they are different creatures with a different purpose.

Essences work by delivering extras into the skin before you move on with the rest of your skincare routine. They tend to have ingredients with a low molecular weight, ie small molecules, so they sink right into the skin – so you could think of them as a pre-serum serum. Cynical Brits might once have sniffed at these (one more step to add to our skincare? Puh-leese!), but now that we've seen how popular these are in Asia, we've taken to them in a big way.

If you're going for the fullest possible version of a skincare routine, you should use essences after a toner, and before a serum. I tend to think that life is too short for all this, and if I use an essence, it will be instead of a toner. You might feel differently.

To use an essence, rather than putting it onto a cotton pad (you lose so much into the pad), spray it into the palm of your hand, pat your palms together, then press the essence into your face.

These are three of my favourite essences from widely available brands:

- **Caudalie Vinoperfect Concentrated Brightening Essence**, £30, uk.caudalie.com. This is one for oilier skins, as it contains glycolic acid along with Caudalie's signature antioxidants from grape seeds, to give skin a light exfoliation; an exfoliating essence, if you like.

- **Allies of Skin Molecular Saviour Probiotics Repair Mist**, £57, cultbeauty.co.uk. This clever brand tends to pack a bunch of benefits into each product. This product has anti-bacterial colloidal silver, skin-boosting probiotics, and moisture-attracting ingredients, too.

- **Laura Mercier Pure Canvas Power Primer Super-charged Essence**, £46, cultbeauty.co.uk. A primer-essence? Well, it's half-way to being make-up. It's soothing, and has skin-supporting peptides plus light-reflecting pearl extracts, which means it gives your skin a fabulous light sheen.

These are two of my favourite essences from specialist brands:

- **Paula's Choice Resist Anti-Aging Brightening Essence**, £41, paulaschoice.co.uk. This is a radiance-booster, with skin-lightening arbutin, hyaluronic acid for hydration, and vitamin C for environmental defence.

- **Exuviance Probiotic Lysate Anti-Pollution Essence**, £54, dermacaredirect.co.uk. A powerful brew, this contains a 10% concentration of probiotics, along with exfoliating polyhydroxy acids, including gluconolactone, and hydrating hyaluronic acid. A treatment in its own right.

The Bottom Line: Cleansing and Toning Your Skin

You need to cleanse your face at least once a day. Use whatever products you like, just do it, and your skin will thank you for it. Adding a toner or essence with skin-enhancing benefits is up to you.

Don't know where to start? Try The Ordinary Squalane Cleanser that I mentioned in the section 'Cream Cleansers and Hot Cloth Cleansers' on page 43. It suits all types of skin, does a great job and is an absolute bargain, too.

RULE TWO: EXFOLIATE YOUR SKIN

After cleansing your skin, what next? Before moving on to using skincare treatment products, there is an intermediate step you should know about: exfoliating your skin. It's not something that you should do every day; but done carefully, it will make an instant improvement to your skin, and will improve the effect of the skincare you use.

What Is Exfoliating?

Your skin is constantly renewing itself, producing new cells in its deeper layers. These new cells work their way to the surface of your face, then die and are shed. You don't even notice them going unless they clump together and come off in flakes. This process of renewal is going on the whole time. Not to the extent that 70 per cent of household dust is made up of dead skin – that popular 'fact' isn't actually true, as most of our dead skin gets washed away in the bath or shower, or sticks inside our clothing and heads to the washing machine. But it is always happening. Exfoliating is the process of clearing away these old dead cells, to keep your skin looking fresh and clear.

Why Bother, If Your Skin Sheds All by Itself?

Fair question – but dead cells tend to collect in patches on the surface of the skin, making the skin look a bit dull. Clearing away these dead cells leaves the surface of your skin that bit smoother, so that it reflects light more evenly and looks smoother and fresher.

Is Exfoliating Better for Some Skin Types Than Others?

If your skin is oily, exfoliating will help keep your pores clear, so they're not blocked by dead cells, which could lead to breakouts, ie acne.

Keeping the skin's surface free from minute bits of skin-debris has knock-on benefits. Any products you use will be absorbed more evenly and will stand a better chance of being effective. This means exfoliating is good for dry skin, too, as moisturisers will sink in better on exfoliated skin. But be sensible. If your skin is dry because the skin barrier isn't in great shape, aggressive exfoliation is going to make things worse. So keep your exfoliation very gentle – just using a flannel will give you a small amount of exfoliation, as will using an acid toner occasionally – and work on building up the skin barrier.

And if your skin issues lie a little deeper than the surface – say, you have flaky patches of skin, or blemishes, then exfoliating can help get the skin back to normal. But be careful how you do it. If you have acne, you don't want to be roughing it up with face scrubs, but a chemical exfoliation with salicylic acid may be helpful to clear blocked pores.

Do I Exfoliate First or Cleanse First?

Most people cleanse first, then exfoliate. Some people prefer to do it the other way round. I quite like using an exfoliating cleanser, which does both at the same time, though not twice a day every day.

How Often Should I Exfoliate?

Exfoliate gently and frequently. There are a number of ways in which you could do this:

- Use a flannel to take off your cleanser every day. This will give you a light exfoliation.
- You could use an acid toner every other day.
- Use a stronger acid exfoliation product that you leave on overnight, once or twice a week
- If you're using a mechanical cleansing brush, I'd keep it to twice a week.
- As for an exfoliating cleanser – again, I'd use it no more than every other day.

I can't stress enough how important it is to be gentle when exfoliating. Most of us think that we need to really scrub our skin in order to get a result – but doing so is just going to stress your skin, create inflammation, and upset the skin barrier.

You are playing a long game when it comes to skincare. You want to create steady, gentle improvements over time rather than surprise your skin with shock-and-awe treatments.

So What Are the Different Ways of Exfoliating?

There are two means of exfoliation: physical exfoliation and chemical exfoliation. Physical exfoliation uses scrubs, cloths, sponges, or cleansing brushes. Chemical exfoliation uses products that encourage dead skin cells to disengage from the surface of the skin, which are either based on enzymes or acids.

FACE SCRUBS

When most people think of exfoliating, they think of face scrubs, products which you rub around your face to remove the surface debris. These are physical exfoliants, as they physically shift the dead cells from the skin. They certainly work, though the drawback to them is that often the exfoliating particles they contain are a bit rough, which can result in tiny scratches in the skin.

If you like using a face scrub like this, use it really gently. Think of it as polishing your skin rather than scrubbing it. And don't use the scrub every day. Your poor face has enough to go through in life without being roughed up in the name of beauty. I know they feel as if they're doing your skin good, but I'm not that keen on them.

There are some physical exfoliants without gritty bits. These are usually gel-based products that you apply to your face in a smooth layer, like a face mask, then leave to dry a bit. When you then come to rub them off, they roll up into little rubbery bits that rub off your skin taking dead skin with them, so it's satisfyingly revolting, but it's quite hard to get an even result. When using these exfoliants, I always find I end up having to wash the residue off my face, and am then finding bits of the stuff around my hairline. So, while I quite enjoy using these, I'm not mad keen on them either.

Using smooth plastic or nylon microbeads as exfoliating particles seemed a great idea when it was dreamed up in the Noughties, and many brands filled their scrubs with them. But as we all now know, the microbeads get flushed down the sink, slip through water-treatment systems, and end up in the sea. Plankton like to eat them, which contaminates the food chain. Microbeads aren't as big a problem as other plastics found in oceans, but they're obviously a really bad thing. They've been banned in the UK since 2018.

EXFOLIATING CLEANSERS

Rather than face scrubs, I'd suggest you try gentler exfoliating cleansers.

Here are some that will go easy on your face:

- **Dermalogica Daily Microfoliant**, £14, dermalogica.co.uk. When you smooth this grainy rice-based powder onto wet skin, it releases a mix of salicylic acid, papain (papaya enzyme), and rice enzymes that give the face a gentle but thorough exfoliation that's both physical and chemical. Curiously addictive, which is why it is a perennial bestseller for the brand.

- **Gatineau Radiance Enhancing Gommage**, £38, gatineau.co.uk. A gommage is a strange thing, a gel that more or less dries on the skin so that it can be gently rubbed away, taking fragments of dead skin with it. Deeply satisfying to use, though you may be picking shreds of it out of your hairline for the rest of the day.

- **Dr Levy 3 Deep Cell Renewal Micro-Resurfacing Cleanser**, £39, cultbeauty.co.uk. This isn't just a cleanser with glycolic acid. If you leave it on for five minutes, like a mask, it gives a deeper glycolic exfoliation. It also contains smooth rice microbeads that help polish your skin as you massage it in and then rinse it off.

FLANNELS AND MUSLINS

Using a damp flannel or muslin cloth to take off your cleanser might seem like just… wiping your face with a flannel. But even doing that is enough gently to remove dead cells off the surface, and can be done whenever you are cleansing your face.

USING A CLEANSING BRUSH

I talked about cleansing brushes in Rule One (see 'Use a Cleansing Brush' on page 52), and about how much more effectively they can cleanse your face than just using fingers, cotton wool, or a flannel. Brushes are also great for exfoliating the face, but I still think it is really easy to over-use them, which stresses out your skin unnecessarily. The one that doesn't is the Foreo, with its silicone bristles which you can nudge really gently around your face.

CHEMICAL EXFOLIATION WITH ACIDS AND ENZYMES

Chemical exfoliation is the grown-up option for getting your skin super-smooth and in great condition. This might sound harsh, like paint-stripping for the skin, but bear with me. Depending on what you use, chemical exfoliation can be gentle, effective, and really beneficial for the skin.

How do you do this? With products that contain active ingredients including a variety of skin-friendly acids or enzymes derived from fruits (see the section 'Exfoliating Ingredients' on page 63) to dissolve the 'glue' that holds your skin cells in place.

They're not going to dissolve the whole way through your skin; just loosen the already dead skin cells on the surface, so that these can be shed, making the fresher, smoother skin below become the new surface.

This description may make you think that chemical exfoliation is thinning the skin (which it is, a fraction) and that this can't be a good idea – but, honestly, it is. The only thinning that is going on is removing already-dead debris off the top of the epidermis, so it's not a problem. Where you want to keep and build thickness in the skin is in the dermis, the lower layers of the skin. Glycolic acid, a chemical exfoliant, helps with this, as do treatment serums containing retinol and other retinoids. See the section 'To Combat Ageing and Boost Skin Renewal: Retinol and Other Retinoids' on page 97 for more information.

Depending on how long you leave chemical exfoliants on the skin for, they can reach a little deeper into the skin, like a mini home face peel. This can keep the skin's surface clear and help to balance out congestion in the skin that causes whiteheads and breakouts. Stronger acid exfoliators can also help to soften wrinkles and improve skin texture by stimulating the skin-renewal processes that produce more supportive collagen and make the skin better hydrated, too.

EXFOLIATING INGREDIENTS

The main exfoliating ingredients are:

- **Alpha hydroxy acids (AHAs).** These acids include glycolic acid and its gentler associates lactic acid, malic acid, and mandelic acid. They brighten and smooth the skin, and improve hydration, too.
- **Beta hydroxy acid (BHA).** There's only one beta hydroxy acid – salicylic acid. As well as exfoliating the surface of the skin, BHA dissolves in oil, so it can reach into blocked pores to clear them. Also, it brings down inflammation and boosts skin hydration.

- **Polyhydroxy acids (PHAs).** These acids include gluconolactone, a powerful antioxidant and mild exfoliant, and lactobionic acid (aka bionic acid), which acts like an AHA but with minimal irritation, and has a moisturising effect.

- **Azelaic acid.** This acid gives a gentler sort of exfoliation (it's also anti-inflammatory, anti-bacterial, helps stop pores blocking up, like BHA, and helps reduce pigmentation, too).

- **Fruit-derived enzymes.** These enzymes include papaya enzyme (papain), which can dissolve protein and decrease inflammation.

Chemical Exfoliants That Do a Brilliant Job

Here are two enzyme-based exfoliants that do a lovely job:

- **Elemis Papaya Enzyme Peel**, £35, elemis.com. The exfoliation power in this leave-on mask comes from papaya enzymes and pineapple enzymes. It's gentle but effective and takes 10-15 minutes to do its work. You might get a bit of mild tingling but even sensitive skins will be fine with it.

- **Kate Somerville Liquid ExfoliKate**, £50, katesomerville.co.uk. There's a 10% acid blend of glycolic, malic, and lactic acids in here, backed up with pumpkin, papaya, and pineapple enzymes for additional smoothing. That makes it sound savage, but again, it's a gentle one.

Here are three of my favourite acid-based exfoliants from widely available brands:

- **Superdrug Naturally Radiant Glycolic Toner 5%**, £9.99, superdrug.com. Also a great product for an introduction to glycolic acid, and a complete bargain.

- **Pixi Glow Tonic**, £18, pixibeauty.co.uk. With 5% glycolic acid, this 'acid toner' has become hugely popular and with good reason – it does the job and is easy for most skins to tolerate.

- **Alpha-H Liquid Gold**, £32, thetweakmentsguide.com. A leave-on treatment product to be used twice a week, at night. I always have this on my bathroom shelf; it gives immediate (well, overnight), noticeable results.

Here are three of my favourite acid-based exfoliants from specialist brands:

- **NeoStrata Glycolic Renewal Smoothing Cream**, £29.50, thetweakmentsguide.com. A night cream with 8% glycolic acid and 2% citric acid, this is easy to tolerate. It will gradually smooth the skin and whittle down pigmentation marks and fine lines.

- **Paula's Choice Skin Perfecting 2% BHA Liquid Exfoliant**, £28, thetweakmentsguide.com. You'll find this product popping up in a number of categories. It's here because of its most obvious role – as an exfoliant. It's good for oilier skins as it exfoliates inside pores, too. There's also a 1% strength if you are curious about it but feeling cautious.

- **Biologique Recherche Lotion p50**, embassyofbeauty.co.uk. This has become a cult classic among beauty aficionados. It combines powerful exfoliating acids – AHAs, BHA, and gluconolactone – to clear, brighten, and strengthen the skin. There's no price given here, because you can't just buy it online – you can only get it after completing the company's skin analysis.

The Bottom Line: Exfoliating Your Skin

Exfoliation is great for your skin, as long as your skin is in good shape – but it is crucial to exfoliate gently. If your skin is super-sensitive or reactive, and reacts badly to exfoliation, don't do it. Concentrate on building up the skin barrier first (see the section 'Question 3: My Skin Is So Sensitive. What Can I Do?' on page 202).

RULE THREE: TREAT YOUR SKIN

So your skin is clean and ready for… what? Before you moisturise your face (Rule Four) and protect it with sunscreen (Rule Five), you have the chance to treat it. That's 'treat' not in the sense of indulging it with something enjoyable (for those sort of pampering treats, see Rule Seven), but rather applying a product with active ingredients that can treat any skincare concerns that are bothering you.

Does My Skin Need 'Treatment'?

If you are wondering whether your skin even needs any 'treatment', tell me this: Are you trying to change your skin in any way – say, reduce wrinkles, or soften pigmentation marks and dry patches, or improve its texture and radiance? The chances are that if you are even reading this, there's something about your skin that's bothering you – something a treatment product can help with.

What Are Serums and What Are They For?

Most treatment products come in the form of serums. Skincare serums have nothing to do with blood plasma, which is what the dictionary is talking about when it mentions the word *serum*. Skincare serums are runny, liquid products rather than gels or creams. Serums contain a higher concentration of active ingredients than moisturisers and are designed to bring about changes in the skin. The easiest way to think of serums is as concentrated booster treatments for your skin.

Serums are lightweight and runny. When you put them on, the skin sucks them up and absorbs them, and you may wonder whether you applied enough, since there is no trace of the stuff left. You probably did apply enough – and if you put on more, you'll just go through the product faster and may end up with a sticky face. Hold the thought that the serum is working its magic just below the surface of your skin, and go about the rest of your skincare regime as usual.

How to Use Serums

Whichever serum you use, put it on to clean, dry skin after cleansing and after any toner or essence you use.

You've likely heard that you should put moisturiser onto damp skin, to 'seal' moisture into the skin. That works if you're using a cream, because that's what a cream is designed to do – sit on the surface of the skin and help keep moisture in.

Serums are different. They are designed to be fully absorbed into the skin, so they need to be applied to dry skin. Applying a serum to damp skin just dilutes the serum and makes it take longer to be absorbed.

If it's a serum you squirt from a pump-dispenser bottle, squirt it onto your fingertips, then dabble it around your face so that it's evenly distributed, and tap it in lightly with your fingertips.

If it's a runny serum from a bottle with a dropper, it's usually easier to put the dose into the palm of your hand, then use your fingertips to apply it from there; or press your palms together, then press them around your face. I find if I put drops on my fingers, they slide off and drip into the basin, and if I try to drip serum straight onto my face, it goes everywhere.

After applying the serum, leave it for a minute or two so that it is properly absorbed before you put anything else on your face.

LAYERING SERUMS

What if you want to use more than one serum? Then you can layer them.

If you like the idea of using serums to treat specific skincare concerns, you might wonder whether you can use only one serum at a time, or whether you can stick them on one after another, and if so in which order. What if you want to use one serum for pigmentation, another for wrinkles, and a third for texture?

You can certainly use more than one serum. In fact, in Asia, it's not uncommon to layer on half a dozen products. Or, like me, you can settle for using one treatment serum in the morning and one at night.

How many serums you use is entirely up to you. It depends on how many serums you can be bothered to use at once; on whether they are lightweight enough to all vanish into your skin, or end up merging into a sticky mess; and on your budget.

But if you're going to use more than one product, the best rule of thumb is to layer them by texture. Start with the thinnest and runniest product, wait until it is absorbed, then add the next one. That means water-based serums should go on before oil-based serums. This feels logical – otherwise, how are the ingredients in the lightweight, runny serum going to battle their way through the heavier product underneath?

The exception to this rule is if you're using a product containing retinol or retinoic acid (see page 97), where the active ingredients will find their way into your skin whatever lies in their path. Also, if you are using retinol or retinoic acid, you may want to 'buffer' your skin by adding moisturising serums beneath them, and moisturiser afterwards. But I'll discuss this more fully in the section 'How to Use Retinoids' on page 100.

WHICH SERUMS CAN YOU LAYER?

You can layer pretty well any serums you want. The exceptions that I'd advise are:

- If you're using an alpha hydroxy acid, be aware that you'll get a stronger results if you don't put anything on afterwards. Any product with water in it – eg serum or moisturiser – will neutralise the acid, so it's stronger if you leave it on its own. If you're wondering what that means for the acid toner you were planning to use before your serum and sunscreen – it's fine, but you'll get more of an exfoliating, brightening result if you use the acid product on its own in the evening.

- Don't use an AHA, BHA, or PHA acid with a retinoid. Your skin is very likely to react, and the result will be redness and irritation.

WAYS OF MAKING YOUR SERUMS MORE EFFECTIVE

How well your chosen serum is able to work depends in part on how well it is getting itself into your skin. Here are four ways to help the serum get into your skin:

- **Exfoliate.** This clears the skin surface of dead cells and improves product absorption.

- **Cleanse.** Cleanse your skin with an electric cleansing brush (see the section 'Use a Cleansing Brush' on page 52). This performs a thorough exfoliation and can improve product absorption considerably.

- **Use electrical currents.** You can use electrical currents to 'push' nourishing products deeper into the skin. Using galvanic currents in this way is something that has been popular in beauty salons for decades.

WHAT IS MICRONEEDLING, AND SHOULD YOU DO IT AT HOME?

Microneedling involves deliberately making hundreds of tiny holes in your face with a spiky roller or pad (often called a 'derma-stamp') covered in fine-tined, super-sharp needles. This may sound like one of the more stupid things that you could possibly do to your complexion, but bear with me, because there are two reasons to make these holes.

First, the skin is a very efficient barrier. One of the main challenges for cosmetic chemists lies in working out how to get their state-of-the-art skin-improving formulations through the defensive barrier of the epidermis to the living cells below, where the ingredients are needed. Using a dermaroller or derma-stamp makes minute holes in the stratum corneum, the tougher, outer layers of the epidermis, to enable serums and their active ingredients better access into the skin. The stratum corneum is only about 0.02mm thick, so you can make these holes using a roller or stamp with very short needles – for example, needles only 0.1mm long – that don't go deep enough to draw blood. You can do this type of microneedling at home.

Second, microneedling – which is also called *medical needling* – can stimulate collagen production in ageing skin. This type of micro-needling requires longer needles, ones that go deep enough to create pinprick bleeding that makes your body produce platelets and growth factors that stimulate collagen production. A practitioner performs this type of microneedling on you; it's not something you can sensibly do at home.

So should you perform the first kind of microneedling at home to help active ingredients get through your skin? Not unless you have been given the needling device, along with instructions and appropriate products to use with it, by a skincare expert. Several dermatologists I've spoken to are not at all keen on home microneedling. They say that it causes unnecessary trauma to the skin, and that few of the products that people apply after needling are designed to go as deep into the skin as they will through the needled holes. For instance, any fragrance in a product is likely to cause irritation if it goes deep into the skin rather than on the surface.

- **Try microneedling.** You could take direct action with a spot of home microneedling. See the nearby sidebar 'What Is Microneedling, and Should You Do It at Home?' for more information on microneedling.

WHAT CAN DIFFERENT SERUMS DO FOR YOUR SKIN?

To choose where to start with treatment serums, first decide what you are looking to achieve. Maybe your main aim is to brighten dull-looking skin, or to tone down pigmentation. If so, start with that. I have divided this 'rule' up to talk about what the different types of treatment serums can do, and why you might want to try them. I've also explained as best I can how they work, and picked out some of my favourites in each category.

So what might you want to do? You could:

- Soften dry skin – with a hydrating serum.
- Protect against environmental damage – with an antioxidant serum.
- Strengthen and brighten the skin – with a vitamin C serum.
- Exfoliate, brighten and hydrate the skin – with an alpha hydroxy (AHA) serum.
- Tackle acne, and decongest and hydrate the skin – with a beta hydroxy acid (BHA) serum or acne serum.
- Firm and strengthen skin – with a peptide serum.
- Supercharge skin renewal – with a growth factor serum or stem cell serum.
- Go for all-round skin renewal – with retinoids such as retinol or retinoic acid.

Does that list make you think, 'But I'd like all of the above'? If so, you *can* use more than one serum at once (see the section 'Layering Serums' on page 67), but you'll have a better idea of whether a serum is doing what you want if you use one or two serums at a time. Or you could use one serum in the morning and one in the evening.

You may also be thinking, 'If retinol is such an all-round wonder, why don't I just cut to the chase and not bother with any of the others?' That's a fair point; and yes, you could certainly do that. Most retinol and retinoid products are designed to be used at night, so you might want to pick another treatment product for the morning.

The following sections tell you about some key serums you might want to try and what they can do for you.

TO SOFTEN DRY SKIN: HYDRATING SERUMS

A hydrating serum is one that puts moisture back into your skin. Our skin is around 60 per cent water, but it can easily become dry. If the skin barrier (the outer layer of the skin, which shields the inner layers of our skin and our insides from the outside world) becomes damaged or 'compromised', then moisture escapes more easily from the skin. That makes skin uncomfortable and less able to do its job as our protective casing. It's not just the moist inner layers of the dermis that the skin barrier is there to protect. Our bodies are tad less than 60 per cent water, and the skin, as our biggest organ, has the job of keeping that water on the inside, and keeping the rest of the world out.

Why Choose a Hydrating Serum?

Choose a hydrating serum to counteract dryness and to stop that tight feeling skin gets when it needs extra moisture. Also, apart from keeping your skin more comfortable, there are compelling cosmetic reasons for keeping skin well hydrated. First, dry skin wrinkles more quickly than well-hydrated skin, so packing in moisture is a preventative measure; and second, plumping up the skin with a hydrating serum has the happy and immediate effect of making fine lines and wrinkles less obvious. (I know I said in the introduction that this 'plumping' effect only makes micro-meters of difference but it is enough to improve the look of the skin.)

How Do Hydrating Serums Work?

Most moisturising serums contain hyaluronic acid (HA), a miraculous hydration-booster that occurs naturally in our bodies and which has become massively popular in skincare products in the past 10 years. In the skin, it helps the skin tissues hold onto water, and plays a crucial role in both making and maintaining the collagen and elastin that keep our skin firm and springy. Each molecule of hyaluronic acid can hold a thousand times its own volume in water, which is how it manages to plump up the skin.

Hyaluronic acid is a type of ingredient called a *humectant*, which means that it draws water to itself. Put it on your skin and it will draw moisture out of the air and into the skin – unless the air around you is very dry, when it may pull the moisture it is looking for out of the lower layers of your skin. To stop this happening, you need to pop a moisturiser over the top of the serum.

Hyaluronic acid molecules are large and tend to sit on the skin's surface rather than being absorbed into it. To get round this hitch, most hyaluronic acid serums combine these large, 'high molecular weight' molecules with hyaluronic acid which is broken up into smaller fragments with a 'low molecular weight' that can sink further into the skin and produce a deeper moisturising effect.

Very similar to hyaluronic acid is sodium hyaluronate, which has the same exceptional ability to bind moisture into the skin. Technically, sodium hyaluronate is the salt form of hyaluronic acid. It's slightly more stable than hyaluronic acid, and its molecules are a shade smaller, so it sinks into skin that bit more easily. But to all intents and purposes it's the same thing doing the same job.

Another helpful hydrating ingredient is vitamin B5, also known as pantothenic acid, which helps to bind moisture into the skin. Moisturising serums often contain vitamin B5 and hyaluronic acid.

Other moisturising ingredients that you will often find piled in to beef up the formulations of hydrating serums include urea and glycerin. These are both great humectants, but they are seen as less novel and exciting than hyaluronic acid. This is why hyaluronic acid tends to get top billing on the product packaging, even if there isn't that much of it in the product formula. To be fair, hyaluronic acid is only needed in tiny quantities, less than one per cent, in hydrating serums. That's why it's down the tail end of the ingredients list, not because the company behind the product has scrimped on including it in the formula.

You will also often find silicones such as dimethicone in hydrating serums. Why? Because they sit on the surface of the skin and help hold moisture inside it.

Do I Need a Hydrating Serum?

I bet you do. You might well think, 'You *would* say that, wouldn't you?' – but seriously, very few people have such well-adjusted skin that it wouldn't benefit from a touch more moisture. Even oily skin needs hydrating, because even though the skin has too much oil, it may still be short on water.

So a hydrating serum is definitely one to consider, particularly as these products can be found at all price points, so you don't have to break the bank to try one.

When Should I Use a Hydrating Serum?

Use a hydrating serum whenever your skin feels dry. If you're wondering whether you can't just use a moisturiser to stop your skin feeling dry – of course you can, but a moisturiser just sits on top of the skin, to try to stop water escaping from the skin. (I'll explain more about this in Rule Four.) A hydrating serum should sandwich an extra dose of moisture into the top layers of the skin.

Do I use hydrating serums? Absolutely, every day.

What Does a Hydrating Serum Feel Like?

Hydrating serums tend to vanish into the face without leaving a trace, but rest assured that they will have settled into the upper layers of your skin. You can think of them as being like a thin layer of absorbent sponge. Once in the skin, they will hang on to water and help keep your skin hydrated. You don't feel them sitting on the surface in the way a cream does, but that doesn't mean that they're not working.

Great Hydrating Serums to Try

Here are three of my favourite hydrating serums from widely available brands:

- **Hada Labo Lotion No 1 Super Hydrator**, £17.45, superdrug.com. Prettily packaged hydrating serum which has glycerin, sunflower seed oil, and hydrolysed collagen in it as well as hyaluronic acid. It does a good job.
- **Vichy Mineral 89 Hyaluronic Acid Booster**, £25, vichy.co.uk. Lovely formula which is easily absorbed, sits nicely in the skin, and will suit anyone.

- **Niod Multi-Molecular Hyaluronic Complex**, £25, cultbeauty.co.uk. If you're not sure what the fuss about hyaluronic acid is all about, this might be the product that helps you see the point. Get past the complicated name ('multi-molecular' means it has big molecules of hyaluronic acid, which sit on the surface of the skin, as well as smaller ones, which sink in deeper to hold water within the skin; there are 12 types of hyaluronic ingredients in here) and just try it and see what it does for you.

Here are three of my favourite hydrating serums from specialist brands:

- **Medik8 Hydr8 B5 Skin Rehydration Serum**, £38, thetweakmentsguide.com. The brand calls this 'liquid rehydration serum', which is very much what it does, with a lovely blend of hyaluronic molecules along with vitamin B5 (panthenol) to help the skin hold onto moisture that bit better.

- **Teoxane RHA Serum**, £55, thetweakmentsguide.com. Another fabulous but expensive hydrating serum. Teoxane is a brand that makes injectable hyaluronic acid gels. RHA stands for Resilient Hyaluronic Acid. The serum combines this ingredient with antioxidants to strengthen and hydrate the skin.

- **Intraceuticals Rejuvenate Hydration Gel**, £73.95, intraceuticals.com/uk. Very expensive – but if you have money to burn, it's pretty fabulous, particularly when used alongside the brand's (even more expensive) Rejuvenate Daily Serum.

TO PROTECT AGAINST ENVIRONMENTAL DAMAGE: ANTIOXIDANT SERUMS

Antioxidant serums can give your skin a layer of protection against ultraviolet light and pollution, so they're genuinely helpful for the skin. If you're wondering whether I mean vitamin C serums (they're the best known of all antioxidant products), I have separated vitamin C into another section below as there are so many of them, and they're quite specific. But vitamin C is just one of many antioxidant ingredients used in skincare which deliver additional, or different, benefits, and you might want to read about why antioxidants are such a vital part of skincare, and what they can do for the skin.

THE TWO-WEEK DEEP HYDRATION COURSE

The hydrating serums I've mentioned in the main text are ones that you'd use every day, week in and week out. But if you want to boost your skin's hydration levels, you could also try the Fillerina Dermo-Cosmetic Filler Treatment (about £87, see fillerina.co.uk for stockists). This is a pricey kit naughtily designed to look as if it is for self-administered injection; in fact, it's a two-week deep hydration course of treatment using special hyaluronic acid gels.

The gels come in a medical-looking bottles with a syringe-type applicators, though there is nothing injectable about them. Using the applicator, you carefully squeeze out a line of the product onto your worst wrinkles for 10 minutes before bedtime, then wipe off the excess before you go to sleep.

I thought this was an elaborate and unnecessary pantomime until I trialled it for a newspaper a few years ago and found it produced a measurable improvement in my skin's hydration levels. So now I am a respectful fan of the whole range, which includes some very nice hydrating creams as well as this gel kit. Yes, it really works.

So Remind Me, Antioxidants Are…?

Antioxidants are the good guys, substances that help counteract a process called *oxidation* which goes on in the skin as it does in the rest of the body. If you think of oxidation as the equivalent of rusting, you can see why you don't want it going on in the skin. When a freshly sliced apple starts to turn brown, that's oxidation.

Oxidation is an issue for skin because it produces molecules called *free radicals* which are damaging to the cells. Free radicals are damaging because they are short of an electron, which leads them to latch on to and seize an electron from nearby cells, setting off a chain of destructive reactions.

In the skin, free radicals can damage the cell membrane; and in short, they speed up the ageing process. Using an antioxidant serum puts a brake on this process, as the antioxidants scavenge up free radicals and keep cells safe.

HOW DRINKING WATER AFFECTS SKIN MOISTURE LEVELS

Every beautician and celebrity and natural health practitioner you ever meet will tell you to drink more water for the sake of your skin. And they have a point. People who drink lots of plain water tend to have clearer, healthier-looking skin than those who don't.

As a result of this most people end up thinking that drinking water will help to 'hydrate their skin' in the same way that drinking water hydrates the body.

In short, it won't. Dermatologists will tell you that skin hydration is not linked to body hydration. If you drink litres of water, it won't start to puff up your skin and seep out of your pores – instead, you will find yourself running for the bathroom. Or put the other way round, if you are thirsty, you don't get in the bath and have a good soak; you drink water. The skin needs to work as an effective barrier, so you have to be severely dehydrated in order for the effects of this to show up on the skin.

So why do people who drink more water look brighter-eyed and clearer-skinned than those who don't? Maybe because people who drink lots of plain water usually have a bunch of other healthy habits, too. They probably eat plenty of vegetables; drink modest amounts of tea, coffee, and alcohol; avoid sugary soft drinks; take regular exercise; avoid smoking; and get enough sleep, too. Put together, all of these things improve the look of your skin (see Rule Six on page 160 for more information).

Also, drinking plenty of water helps improve your digestion, and gut health has a huge effect on the skin.

Antioxidants are what give colourful fruit and vegetables their hue – for example, the red lycopene in tomatoes, the orange beta carotene in carrots, and the purple anthocyanins in blueberries are all antioxidants. Eating plenty of antioxidants helps limit the damage done by oxidation in the body, and using antioxidants topically – ie, applying them to the outside of the skin – is also highly beneficial. Many vitamins – such as vitamin A, vitamin C, and vitamin E – are antioxidants.

'EATING' YOUR WATER

No, not attempting to chew the stuff, but eating plenty of foods that have a high water content, such as vegetables, soup, and fruit. This is a theory put forward by Dr Howard Murad, a well-known American dermatologist, who says that consuming water in foods leads to better absorption of water in the body, because the 'cellular water' absorbed from food will be taken up more slowly and completely by the body, whereas water you gulp down by the glassful will just pass straight through you.

In his book, *The Water Secret: The Cellular Breakthrough to Look and Feel 10 Years Younger*, Dr Murad explains why he feels that eating water is not just vital for our skin, but for our health, too – because, he says, it is our cells' ability to remain hydrated and retain water that determines the state of our health and looks. Is there anything to this theory? I'm not convinced, but consuming more vegetables has got to be a good idea for any of us.

Key Antioxidants Used in Skincare

The following list explains the key antioxidants used in skincare:

- **Vitamin A.** This vitamin improves many aspects of skin repair. See 'To Combat Ageing and Boost Skin Renewal: Retinol and Other Retinoids' on page 97.

- **Vitamin C.** This vitamin can stimulate collagen production and reduce pigment formation. See 'To Strengthen and Brighten the Skin: Vitamin C Serum' on page 80.

- **Vitamin E.** This vitamin helps boost healing in the skin.

- **Polyphenols.** These plant-based vitamins are found in chocolate, fruit, and grapeseed extract. They help improve the skin's ability to defend itself against the environment.

- **Glutathione.** This powerful antioxidant has a reputation for helping to lighten pigmentation.

- **Resveratrol.** This antioxidant from grape skins (and which is present in red wine) makes the mitochondria, which create energy within the skin cells, work more effectively.

- **Idebenone.** This super-powerful antioxidant can help neutralise free radicals.

- **Ubiquinone.** Also known as coenzyme Q10 (CoQ10), this antioxidant helps prevent fatigue in skin cells.

- **Epigallocatechin-3-gallate.** This antioxidant from green tea can help reduce inflammation and prevent cell damage.

- **Niacinamide.** This form of vitamin B3 reduces inflammation and improves skin texture and tone by improving the skin barrier. It is great for treating rosacea and acne-prone skin.

- **Bakuchiol.** This is one of the newest and trendiest ingredients in active skincare, and it's often hailed as a 'retinol alternative' because it has been shown, in a couple of studies, to give similar results to retinol in terms of softening wrinkles and improving skin health, but without the irritation. It's an antioxidant rather than a retinoid, and it looks a promising ingredient for people who find their skin can't handle retinol.

Why Bother with an Antioxidant Serum?

Reading this, you may wonder how you've survived this long without an antioxidant serum. Well, our bodies *do* have perfectly good mechanisms for producing our own antioxidants to clear up free radicals. But as with most processes in the body, as we grow older, our production of antioxidants slows down and becomes less effective.

Using antioxidant skincare is also helpful because our environment and our lifestyle can influence the amount of free radicals our bodies produce. Perfectly normal bodily functions, such as processing food and taking exercise, make our bodies produce some free radicals. Pollution and exposure to sunshine can increase the rate of production; and stress, a bad diet, drinking too much alcohol, and not getting enough sleep all make the situation worse.

Using an effective antioxidant helps provide a shield for your skin, which also helps to repair the skin from inside. Antioxidants scavenge up the free radicals which are accelerating the ageing processes in the skin, reduce inflammation, and help give skin back its glow.

Do I Need Antioxidants?

Most certainly. Your skin will thank you for extra antioxidants. They're not a magic bullet – using an antioxidant serum won't suddenly change the look of your skin, but it will be nourishing your skin and both protecting your skin from future damage and helping repair damage that has already been done. Well worth a try.

Should I Use Vitamin C or an Antioxidant Serum?

Whether you should use vitamin C or an antioxidant serum depends what you want that product to do. A vitamin C serum is a good starting point – but if you want a product to reduce inflammation in spotty skin, you might be better off with a niacinamide-based serum. And if you just want a shedload of antioxidants, to see what they can do for your skin, try a product like the NeoStrata Skin Active Antioxidant Defense Serum, below, which combines eight powerful antioxidants. The free radicals won't stand a chance.

How to Use Antioxidant Serums

Apply the serum straight to dry skin after cleansing, before any other serums and allow it to sink into the skin before applying anything else.

Great Antioxidant Serums to Try

Here are three of my favourite antioxidant serums from widely available brands:

- **The Ordinary Buffet**, £12.70, cultbeauty.co.uk. Another cracker from this excellent range which provides useful skincare ingredients at bargain-basement prices.
- **Caudalie Vinoperfect Radiance Serum**, £46, uk.caudalie.com. Caudalie's USP is the antioxidants found in grape seeds, and their key ingredient here is a trademarked one called Viniferine, with a major reputation for brightening dark spots.
- **Elizabeth Arden Prevage Anti-Aging + Intensive Repair Daily Serum**, £170, elizabetharden.co.uk. Prevage has been around long enough to become a classic and gain the brand a legion of fans. It is based on idebenone, one of the most powerful antioxidants in existence, which has a proven ability to make skin look younger.

Here are three of my favourite antioxidant serums from specialist brands:

- **Paula's Choice Resist Anti-Aging Ultra-Light Antioxidant Serum**, £35, paulaschoice.co.uk. This is the ultra-light version of the brand's terrific antioxidant serum with niacinamide and restorative quercetin, as well as vitamins C and E.

- **NeoStrata Skin Active Antioxidant Defense Serum**, £57, thetweakmentsguide.com. Why just have one antioxidant, asks NeoStrata, when you could choose a serum like this, which packs in eight powerful and well-researched antioxidants for comprehensive skin protection? Persuasive talk – and the serum is nice to use, too.

- **Alphascience Phytic Rejuvenate & Glow Serum**, £75, efskin.com. Phytic acid is a powerful antioxidant, and this serum can be used twice daily to neutralise pollution and fade dark spots. It is good for oilier, blemish-prone skin.

TO STRENGTHEN AND BRIGHTEN THE SKIN: VITAMIN C SERUM

We all know of vitamin C as a vital component in our diets, and if you have more than a passing acquaintance with skincare, you'll probably have heard that vitamin C is an extremely useful ingredient in skincare, too. Here's why.

What Vitamin C Can Do for the Skin

Vitamin C is a brilliant anti-ageing ingredient for the skin, because it brightens dull and discoloured skin, fades age spots by inhibiting pigment formation, helps to strengthen the skin against the damage that UV light inflicts, and also boosts the production of collagen and elastin in the skin. Vitamin C is an antioxidant, so it tackles free radicals, the unstable molecules that accelerate ageing in the skin, and it has been well proven, clinically, to work wonders in the skin – *if* it is well formulated and used at a high enough concentration.

That 'if' is crucial. Vitamin C is a tricksy ingredient, as it oxidises easily when it sees UV light, so it needs to be carefully formulated and then contained in dark or airtight packaging. Vitamin C products often have a low pH of around 3.5, which keeps the ingredient stable, but it does mean they're acidic and may sting a bit when you apply them; any stinging doesn't usually last long.

To get the most benefit from a vitamin C product, look for a serum with 10–20% vitamin C in it. 20% concentration is about as much as the skin can absorb; and the higher the concentration, the more likely it is that the product will irritate your skin.

Because of the complexity of formulating them, effective vitamin C products are usually on the pricier side. This is not always the case; as ever, The Ordinary has a great-value strong vitamin C product, *but* it feels very sharp on the skin, and if you have sensitive skin, you should use it with great caution.

Why Collagen-Building Is Crucial to Keep Skin Firm

Collagen is the vital protein that gives structure to our skin. It is what keeps skin firm and youthful-looking, providing skin's natural scaffolding. As we age, we produce less collagen, and what we have is broken down more easily. So having more collagen is a good thing as far as your skin is concerned.

There are many 'collagen creams' around which sound like a good idea but are not very helpful because, like hyaluronic acid, collagen is a large molecule that will only sit on the surface of the skin. To stimulate collagen production, which takes place within specialized cells called fibroblasts in the dermis, the deeper layers of the skin, you need specialized products – preferably ones with a proven ability to stimulate the fibroblasts into action. This is something that a good-quality vitamin C serum can do.

Vitamin C comes in various forms on the ingredients label – there's retinyl ascorbate, L-ascorbic acid (which may ring a bell from long-ago chemistry lessons), tetrahexyldecyl ascorbate, sodium ascorbyl phosphate, and ascorbyl palmitate. All have a good deal of scientific research behind them, though what you really want to look for is a product that has been put through clinical trials that show it produces good results in the skin.

How well a vitamin C product performs isn't only about the pH and the percentage of vitamin C it contains: it also depends on what that vitamin C is combined with. Several brands add ferulic acid to their vitamin C serums, because ferulic acid is an antioxidant that has a synergistic effect and boosts the performance of other antioxidants. So you get a 1+1=3 type effect, where the finished product works even better than the sum of its parts would suggest.

Do I Need a Vitamin C Serum?

Respectfully, I'd suggest you probably do. Every skin, even reactive skin, can tolerate a vitamin C serum, and every skin can benefit from it. So it should be up at the top of your lists of Products to Consider.

How to Use Vitamin C in your Skincare Routine

The simplest way to introduce vitamin C into your skincare routine is to apply a vitamin C serum to clean, dry skin after cleansing in the morning. Follow it with hyaluronic acid serum if your skin feels dry, then apply sunscreen. There's no reason you can't use vitamin C serums at night as well.

> If you want to use a vitamin C product at night and also want to use a retinoid product at night, use them on different nights.

Great Vitamin C Products to Try

Here are some of my favourite vitamin C products from widely available brands:

- **The Ordinary Vitamin C Suspension 23% + HA Spheres**, £4.90, boots.com. Most vitamin C products are for use in the morning; this one, which is a 'suspension' in a silicone-y paste rather than a liquid serum, feels gritty and tingly as it goes on, so it's best used at night. Use with caution, or mixed with moisturiser, if you have sensitive skin.
- **Balance Me Vitamin C Repair Serum**, £32, balanceme.com. This award-winning brightening serum also offers hyaluronic acid, so it hydrates as well as softening uneven pigmentation.

- **DCL C Scape High Potency Night Booster 30**, £108, cultbeauty.co.uk. This is strong stuff. It's brilliant, but even my skin, which is used to active ingredients, found it a bit of a surprise. It feels slightly gritty when it goes on, and it tingles – which is fine – but the tingling is quite pronounced and goes on for quite a while. I've now learned to put it on a good half-hour before bedtime, otherwise I find I'm lying there trying to get to sleep and being distracted by the slight itchiness it brings.

Here are some of my favourite Vitamin C products from specialist brands:

- **Medik8 C-Tetra**, £35, thetweakmentsguide.com. Vitamin C serums – or rather, properly formulated, effective, vitamin C serums – are one of the bedrocks of Medik8's business. This is their 'starter' vitamin C, and very nice it is too, based on tetrahexyldecyl ascorbate, an oil-soluble form of vitamin C, and gentle on sensitive skin. If you want something more potent, Medik8 now has a C-30 serum (£44 medik8.com), where the active ingredient is 30% ethylated ascorbic acid. This is pretty strong stuff, so approach it with respect.

- **Paula's Choice C-25 Super Booster**, £50, paulaschoice.co.uk. A great serum from this brilliant brand, based on 15% L-ascorbic acid (plus ferulic acid and vitamin E) to brighten dull skin, fade dark spots, and boost collagen production.

- **SkinCeuticals CE Ferulic**, £140, and **Phloretin**, £150. skinceuticals.co.uk. The CE Ferulic serum is an industry classic and is very popular with serious skincare clinics. Combining vitamin E and ferulic acid – which, like vitamin C, are both antioxidants – gives a 'synergistic' effect by which the combined product is even more effective than you'd expect from putting these ingredients together – a 2+2+2=10 sort of effect. I find the Ferulic serum a tad oil-rich on my skin, so I prefer the sister-product, Phloretin, which has a lighter texture but an even higher price-point.

- **ZO 10% Vitamin C Self-Activating**, zo-skinhealth.co.uk. A terrific vitamin C product from a range which is only available through clinics – ZO Skin Health doesn't sell directly to the public, which is why there's no price given. In the clinic, an aesthetician will analyse your skin and recommend specific products for you, so take a look through the company's website if the idea appeals.

TO EXFOLIATE AND BRIGHTEN DULL SKIN: HYDROXY ACID SERUMS

None of us wants dull skin, and one of the swiftest and surest ways to improve skin that has lost its glow is with a product containing hydroxy acids such as alpha hydroxy acids, beta hydroxy acid, or polyhydroxy acids.

What Are Hydroxy Acids?

Hydroxy acids are substances that can help the skin in several ways. There are three main types of hydroxy acids:

- **Alpha Hydroxy Acids (AHAs).** These are the acids you find in 'acid toners'. This group includes lactic acid, malic acid, mandelic acid, phytic acid, and glycolic acid. Phytic is the gentlest of these, and is used more as an antioxidant than as an exfoliant. Lactic, mandelic, and malic acids are the sort you will find in the gentler type of acid toners, and glycolic acid is the strongest – or, technically, it has the smallest molecules, which can wiggle further into the skin, so it can have a greater effect more quickly than the other acids.

> Alpha hydroxy acids make your skin more sensitive to ultra-violet light, so you must protect your skin with sunscreen while using them. But then I hope you're using sunscreen every day already – or that you will be once you've read Rule Five, which is all about protecting your skin from UV rays.

- **Beta Hydroxy Acid (BHA).** There is only one of these: salicylic acid. This acid is exfoliating and is great for acne-prone skin. I'll talk about salicylic acid in detail in the section 'What Is Beta Hydroxy Acid and What Can It Do for My Skin?' on page 88.

- **Polyhydroxy Acids (PHAs).** These acids are sometimes called polyhydroxy bionic acids (PHBAs). They include lactobionic acid and gluconolactone, which are similar to alpha hydroxy acids but gentler, so they're good for sensitive skins, and they don't make the skin more sensitive to the sun in the way that alpha hydroxy acids do.

How Hydroxy Acids Help the Skin

All these hydroxy acids are best known for their exfoliating effects, which give a chemical exfoliation rather than a physical exfoliation. The acids gradually dissolve the bonds – the inter-cellular glue, if you like – that keep the outermost layer of dead skin cells stuck to the surface of your skin.

Dissolving the top layer of skin with an acid sounds drastic, but it is a much gentler way to exfoliate than physically scrubbing off those cells with an abrasive face scrub. So using a product containing hydroxy acids, such as an acid toner containing AHAs, will help keep skin clear and glowing because that smoother outer surface of your skin will reflect the light better and look more radiant.

Hydroxy acids are also anti-inflammatory, so they can be helpful for calming acne, and work on softening pigmentation. Another benefit is that they're humectants, drawing water into the skin and helping moisturise it. Better still, glycolic acid can stimulate collagen production, so it can also soften wrinkles.

Do I Need to Use an Alpha Hydroxy Acid Product?

You could try one and see if you like it. Many of us find them seriously addictive, for the hydration and glow that they give. If you have sensitive skin, be sensible – you may do better to concentrate on improving your skin barrier than chasing an acid-boosted glow until your skin is in better shape.

Where Do I Start with Hydroxy Acids?

Start with a gentle acid toner. Introduce the toner gradually – for example, just use it twice a week at first, and see how your skin is with it. If there is no irritation or redness, you could start using the toner every other day.

I know many people like to use acid toners every day, but I'd strongly advise you not to. I've been repeatedly told by skin experts that too many of us are using AHAs too much for our own good, and overuse can damage the skin barrier and contribute to pigmentation issues, especially in darker skin. You'll see an impressive glow and radiance to your skin when you start using AHAs, and it will be tempting to use them more often, in pursuit of more glow, but resist that urge – the skin doesn't work like that, and you're more likely to end up with inflammation and irritation from over use.

How to Add Glycolic Acid to Your Skincare Routine

If you want to step up to using a glycolic acid product which is more potent than an acid toner, the easiest way is to use it in the evening, twice a week. This is what I do – using a glycolic lotion twice a week, on nights I am not using retinol – and I find that it is enough. After cleansing, give your skin a wipe-down with your chosen alpha hydroxy acid lotion or tonic and leave it on. That's it. It will tingle, but this shouldn't go on for long. If you feel it is too tingly, put a moisturiser on top of it, as that will neutralise the acid and soften its effects. Or you could try a night cream containing glycolic acid, which can be used every night.

As above, if you find your skin is becoming red and irritable, do the sensible thing and stop using the alpha hydroxy acid product until your skin is back to normal.

Will Using Alpha Hydroxy Acids Thin My Skin?

Yes, it will, but don't worry about it – because the only part of the skin that is being thinned out is the dead top layer on the surface of the skin. These skin cells are continually being renewed from below; and at the same time, the acids help to trigger skin regeneration and boost collagen production in the lower layers of the skin, which makes the skin firmer and thicker overall. So using the acids is very slightly thinning the epidermis by removing the dead cells on the surface, but improving the health and thickness of the dermis, the lower layers.

Great Alpha Hydroxy Acid Products to Try

Here are three of my favourite alpha hydroxy acid products from widely available brands:

- **Superdrug Naturally Radiant 5% Glycolic Tonic**, £9.99, superdrug.com. A great product for an introduction to glycolic acid, and a complete bargain.

- **Pixi Glow Tonic**, £18, pixibeauty.co.uk. With 5% glycolic acid, this hugely popular 'acid toner' is a good one to start with.

- **Alpha-H Liquid Gold**, £33.50, thetweakmentsguide.com. Leave-on liquid to be used twice a week, at night. I always have this on my bathroom shelf; it gives immediate (well, overnight), noticeable results.

Here are three of my favourite alpha hydroxy acid products from specialist brands:

- **Biologique Recherche Lotion p50**, embassyofbeauty.co.uk. Another cult classic, which combines powerful exfoliating acids – AHAs, BHA, and gluconolactone – to clear, brighten, and strengthen the skin. There's no price, because you can't just buy it online – you can only get it after completing the company's skin analysis.

- **NeoStrata Glycolic Renewal Smoothing Cream**, £29.50, thetweakmentsguide.com. A night cream with 8% glycolic acid and 2% citric acid, this is easy enough to tolerate. It will gradually smooth the skin and whittle down pigmentation marks and fine lines.

- **Paula's Choice Skin Perfecting 8% AHA Lotion Exfoliant**, £29.50, paulaschoice.co.uk. This lightweight lotion will both exfoliate and hydrate the skin. Massage it in morning or evening and let it go to work.

TO EXFOLIATE AND DECONGEST SPOTTY SKIN: BETA HYDROXY ACID (BHA) SERUM

I'll talk in more detail about treating acne later in this section and also in Part Three (which starts on page 181), but while I'm on the subject of hydroxy acids, here's one that is really useful for anyone who suffers with congested skin.

What Is Beta Hydroxy Acid and What Can It Do for My Skin?

There is only one beta hydroxy acid (BHA), which is salicylic acid.

Like alpha hydroxy acids, beta hydroxy acid has an exfoliating effect on the skin, so you could call it another exfoliating acid. Where beta hydroxy acid is different from alpha hydroxy acids is that it is not soluble in water, like the alpha hydroxy acids, but it is soluble in oil. That means that salicylic acid can actually weasel its way into clogged, oily pores and clean them out while also exfoliating the surface of the skin, which is excellent news for anyone plagued by skin that just will block up and break out if it gets half a chance.

Some skin therapists say that it has a drying effect on the skin, which puzzles me because – as Paula Begoun, founder of the Paula's Choice brand has pointed out to me – the original research done on BHA (and on AHAs, for that matter) was all to do with their ability to improve the hydration of the skin. BHA can reduce skin oiliness, so that may be what they mean. I use BHA regularly, and it always makes my skin feel more hydrated, rather than less.

Salicylic acid is also anti-inflammatory, so it calms down redness in blemishes while going about its clean-up routine.

Do I Need a Beta Hydroxy Acid Serum?

If your skin tends to get lots of blackheads, a beta hydroxy acid product could be your new best friend. If you have sensitive skin but still want to try the product, you could start with a product that has a lower concentration of BHA.

How to Use a Beta Hydroxy Acid Serum

After cleansing, put some beta hydroxy acid lotion onto cotton wool and wipe it over the oilier areas of your face. Allow it to dry before applying other products. Use it twice a week at first to assess how your skin gets on with it before using it more frequently. I know Paula Begoun uses the product every day, but I'm more cautious with it.

Great Beta Hydroxy Acid Products to Try

Here are three of my favourite beta hydroxy acid products from widely available brands:

- **Garden of Wisdom Salicylic Acid 2% Serum**, £10, victoriahealth.com. If you're trying salicylic acid for the first time, you've little to lose by trying this.

- **Nip+Fab Teen Skin Fix Breakout Rescue Pads**, £9.99 for 60, nipandfab.com. Nip+Fab does a great range of acid-soaked pads in different strengths and acid-combinations. These salicylic-acid pads are easy to use and great value.

- **Clinique Anti-Blemish Solutions Clinical Clearing Gel**, £22, clinique.co.uk. Wipe over spotty parts of the face after cleansing so that the salicylic acid can ease its way into sticky pores and clear them.

Here are three of my favourite beta hydroxy acid products from specialist brands:

- **Paula's Choice Skin Perfecting 2% BHA Liquid Exfoliant**, £28, thetweakmentsguide.com. This is my go-to salicylic (yes, even at my advanced age, I still get spots; and yes, this product is popping up everywhere, isn't it?). There's also a 1% strength available at paulaschoice.co.uk if you want to start gently.

- **Alpha H Clear Skin Tonic**, £34, thetweakmentsguide.com. Another terrific exfoliating skin tonic with 2% BHA – ie salicylic acid – which is great for congested skin. Like alpha hydroxy acids, BHA has a hydrating effect on the skin, and this product has botanical extracts – chamomile, arnica, thyme, and cucumber – which help enhance the anti-inflammatory effects of salicylic acid.

- **Zenii Salicylic Acid Exfoliator**, £40, skincity.co.uk. This lotion is one to use more as a treatment than a serum. Wipe it over the skin, leave it for a couple of minutes (between one and five minutes, depending on how well your skin is used to the product, then rinse it off before applying the rest of your skincare routine.

TO BUILD COLLAGEN AND REDUCE WRINKLING: PEPTIDE SERUMS

A decade ago, peptides were hugely popular as anti-ageing skincare ingredients. Since then, they have been overtaken in popularity by ingredients such as retinol. But peptides are still very much around and have a great deal to offer.

What Are Peptides and What Can They Do for the Skin?

Peptides are chains of amino acids, which are the building blocks of proteins. Peptides act as chemical messengers in the skin. Send the right peptides into action, the theory goes, and they will act like tiny keys to turn on particular biochemical processes in the skin. Find the right key, or peptide, to boost a process – such as collagen production – which is slowing down with age, and you could be looking at a great result.

One oddity about peptides is that they are large molecules that can't penetrate the skin, yet many of them are well proven to have beneficial effects. How so? Partly, it seems that they have a 'trickle-down' effect. When they're applied to the skin, they have enough of an effect of the top layers of skin that messages are sent on deep into the skin, to get to work creating more collagen, or strengthening the elastin which gives skin its spring. But increasingly, brands are turning to sophisticated delivery mechanisms that take peptides across the skin barrier so that they can go to work faster and more effectively.

What Types of Peptides Are There?

There are many peptides used in skincare. These are some of the most popular:

- **Matrixyl 3000.** Otherwise known as palmitoyl pentapeptide, this peptide has been shown to boost collagen production in the skin.
- **Copper peptide.** This has a big following for helping to smooth and improve the skin and for improving collagen production.
- **Argireline (acetyl hexapeptide-8).** This is a type of neuropeptide (a category of peptides that affect nerve transmissions in the skin). It can inhibit muscle contractions in the skin, so it's meant to act like a kind of topical wrinkle-relaxer.

Do I Need a Peptide Serum?

You probably do, even if you may think that you already have more than enough going on with your skincare. If you want something inexpensive to start with, The Ordinary has a great product that combines Matrixyl 3000 with Matrixyl Synthe'6, another well regarded peptide, for less than £10. Or, you could go for a proven peptide serum, such as the perennially popular Protect & Perfect Serum from No7. That range is actually formulated for 30–40-year-olds, so if you are older than that, try the Lift & Luminate range or the Restore & Renew range. These ranges have the same dose of Matrixyl 3000+ (a variant on the normal Matrixyl 3000) as Protect & Perfect, but with other ingredients that are helpful to older skin.

Peptides can be helpful to all skin types, but you will get better results if you use them alongside other proven wrinkle-busters such as retinol, rather than relying on them to do all the work by themselves.

How Should I Use a Peptide Serum?

Pick your peptide product, use it according to the instructions, and see what happens. Peptides should be well tolerated by all skin types.

Great Peptide-Based Serums for Wrinkle-Busting

Here are three great peptide-based serums from widely available brands:

- **Olay Regenerist 3 Point Lightweight Firming Serum**, £31.49, boots.com. The Regenerist range is powered by pentapeptides and an 'advanced amino-peptide complex'. That's the science; the point is, it is well proven and, thanks to regular tweaks to update the formula, is as popular as ever.

- **No7 Protect & Perfect Intense Advanced Serum**, £34, boots.com. Since this serum shot to national prominence in 2007, it has become something of a national treasure. Also, it is scientifically sound, based on the powerhouse peptide Matrixyl 3000+ (No7's specially 'tweaked' version of Matrixyl 3000) and has been shown genuinely to reduce fine lines in the way a prescription skincare product would.

- **Niod Copper Amino Isolate Serum 2:1**, £38, niod.deciem.com. Copper peptides are the magic ingredient in the latest version of this popular serum, and they have, excuse the pun, copper-bottomed credentials for producing an anti-ageing effect on the skin.

Here are three great peptide-based serums from specialist brands:

- **Medik8 Liquid Peptides Drone-Targeted Peptide Complex**, £43, thetweakmentsguide.com. There's a whole heap of peptides in here along with a clever delivery system that the brand says delivers each of them into the layer of skin where they will most help to rejuvenate, or stimulate collagen, or minimise skin wrinkling.

- **NeoStrata Tri-Therapy Lifting Serum**, £75, thetweakmentsguide.com. This clever serum targets slack skin and fine lines with a patented ingredient, Aminofil, which uses peptides to build volume within the skin. There's hyaluronic acid for added hydration, too, and exfoliating gluconolactone to help keep the skin smooth.

- **PCA Skin Exlinea Peptide Smoothing Serum**, £95, pcaskin.co.uk. A bunch of wrinkle-softening peptides form the backbone of the product, and are backed up by hyaluronic acid and firming extracts, in a serum that's gentle enough to use morning and evening.

TO FINESSE SKIN RENEWAL: GROWTH FACTOR SERUMS

Serums containing growth factors aim to act as serious skin-regenerators. They tend to cost a good deal, because they're on the cutting edge of skincare science, and they are tricky to manufacture. They're subject to a fair bit of controversy within the skincare industry, too.

What Are Growth Factors?

Growth factors are substances which occur naturally in the skin. They're made by the fibroblasts, the cells that make collagen. When the skin is wounded, for example, our bodies produce growth factors which encourage the production of collagen and elastin as part of the wound-healing process. As with other aspects of the skin's ability to repair itself, we have fewer growth factors in our skin when we're older.

What makes growth factors fascinating is that they can prompt repair in the skin, and reduce inflammation, fade scars and generally make older skin cells behave like lively younger versions of themselves.

What Kinds of Growth Factors Are We Talking About?

The main types of growth factors that find their way into skincare products are Epidermal Growth Factor (EGF), which stimulates the growth of skin cells, and Transforming Growth Factor-Beta (TGF-β), which speeds up wound healing by stimulating collagen production and improving skin hydration.

The growth factors that you find in skincare come in various different forms. One popular form of growth factor is human-like growth factor grown within plants. Other forms are lab-created versions with identical chemical structures to natural growth factors; others still are derived from human sources.

Why Are Growth Factors Controversial?

Human sources? Yes, that's part of what makes them controversial, as those human sources have in the past included skin from infant circumcisions. Once the skin fragment has been obtained – and only one fragment is needed to start the whole process – the fibroblasts within it are cloned in the lab, and the growth factors that these fibroblasts release are harvested for use in skincare.

The other controversial issue is the enduring question of whether substances which promote cell division and growth – which is helpful for ageing skin – might not be so helpful if that skin is in a pre-cancerous state. Growth-factor skin care hasn't been shown to cause problems here, though studies have yet to prove that this can't happen, either.

How Do Growth Factors Work in the Skin?

Like peptides, growth factors consist of chains of amino acids; but growth factors are complete proteins, whereas peptides are shorter chains that form the subcomponents of proteins. Growth factors work in a similar way to peptides, by slotting into receptor-sites on the skin cells and stimulating the cell into a particular behaviour – like making more collagen.

That's the theory, but one issue with growth factors is that they are large molecules, far too large to slip through the skin. So they aren't absorbed into the skin, yet many studies have shown that growth-factor serums have created remarkable improvements in the skin. The most accepted theory here is that even though growth factors aren't getting through the skin barrier, they're able to interact with the top layers of skin and set off a cascade of reactions that, ultimately, achieve results such as collagen production in the dermis, the lower layer of the skin.

There are brands who have shown that their growth factor serums work, and that they improve the skin, though how exactly they work is still subject to debate, and more scientific studies need to be conducted on this complicated science.

Do I Need a Growth Factor Serum?

It's more of a case of want, rather than need, when it comes to growth factors. Serums with growth factors are expensive, but you might want to consider them if, say, your skin can't tolerate retinol.

How to Use a Growth Factor Serum

Apply the serum as directed, morning and evening. As for when to use the serum – you could use it the whole time; or as a treatment course for when your skin is in recovery mode, say, after a sunny holiday or after a cosmetic procedure.

Great Growth Factor Serums to Try

These growth factor serums are all expensive. Growth factors are relatively expensive to source and to formulate, so they are not yet available in mass-market versions.

Here are two specialist growth factor serums:

- **Bioeffect EGF Serum**, £125, bioeffect.co.uk. A lovely product that has produced remarkable results in studies. Sceptics say the superior form of hyaluronic acid in the product helps no end, but fans swear that it's the EGF, grown inside barley plants in volcanic ash in a giant greenhouse in Iceland, that's working the magic.

- **AQ Skin Solutions Active Serum**, £157,
  aqskinsolutions.co.uk. The fibroblast-derived growth factors
  in here are grown in the lab, to encourage the healthy growth
  of your own skin cells and make cells behave like livelier,
  younger versions of themselves.

Stem Cell Skincare

In skincare, stem cells are a hot-sounding ingredient, but – there
are a few 'buts'.

I say 'hot-sounding' because, if you have heard of stem cells, it
is usually in the context of cutting-edge scientific research. Stem
cells are cells in our body which can turn into any other kind of cell
and repair damage in the body. There are concentrations of stem
cells in the bone marrow, in fat tissue, and in umbilical cords.

In medicine, stem cells are the subject of intense research for
their potential to, for example, replace or rejuvenate damaged
tissue, or to understand diseases better. Transplants of stem cells
are used – live – to tackle diseases such as leukaemia. In cosmetic
medicine, stem cells extracted from fat tissue are reinjected – again,
fresh and live – into the facial tissues to rejuvenate them.

You also find stem cells in plants, and these are what are used
in skincare. Why? Actually it's hardly worth going into the why,
because the point is, however good a story brands spin around why
their apple stem cells, for instance, are amazing for our skin, plant
stem cells do not have a stimulating effect on human stem cells.
They just don't. There is no inter-species stem cell interplay going
on. Many stem-cell serums and creams show good results in testing,
but this is generally agreed to be because the plant-derived stem
cells they contain work as antioxidants.

However – there's always a 'however' in skincare, isn't there?
– the Dr Levy brand, which makes very advanced and very
expensive serums (which admittedly do get great results), says that
its ArganCellActiv formula, which has been patented, and which
you'll find in the Dr Levy Stem Cell Intense Booster Serum (£280,
cultbeauty.co.uk), is proven to stimulate stem cells in skin, right
down in the dermis.

Then there's a range called Calecim, which uses mammalian stem cells taken from the lining of the umbilical cord of New Zealand red deer. These stem cells are cloned in the lab, and then the animal elements are filtered out, leaving just epithelial stem cells, the sort that can stimulate skin cells. Making these cells into a culture produces growth factors and cytokines (tiny proteins that act as intercellular messengers). The brand's clinical studies suggest that human skin responds to these. Yes, it sounds like science fiction; and again, the technology is patented, and it's very expensive. The Calecim range is becoming popular in cosmetic medical clinics in the UK, which use a professional-strength version of the products to help with skin healing after aggressive procedures. And of course there's a home-care range too (Calecim Multi Action Cream, £175, thetweakmentsguide.com), for improving elasticity and firmness in mature skin.

Whatever next? Follow me on social media – @alicehartdavis – and I'll do what I can to keep you posted.

WHAT ABOUT 'GENE CREAMS'?

Ah yes, the creams based on the shortcomings in your DNA. Already, several companies (like ALLÉL, Younom, GENEU, and Nomige) will take a swab of saliva from the inside of your cheek and, from the DNA this contains, analyse how some of your key skin-related genes are functioning. Then they create a special cream for you with ingredients to compensate for the weaknesses in your skin-gene profile.

This type of personalised product is widely predicted to be the future of skincare. But – there's always a 'but' – there are hundreds and hundreds of genes that relate to skin ageing, and these swab-tests only look at half a dozen of them. So although they're moving in the right direction, and the latest brands such as Nomige (nomige.com) keep close tabs on customers and personalise the regime until they get results, custom-made creams are not yet the answer to your skincare dreams.

TO COMBAT AGEING AND BOOST SKIN RENEWAL: RETINOL AND OTHER RETINOIDS

Unless you are new to skincare or have been hiding under a stone for the past 10 years, you will surely have heard of retinol. It is frequently touted as a wonder-ingredient for skin, but people are often scared to try it, because it has a reputation for making the skin dry and flaky.

Retinol is one of a group of skin-improving ingredients called retinoids. Here's what you need to know about retinol and its close relations.

What Is Retinol?

Retinol and the other family members of the retinoid tribe are all derived from vitamin A. There are few topics on which skin experts agree – but here's one: retinoids are the gold-standard treatment to make the skin look fresher, less wrinkled, more even in tone, and smoother.

If that's the case, why aren't we all using retinoids already? That's a good question. They have such well-documented powers to improve the skin, there's a strong argument that we should all be using them, most of the time. Retinoids help normalise skin function, so if you're young and spotty, they will reduce oil production. If your skin has pigmentation patches, a retinoid will rein them back. If you have older, wrinkled skin, a retinoid will smooth the surface and soften those wrinkles.

Strong, Stronger, Strongest: Meet the Retinoids

So which retinoid does what, and where does retinol fit into the retinoid family tree? Here's a round-up of retinoids, from the strongest to the weakest.

- **Retinoic acid.** Also known as tretinoin, retinoic acid is the strongest and most effective retinoid and has a marked rejuvenating effect on skin. Our skin cells have receptors for retinoic acid and know exactly what to do with it. It is also only available on prescription, because it is so potent. It is best if you are supervised by a doctor or dermatologist while using tretinoin. Side effects, if you use too much tretinoin too quickly, include redness, irritation, dryness, and peeling, so you need to go slowly with it to get the results without too much upset along the way.

- **Hydroxypinacolone Retinoate (HPR).** This is an 'ester of retinoic acid' which can bind straight onto the retinoid receptors in our skin cells. (An ester is a chemical compound derived from an acid, with a slightly different chemical formula.) This binding means it has a very direct effect, without having to go through any conversion processes in the skin, so it's strong stuff.

- **Retinaldehyde (retinal).** This is also powerful stuff, and needs to go through only one conversion step in the skin before it becomes retinoic acid and hits those receptors on the skin cells to trigger skin regeneration. It gives results around 11 times faster than retinol, yet it is no more difficult to tolerate than retinol.

- **Retinyl retinoate.** Before we get to retinol, on the sliding scale of strength and effectiveness, there are newly created types of retinoid molecules, which have been tweaked in the lab to give them cosmetic super-powers. One of these is retinyl retinoate, which is gentler on the skin than retinol, but produces results that are eight times as good as retinol. R-retinoate needs to go through one conversion step, after which some of the product becomes retinoic acid, and the rest becomes retinol; the retinol goes through two conversion steps to become retinoic acid itself.

- **Retinol.** This is the retinoid we hear most about, as it is widely available in over-the-counter skincare. Once it's on the skin, retinol has to be converted into retinaldehyde, and then into retinoic acid in order to work its magic. So it will give you skin-renewing results, but more slowly, and with fewer side effects, than retinoic acid.

- **Retinyl propionate, retinyl palmitate, retinyl acetate.** These are all esters (slightly different chemical forms) of retinol, and they're the runts of the retinoid family. They needs to go through one conversion process in the skin to become retinol, then two more conversions to become retinoic acid. Some scientists say retinyl propionate looks promising for low-level skin renewal, but most agree that retinyl palmitate and acetate are unlikely to give noticeable rejuvenating effects. So they sound good in theory, like a gentle way to start with retinoids, but you'll be lucky if you see results with them.

What Can Retinoids Do for the Skin?

Retinoids can transform the skin, because they kick-start collagen production and at the same time reduce the rate of collagen breakdown in the skin. So your existing collagen lasts longer, and new collagen is made faster.

Retinoids also speed up the rate at which ageing skin cells renew themselves, which has an exfoliating effect on the skin. When the cells that line the hair follicles start shedding too fast – which clogs up the cells and provokes acne – retinoids slow the process down. They reduce oiliness, so they help to unclog blocked pores, and quieten down the production of excess pigment in the skin. Put together, all these effects make the skin look clearer, smoother, more even in tone, and less wrinkled, so products containing retinol and other retinoids are a great addition to any skincare regime. They will keep older skin looking fresh, and are also very helpful for younger skin suffering from acne.

Do I Need Some Sort of Retinoid Product?

Yes, it would probably be helpful, for all the reasons above – unless your skin finds retinoids too challenging to cope with.

Which Type of Retinoid Is Best for Me?

Before you decide that what you need is the strong stuff (ie prescription-strength retinoic acid), the other thing to know about retinoids is that piling on too much too fast will irritate the skin. Classic side effects of using retinoids can include redness, dryness, itchiness, and skin peeling – not things that any of us would voluntarily step up for.

How to get the benefits without the side effects? Start slowly (see the next section) and build up your skin's tolerance, and choose a product that is formulated to make the journey easier for you. This could be a retinol that is mixed with hydrating ingredients that soften its impact, or a product with 'encapsulated' retinol which is released slowly into the skin, or one of the newer retinoids like hydroxypinacolone retinoate and retinyl retinoate, which are very effective, yet gentler on the skin and much easier to get on with than traditional prescription retinoids.

How to Use Retinoids

The key thing when introducing a retinoid to your skin is: go slowly. Use it twice a week for the first week *and no more*. A retinoid is active stuff: your skin needs a while to become accustomed to it, and you need to work out what sort of dose your skin can tolerate.

The twice-a-week start is also vital because if your skin is going to find your chosen retinoid irritating (and it may well do), it will take 72 hours for this irritation to show up in your skin. So if you just wait 48 hours, think it's all fine, then apply another dose, all may be fine until that third day, when suddenly your skin goes haywire, you think 'Oh no!', and the reaction carries on for longer than you expect, because you have already given yourself a second dose of it.

So start carefully and gradually, using a small amount, and you'll soon find out how your skin feels about retinoids. If you're fine with using the retinoid twice a week without your skin looking dry, red, scaly, or irritated, then step up to three times a week.

If you are finding a retinoid dries out your skin, and you may well do, then wait until the retinol or retinoid is absorbed, then pop a moisturiser over the top of it. Some people reckon that 'buffering' the retinoid by using a moisturiser along with it will soften its effects. Doing this won't stop the retinoid from getting into your skin and doing its job, but the moisturiser will take the edge off the dryness and irritation.

Do use your head and be sensible with retinoids. If your skin is protesting, just stop using the product for a few days, or a few weeks, then try again. Because your skin needs to acclimatise itself to a retinoid, you need to creep up on it; then, when it has adjusted, you can push it a bit more, to stimulate further improvement. You're playing a long game when it comes to skincare in general and retinoids in particular, so take it at your own pace.

BUILDING MY OWN RETINOID TOLERANCE

Everyone's skin is different. In the first draft of this book, a couple of years back, I wrote that I didn't tolerate straightforward retinol very well, and that using a product containing 0.5% retinol, every second night, was my limit.

Reading that again more recently made me smile. I can now manage a medical grade 1% retinol every other night, or a prescription product with 0.025% retinoic acid every night, but it has taken me a while to get there. But then, as a diehard fan of retinoids, I also use – and enjoy – other retinoids like hydroxypinacolone retinoate and retinyl retinoate, which are easier to tolerate.

Why don't I just stick with one product? I'm always curious to try new products, to find out what they are like to use, so that I can pass that knowledge on to you – and also to see what they can do for my skin.

And yes, I can still get it wrong and overdo it and end up with peeling skin. My neck, I've discovered, is much less tolerant of retinoids than my face. The answer, as always, is to back off, let my skin recover, and go more slowly.

Choosing a Retinoid: It's Not Just About Numbers

When choosing a product – let's say it's retinol – you'll probably want to look first at the percentage of retinol to get a rough idea of the sort of the result the product might deliver. But keep in mind that the choice is more complicated than that. How well that active ingredient can get at the skin also depends on the formulation of the product. So it is not necessarily the case that a higher percentage on the product label will mean a better or more effective product.

Why not? Moisturising agents or oils in the formula will buffer the effects of the retinoid, so something that shouts '2 per cent retinol' yet puts it in an emollient formula will feel less challenging and may not deliver as much effective retinol to your skin as a 0.3 per cent retinol with nothing in the formula to hold it back.

Or it might be that the percentage touted on the packaging is actually talking about a 'retinol complex' – in other words, retinol and other ingredients – rather than just retinol. No7 has run into criticism for doing just this with its newest product, the Advanced Retinol 1.5% Complex. 1.5% is the percentage of all active ingredients in the formula. How much retinol is in there? 0.3%, which is the maximum concentration advised by EU skincare regulations. 0.3% retinol is also the concentration which No7's research found to hit the 'sweet spot' of achieving decent results while remaining easy to tolerate for most people. Yes, it's a minefield.

So how do you choose? Pick a product from a reputable brand (see my suggestions, below), and read the small print to understand what you're actually getting in terms of the active ingredient.

When to Use Retinols and Retinoids

Most retinols and retinoids should be used at night. One reason is because most retinoids are sensitive to daylight, which makes them break down and lose their effectiveness. Another is that night time is repair time as far as the skin's internal biology is concerned.

But having said that, there are a handful of great new retinoid products which are fine to use by day because the retinoids in them have been engineered – tweaked in the lab – so as not to be vulnerable to daylight.

Whichever product you choose, follow the instructions, which probably will tell you to apply the product to a cleansed, dry face in the evening and to use it sparingly. I'd suggest using the product on your neck and the backs of your hands, too, since these areas usually need even more help than the face.

If you're not already in the habit of wearing a sunscreen during the day, you need to step up and do this, because using a retinoid may make your skin more reactive to daylight. You'll also want to protect the fresher, new skin that the retinoids are helping to give you.

> The idea that retinol 'speeds up' skin cell turnover may sound like a bad idea – after all, isn't too much cell proliferation associated with cancer? But what retinol and other retinoids do, more accurately, is normalise skin cell turnover. So in older skin, where skin cell turnover has slowed down, retinol will speed up turnover. But in skin that's producing skin cells too fast (hyperkeratosis), retinol can slow this down.

Great Retinol Products to Try

Here are some of my favourite retinol and retinoid products from widely available brands:

- **The Ordinary Granactive Retinoid 2% Emulsion**, £8, theordinary.deciem.com. If you want to start your journey into retinoids at the budget end of the spectrum, you could do worse than try this, which is gentle on the skin but which gives decent results. A 'granactive' retinoid is an ester of retinoic acid… which means it's hydroxypinacolone retinoate (HPR). In this formula, it is softened with hydrating glycerin and soothing bisabolol.

- **No7 Advanced Retinol 1.5% Complex Night Concentrate**, £34, boots.com. You know that an ingredient has reached a tipping point in popular awareness when No7 includes it in its signature skincare range. It's taken No7 a while to get round to retinol, but this product with 0.3% retinol has been through enough trials to reassure fans of the brand – and sceptics – that it really does the job it claims to do, and softens wrinkles without being difficult to tolerate. If you're wondering about the strength, it's 0.3% pure retinol made up into a 1.5% 'retinol complex'. Irritating marketing, but it's a good product, and easy to tolerate for the majority of people.

- **Dr Sam's Flawless Nightly Serum**, £39,
  drsambunting.com. Along with a 2% granactive retinoid, this
  serum also contains niacinamide (which improves the health
  of the skin barrier and clears pores), azelaic acid (which helps
  bring down redness and pigmentation) and bakuchiol, a
  plant-derived skincare ingredient which works in a similar
  way to retinol, but more gently. Great stuff.

- **Murad Resurgence Retinol Youth Renewal Serum**,
  £75, murad.co.uk. Nice-to-use and easy-to-tolerate product
  from Hollywood dermatologist Dr Howard Murad. There's a
  cream version if this serum isn't moisturising enough.

Here are some of my favourite retinol and retinoid products
from specialist brands:

- **Medik8's Retinol 3TR**, from £26, thetweakmentsguide.com.
  Medik8 is big on retinols and retinoids. This is a great one to
  start with. The TR stands for time release, which means it is
  easier to tolerate as the retinol is drip-fed into your skin cells
  overnight, rather than all being dumped in at once. Then you
  can step up the strength, or progress to their R-Retinoate or
  Crystal Retinal products, which take your retinoid journey up
  towards prescription levels.

- **SkinCeuticals Retinol 0.3**, £65, skinceuticals.co.uk. A
  well-formulated, time-release retinol so well known that it has
  become a popular classic.

- **Skinbetter+ Intensive AlphaRet Overnight Cream**,
  £110, thetweakmentsguide.com. A skincare unicorn, in that
  you wouldn't expect to find a bioengineered retinoid and
  glycolic acid combined in one product, but here they work
  beautifully together for powerful skin rejuvenation, supported
  by a bunch of peptides. Also, nice to use.

Here are some of my other favourite retinol and retinoid
products from specialist brands. You can buy these ones only via
clinics, after a consultation with one of their advisers to decide
which product is most appropriate for you.

- **Environ Youth EssentiA System**, environskincare.com.
  The Environ system is based around the skin-regenerating
  powers of vitamin A and enables you to start gently and build
  up your tolerance under professional supervision. Works
  beautifully. Find a local clinic through their website, and off
  you go.
- **ZO Skin Health retinol products**, zo-skinhealth.co.uk. A
  great range of serious medical skincare created by Dr Zein
  Obagi (yes, the same Dr Obagi who founded Obagi Medical,
  another great range of powerful products). You can only buy
  these products via a skincare professional who works with the
  brand and who can assess your skin and choose appropriate
  products for you. Again, go via the website.

Another source of retinoid products is Dermatica (dermatica.co.uk).
This is a brilliant new online dermatology service where you can
upload photos to be scrutinised by a consultant dermatologist, who
will then advise on which ingredients should be compounded into
your personalised prescription product. Yes, prescription – so your
product will likely contain actual tretinoin. Yes, it's a game-changer
of a service. From £20 a month.

TO REDUCE PIGMENTATION: ANTI-PIGMENTATION SERUMS

The way pigmentation spots build up on the skin over time is one
of the most maddening and predictable signs of ageing. Then there
is melasma, a kind of pigmentation which is driven by hormones
and which builds up in the lower layers of the skin. Or you might
be struggling with post-inflammatory hyperpigmentation, which is
the kind of darker marks that crop up where the skin has been
damaged, for example by acne scarring.

I'll talk more about treating each of these kinds of pigmentation
in Part 3 of the book (see page 181). In this section, I'll go over the
particular treatment serums that can help to reduce pigmentation
and make the skin tone look more even.

What Are Anti-Pigmentation Serums?

Anti-pigmentation serums are products often sold as 'brightening'
serums which improve the look of pigmented skin. They do this by

slowing down the production of pigment in the skin – by using ingredients which reduce the rate at which the melanosomes (the parts of cells in the skin that make pigment) create pigment, or they slow down the rate at which this pigment is transferred into the skin cells.

What Are the Key Ingredients in Anti-Pigmentation Serums?

The main ingredients that you'll find in anti-pigmentation serums include the following:

- Vitamin C
- Azelaic acid
- Liquorice extract
- Kojic acid
- Niacinamide
- Alpha hydroxy acids, such as lactic acid and glycolic acid
- Retinol
- Tranexamic acid

How Do These Ingredients Help with Pigmentation?

These ingredients work in different ways, which is why you may find a combination of them in anti-pigmentation products.

First, there are the melanin inhibitors, which include vitamin C serums (see the section 'To Strengthen and Brighten the Skin: Vitamin C Serum' on page 80), azelaic acid, liquorice extract, kojic acid, and arbutin. Melanin inhibitors stop the melanosomes, the melanin-producing cells in the skin, from creating so much pigment in the first place.

Then there's niacinamide, a version of vitamin B3. Niacinamide helps reduce pigmentation by blocking the transfer of melanin from the melanocytes that make it to the keratinocytes, the skin cells where it sits and shows up. Tranexamic acid, the newest ingredient in the anti-pigmentation catalogue, also reduces melanin transfer, as well as reducing melanin production.

Alpha hydroxy acids, which include glycolic acid and the gentler lactic acid, can help reduce pigmentation marks in the skin, too. These exfoliating acids have a peeling action on the skin, encouraging the shedding of outer, pigmented layers so that fresher, clearer skin grows through from underneath.

How to Use Anti-Pigmentation Serums

Use anti-pigmentation serums religiously, as directed on the product packaging. Those instructions will probably tell you to use it once a day, at night, after cleansing; but if they say twice a day, do as you're told. These serums are not as strong as prescription-strength products, but many of these have clinical data behind them to show that they really do work if you use them consistently. Many prescription-strength anti-pigmentation products contain hydroquinone, the gold-standard, prescription-only pigment-busting ingredient.

Whatever you are using to treat pigmentation, you absolutely must follow it with sunscreen. Why? Because nothing stirs up the melanosomes into a frenzy of pigment-creating activity like UV light – that's daylight, not just bright sunlight. So make sure you protect your skin.

Which Skin Types Are These Ingredients Good For?

All these ingredients are good for all skin types. I mention this because darker skins suffer more with pigmentation than paler ones. What you want to avoid is anything calling itself a skin-lightening cream, because such products may contain dubious bleaching agents. Also, people with darker skin tones should be cautious with alpha hydroxy acids; using too much can provoke hyperpigmentation.

Great Pigmentation-Reducing Serums to Try

You could start with the vitamin C serums listed in the section 'Great Vitamin C Products' on page 82, which all help with brightening the skin. If you want something more specific, here are three great pigmentation-reducing serums from widely available brands:

- **No7 Lift & Luminate Triple Action Serum**, £27, boots.com. As well as tightening the skin, this serum will give decent brightening and pigment-smoothing results if you use it consistently and with dedication.

- **Murad Rapid Age Spot Correcting Serum**, £75, murad.co.uk. Another good over-the-counter pigment-quelling serum, with clinical trials behind it to show how well it works.

- **Clinique Even Better Clinical Dark Spot Corrector**, £98, clinique.co.uk. Proven in clinical trials to work as well as a prescription skin-lightening ingredient, this serum is gentle enough to be used twice a day.

Here are three great pigmentation-reducing serums from specialist brands:

- **iS Clinical White Lightening Serum**, £64, skincity.co.uk. iS Clinical is one of the rare brands that subjects its finished products to clinical trials, so buyers can be sure the products will do what they claim. This serum is one of iS Clinical's bestsellers.

- **SkinCeuticals Discoloration Defense Serum**, £85, skinceuticals.co.uk. One of the first treatment products to include tranexamic acid, this serum has shown, in a clinical study, that it significantly improves discolouration on the skin. What else is in here? Brightening niacinamide and exfoliating sulfonic acid, too.

- **Elequra Radiance Accelerator**, £98, thetweakmentsguide.com. As names go, 'Radiance accelerator' is rather underplaying the powers of this lovely, powerful, future-tech serum. It has two types of vitamin C in it along with retinol and periwinkle extract. These ingredients work as a tag team to deliver rejuvenating and collagen boosting effects as well as skin-brightening.

Here is an online prescription option for pigmentation-reducing serum:

- **Dermatica personalised prescription products**, dermatica.co.uk. Brilliant new online dermatology service where you can upload photos to be scrutinised by a consultant dermatologist, who will then advise on which ingredients should be compounded into your personalised prescription product. From £20 a month.

TO CLEAR BREAKOUTS: ANTI-ACNE SERUMS

Because blemishes, spots, and breakouts are not limited to the teenage years, I'm including a section on serums that can help to keep such problems under control. There's more on building a regime to support blemish-prone skin in Part 3; see the section 'Question 5: Help, I've Still Got Spots! What Can I Do About Adult Acne?' on page 212.

> Since acne is a hormonally-driven condition, you may need more help than an over-the-counter product can give. If so, seek specialised advice from a dermatologist who can provide prescription-strength skincare.

What Is an Anti-Acne Serum?

The anti-acne serums I'm talking about here are over-the-counter products that can help to reduce oiliness in the skin, calm down existing spots, and help to prevent new ones by deep-cleaning the pores.

What Are the Main Ingredients in Anti-Acne Serums?

Most products that are designated as blemish-busters will contain one or more of the following ingredients:

- Beta hydroxy acid (BHA), ie salicylic acid
- Alpha hydroxy acids (AHAs), such as lactic acid or glycolic acid
- Niacinamide
- Benzoyl peroxide
- Azelaic acid
- Retinol or other retinoids

How Do These Ingredients Help to Clear Breakouts?

Here's how the ingredients in anti-acne serums help to clear breakouts:

- Salicylic acid dissolves in oil, so it can work its way into blocked pores to clear them out while exfoliating the surface of the skin, too. Plus, it's anti-inflammatory, which helps reduce the redness and swelling in breakouts.

- Alpha hydroxy acids including lactic acid and glycolic acid have a superficial exfoliating effect on the skin, which helps to keep pores clear.

- Niacinamide is anti-inflammatory and also reduces oil production in the skin, both of which are helpful for anyone who suffers with oily skin and breakouts. It also helps repair the skin barrier and improve skin hydration.

- Benzoyl peroxide sinks through oil and sebum into the follicles, where it helps clear out clogged pores by exfoliating them. At the same time, it kills bacteria that are driving the flare-up of spots, and takes down inflammation.

- Azelaic acid is anti-bacterial as well as anti-inflammatory. It also slows down the overproduction of skin cells which contributes to clogging up the pores, so it's a terrific ingredient for tackling acne.

- Retinol helps to normalise oil production in the skin, so it will reduce oiliness in oily skin. Beyond that, it helps keep skin exfoliated and improves skin repair to heal the damage from acne lesions.

Do I Need an Anti-Acne Serum?

You could just add a salicylic acid toner into your morning routine, and use a retinoid in the evening. But if you'd like to use a specific anti-acne serum, then by all means give it a try.

How to Use Anti-Acne Serums

Follow the instructions on the packaging. With any new product, introduce it cautiously, particularly if that product contains either benzoyl peroxide or retinol, as either of these may make the skin dry and irritated.

Great Anti-Acne Serums to Try

Here are three products from widely available brands, that can help you reduce acne:

- **Acnecide**, £10.49, boots.com. This spot-busting gel contains 5% benzoyl peroxide. It's effective, though it's drying on the skin and may stain your pillowcases. It's available from the pharmacy section within Boots stores, or online.

- **Nip+Fab Salicylic Fix Day Pads**, £12.95, nipandfab.com. Wipe-over-your-face pads with salicylic acid to keep pores clear, and give a gentle exfoliation of the skin along the way.

- **La Roche-Posay Effaclar Duo+**, £17, boots.com. A hydrating gel (yes, even a spotty skin needs hydration) that contains calming niacinamide and salicylic acid to help clear blemishes.

Here are three products from specialist brands, that can help to reduce acne:

- **NeoStrata Targeted Clarifying Gel**, £23, thetweakmentsguide.com. A thick gel rather than a serum, to pop straight onto spots (rather than to smear all over your face). It contains salicylic acid and vitamin A for targeted spot-busting.

- **Exuviance Night Renewal Hydragel**, £39, thetweakmentsguide.com. This brilliant moisturising gel contains mandelic acid, which is more gentle on the skin than salicylic acid but which also dissolves in oil, so it can help reduce spots. Repairs and hydrates oily skin at the same time.

- **iS Clinical Active Serum**, from £70, isclinical.co.uk. 'Active' serum sounds a bit general, but this is really good on acne (as well as on pigmentation) thanks to the natural source of salicylic acid that it contains.

TO CALM IRRITATED AND REACTIVE SKIN: ANTI-INFLAMMATORY SERUMS

If your skin gets inflamed and red very easily, you may have found that it is easier to avoid skincare products altogether rather than risk stirring things up. But irritated skin needs help – first, to calm the irritation, then to rebuild the skin barrier so that your skin is more resilient and less easily irritated. There are many products that can help you do this. This section is just talking about anti-inflammatory serums. For more detail on strengthening and repairing the skin barrier, see the section 'Why Do We Need Moisturiser?' on page 115.

What Is an Anti-Inflammatory Serum?

'Anti-inflammatory serum' is a bit of a general term, but I'm talking about any products that have the potential to take the redness, the itch, the sting, or the prickly discomfort out of reactive skin, to calm it down and make it feel better. Irritated and reactive skin means that the skin barrier is stressed and not in good shape – 'compromised', as a dermatologist would put it – so that it is letting moisture escape. So soothing, hydrating products that can help repair the barrier will have a knock-on calming effect on the skin.

What Ingredients Do Anti-Inflammatory Serums Contain?

There's a bunch of ingredients with calming, soothing properties which frequently appear in anti-inflammatory serums. These include:

- **Niacinamide.** This form of vitamin B3 is anti-inflammatory, so it calms the skin. It is really helpful for repairing a damaged skin barrier because it encourages the skin to make more ceramides.

- **Ceramides.** These are a type of lipid, or fat, that's found in the skin. They're vital for skin texture because, along with cholesterol and essential fatty acids, they make up the skin's 'lipid layer' – the fatty 'mortar' that surrounds the 'bricks' of skin cells in the outer layers of the epidermis. This lipid layer is what makes our skin such a good waterproof barrier against the outside world.

- **Hyaluronic acid.** These hydrating molecules hold up to a thousand times their own weight in water, which is great news for skin that's stressed, sore, and probably dehydrated. Well-hydrated skin functions better, so improving hydration helps to rebuild the skin barrier.

- **Glycerin.** This is a humectant – an ingredient that draws water into the skin, to help hydrate it and make it feel more comfortable.

- **Panthenol.** Also known as vitamin B5, this works as a soothing, healing agent on the skin.

- **Vitamin E.** This vitamin is anti-inflammatory and works as an antioxidant; it's also fat-soluble and hydrating. So it's a really useful ingredient for repairing stressy, red, or damaged skin.

How Anti-Inflammatory Calming Serums Work

These serums work in a couple of different ways:

- They calm down inflammation in the skin, which reduces visible redness and makes skin feel more comfortable.

- They hydrate the skin, so that it is more comfortable on the inside, and able to function better.

- They help to repair the skin barrier. This has two benefits: first, moisture in the skin doesn't escape so easily into the air around you (which dries the skin out and stresses it); and second, dirt, bacteria, or anything that might irritate your skin can't get into it so easily.

Why Is Your Skin Irritated?

There may be many reasons for your skin being irritated, but make sure you're not using skincare products with obviously irritating ingredients. That means peering at the small print on the back of the label (or looking it up online, where the ingredients are often easier to read). You want to avoid:

- **Parfum.** This is the catch-all term for fragrance, which is irritating to the skin.

- **Essential oils.** These oils are also often irritating to the skin.

- **Alcohol.** Alcohol is irritating and drying to the skin.

Do I Need an Anti-Inflammatory Serum?

If you are suffering with reactive, stressed, irritated skin, one of these could be worth a try.

How to Use a Calming Anti-Inflammatory Serum

Apply the serum to clean skin. The packaging may say 'use morning and evening', but you might do better to wait a day or so to see how your skin likes the serum before ladling on a second dose.

Great Calming Anti-Inflammatory Serums to Try

Here are three serums from widely available brands that can help calm inflammation:

- **Avene Tolerance Extreme Cleansing Lotion**, £15, boots.com. The whole Tolerance range is a great one to know if you have irritable skin. Use this to hydrate and calm skin without stressing it out further.

- **La Roche-Posay Rosaliac Anti-Redness Intense Serum**, £19.50, boots.com. Also a great anti-redness range to earmark. This lightweight serum is cooling as well as soothing and anti-inflammatory.

- **Murad Sensitive Skin Soothing Serum**, £52, murad.co.uk. Full of lightweight hydrating hyaluronic acid, moisturising glycerin, and 'glycolipids' which help repair skin-cell membranes and soothe irritated skin.

Here are three serums from specialist brands that can help calm inflammation:

- **Medik8 Calmwise Serum**, £32, thetweakmentsguide.com. Medik8's whole Calmwise range is dedicated to soothing distressed skin. This serum contains teprenone, a patented anti-redness ingredient which has been shown in trials to reduce redness by up to 30 per cent after a month of use.

- **Epionce Lite Lytic TX**, £52.50, epionce.co.uk. Soothing, healing, and calming for frazzled skin; good for rosacea, too.

- **Exuviance Anti-Redness Calming Serum**, £54, skincity.co.uk. An impressive 67% of testers found this serum reduced redness straightaway, thanks to its combination of soothing active ingredients and botanical extracts.

The Bottom Line: Treating Your Skin

If you want to make some changes in your skin, pick the most appropriate treatment products and use them diligently.

Don't use too many products at once, or you may confuse and upset your skin. Start by choosing one product for the morning and one for the evening. Then maybe add another for hydration, and see how that works for you before chopping and changing.

RULE FOUR: MOISTURISE YOUR SKIN

Everyone knows that you need moisturiser. If you own one skin-care product, this is it, right? It makes the skin feel more comfortable, and helps to keep it soft and smooth. But why do you need a moisturiser, and what exactly is it doing for your skin?

Why Do We Need Moisturiser?

In theory, we shouldn't need moisturiser, since our skin has an in-built ability to moisturise itself. That's due to 'natural moisturising factors' and sebum.

Natural moisturising factors (NMFs) are a mixture of salts and amino acids (the building blocks of proteins) which help the cells in the skin hang on to water. Sebum is a thin oil produced by the skin's sebaceous glands; it sits on the surface of the skin as part of the skin's 'acid mantle' (see the section 'What Is the Acid Mantle?' on page 117), keeps the surface of the skin supple, and prevents the moisture in the skin from evaporating into the surrounding air. At least, that's how things should work; and when everything is nicely balanced like this, say, in a child's skin, the skin does its job properly. It provides a barrier between you and the world; keeps moisture in; and keeps dirt, bacteria, and pollutants out.

So, if it is built to look after itself, why does skin become dry? It's mostly thanks to modern life and our habit of washing. Wetting the skin may soften and hydrate it while the water is actually on your skin, it but as soon as you dry off, skin often starts to feel tight and dry. The acid mantle is easily disrupted by soap or detergent, and then those natural moisturising factors, which are water-soluble, can be washed out of the skin. That disrupts the skin barrier and makes it less effective.

Not that you shouldn't wash your face – keeping skin clean is always a good idea – but it is much kinder to your skin to use gentle products. That's the big argument in favour of cleansing with lotions, creams, balms, and oils rather than with foaming wash-off products, whatever your skin type. (If you're thinking, didn't I say I loved foaming face washes with added acids in the section 'Facial Washes with Added Acids' on page 46 – yes, I did, as long as they're the right sort of foaming face washes, with gentle cleansing agents which don't rip all the oils out of your skin.)

When you wash your face, and your skin starts to feel a bit tight, a vicious cycle begins. In healthy normal skin, the skin cells fit together snugly, packed in like bricks in a wall and surrounded by a liquid 'mortar' of moisturising substances including the vital skin lipids – ceramides, fatty acids, and cholesterol – as well as natural moisturising factors.

In the skin barrier, the uppermost layers of the epidermis, the skin cells are older and squashed flat, sandwiched together with those protective lipids, like flaky pastry with layers of melted butter in between it. It makes a good seal.

But when your skin becomes dry, the cells' contents shrink. Small gaps appear between them, and the barrier, in official language, becomes 'compromised' – it can't do its job so well and allows more water to escape, making itself drier still; and it allows dirt and bacteria to get in.

A dry environment will also help to pull moisture out of the skin into the surrounding air. The weather affects your skin, too – wind and cold air conspire to dry skin out. Central heating dries the air, as does air-conditioning, and dries your skin out at the same time. In a normal skin, up to 15 per cent of the outer layers of the skin – the stratum corneum – is made up of water. When that level falls to 10 per cent or lower, skin looks dry and flaky. So it's a delicate balance, and the right moisturiser can help even things up.

What Can Moisturiser Do?

What moisturiser does is settle on the outer layers of the skin and prevent the water that is in your skin escaping out into the air. Moisturiser keeps the surface of the skin soft and supple, which helps the skin work properly as a barrier.

WHAT IS THE ACID MANTLE?

The acid mantle is a super-thin layer of oil (sebum) and sweat which covers the outside of the skin and – yes – it's there as an extra line of defence against anything that's trying to get into the skin, like water, bacteria, or dirt. Sweat contains lactic acid, which gives the mantle – and our skin – a naturally slightly acidic pH of 4.5–6 (pH 7 is neutral).

Why Bother with Moisturiser?

There are four main reasons that you might want to use a moisturiser:

- Your skin will look better.
- Your skin will work better when moisturised.
- Your skin will feel better.
- Moisturised skin wrinkles more slowly.

YOUR SKIN WILL LOOK BETTER

If your skin is better moisturised, it will look smoother, plumper, and less wrinkled. It will also feel softer. This transformation isn't magic; it is something that any half-decent moisturiser can do, and do almost instantly. Often, when you see creams claiming an amazing instant plumping effect, it's not because they contain some miracle anti-ageing elixir, but because they're doing a great job of hydrating dry skin, and what you see is simply your skin cells plumping themselves up. Think of a dried-out sponge absorbing water and becoming thicker and springier – it's that basic an effect.

Plumping up the skin cells like this reduces the appearance of lines and wrinkles, too. So, yes, a lot of 'miracle creams' which achieve an instant effect on the skin do so not by virtue of their new magic ingredients, but by the good old-fashioned principles of moisturisation. Plumped-up, hydrated skin cells also make the outer layers of the skin appear more translucent and reflect the light more evenly, which also makes the skin look smoother.

YOUR SKIN WILL WORK BETTER WHEN MOISTURISED

When the skin cells are hydrated, they make your skin a better barrier between you and the outside world. That's what your skin is there to do. Hydration improves communication between skin cells, too, and allows cell-repair processes like producing new collagen and elastin to happen more easily.

YOUR SKIN WILL FEEL BETTER

On a less functional and more personal level, using moisturiser will make your skin feel more comfortable. Also, the mini-ritual of smoothing it on is one tiny indulgence that can cheer up the day; it feels nice, and you are nurturing your skin.

MOISTURISED SKIN WRINKLES MORE SLOWLY

Another benefit of using moisturiser is that it slows down the rate at which skin wrinkles. Most of us have probably noticed over the years, even if we haven't really thought about it, that dry skin becomes crepey and wrinkly more quickly than oily skin. One of the few compensations of having an oily skin – which usually means worse acne in your teens – is that as you get older, your wrinkles don't become entrenched as fast as they do on the faces of your dry-skinned friends.

This effect has been scientifically proven, too, in a study by cosmetic giants Procter & Gamble, published in the British Journal of Dermatology in 2010. (The study was carried out not just for the benefit of humankind, but to help us see why we should use the company's moisturisers – but leave that aside.) The study followed 122 women aged between 10 and 72 for eight years and found that how fast their skin wrinkled depended on how well-hydrated it was at the start of the experiment. Dr Greg Hillebrand, lead author of the paper, pointed out that a 28-year-old woman who uses face cream will have 22 per cent more wrinkles by the time she is 36. But if she doesn't use moisturiser, she will have 52 per cent more wrinkles.

So How Does Moisturiser Work?

Moisturisers combine several key types of ingredients to put moisture back into your skin and keep it there:

- **Humectants.** Humectants attract water into the outer layers of the skin (the epidermis) to soften these layers and plump them up, which makes fine lines look instantly less obvious. Some humectants, such as glycerin and urea, are old-fashioned and cheap but serviceable. Other humectants, such as hyaluronic acid, are newer, more fashionable, and more expensive.

- **Occlusives.** Occlusives form a film on the skin to keep moisture in and stop it escaping into the outside air. Oils and lanolin are examples of occlusives.

- **Emollients.** Emollients smooth over the surface of the skin to fill in the tiny cracks in the skin barrier. Some emollients – such as oils, shea butter, and lanolin – act as both occlusives and emollients. Other emollients, such as plant oils and fatty acids, don't act as occlusives.

Humectants, occlusives, and emollients form the basics of moisturisers, but few cosmetics companies stop there these days. Even the cheaper types of mass-market moisturiser will include other ingredients with added benefits, such as antioxidant vitamins, soothing natural extracts, and sunscreen. Sophisticated and expensive products contain increasingly sophisticated and expensive added ingredients, such as peptides (see the section 'What Are Peptides and What Can They Do for the Skin?' on page 90) to stimulate collagen production, natural moisturising factors to help the skin to regulate its moisture levels, or even enzymes to help repair the skin's DNA – in short, every skin-improving, 'anti-ageing' ingredient you have ever heard of.

Hydrating Serums, or Moisturisers?

If you've read about the benefits of lightweight hydrating serums made with hyaluronic acid (see the section 'To Soften Dry Skin: Hydrating Serums' on page 71) and decided that you're going to try one, you may be wondering whether you actually need to add a moisturiser on top of it. Isn't your skin going to have plenty of hydration already just from the serum?

BEFORE YOU CHOOSE A MOISTURISER...

How do you decide which moisturiser to use? That will depend on:

- **Your skin type.** Your skin may be dehydrated or oily (or both), or reactive.

- **Your personal preference.** Do you like a product that feels light and fresh or one that feels rich and creamy? With or without fragrance?

- **How your skin is feeling.** This can vary season to season, or even day to day, depending on what you have been up to and the environment you have been in. In the winter, your skin may feel drier and in need of more moisture, but it will also feel it needs cossetting when you've been outside all day in the wind, or after a hot holiday.

- **What you want the product to do.** You might say, duh, I want it to moisturise my skin. There are many moisturisers that will do just that and only that, but there are also moisturisers with anti-ageing ingredients, or sun protection, or which are tinted, or which do all of the above at once.

- **How you want the product to make you feel**. That may sound a bizarre consideration, but do you mind whether your moisturiser is basic and functional? Or would you prefer it to feel like a pampering treat every time you pick it up? Does it matter if it is in an ugly jar or does it need to look pretty on the bathroom shelf. (I'm serious. Even if they are full of the very latest cosmetic technology, products in boring, functional packaging or in clinical bottles, won't give you that moment of joy every time you look at them which other products will.)

- **Your budget** (see the section '4. But Expensive Products Are Often Better Than Cheaper Ones' on page 3). There are plenty of very basic moisturisers which cost less than £10 and which will have a basic moisturising effect on your skin, and there are others which cost a great deal more and have fantastically complex formulations of the latest cosmetic technology to help regenerate and energise the skin. The latter will doubtless feel nicer to use, smell nicer, and have way better packaging. Are they 'better' for your skin than cheap moisturisers? Usually, but not by as big a factor as you might expect, given their price.

(continues)

BEFORE YOU CHOOSE A MOISTURISER... *(continued)*

- **Your views about skincare**. You may prefer skincare that is 'free from' certain ingredients (see the section '14. 'Nasties' and 'Toxic' Ingredients' on page 21 for information on paraben-based preservatives, mineral oils, and sulphates). Maybe you want products that are vegan, or organic products. (I'm trying to avoid using the terms 'natural' or 'clean'. If you've read this book from the start, you'll have seen my views on these on page 17.) You may want to seek out brands with a particular emphasis on sustainability.

- **The sort of person you are.** Do you just want to get up, wash your face, slap on one cream, and be done with it? If so, you'll want an all-in-one wonder-worker (they do exist; see below). Or do you prefer to start laying down layers of different treatments serums onto your skin and topping the lot off with sunscreen? If this is the case, you may not want a moisturiser at all.

I'd say you probably do need a moisturiser as well – unless you're using a moisturising sunscreen, which will do the job, or unless you have oily skin and really feel that a hydrating serum is enough. Why? Just because hydrating serums usually sink into the skin and appear to vanish. A moisturiser added on top will keep the surface of your skin feeling smooth and comfortable. Also, if you are in a dry atmosphere, which tends to suck moisture out of the skin, a moisturiser will form a barrier on the skin to prevent this.

Which Moisturiser Should I Use?

If I had £1 for every time I've been asked this question, I'd be laughing. The trouble is, it's almost impossible to answer, because finding the ideal moisturiser for you depends on so many factors.

What you want is a product that feels nice to use, makes your skin feel great, and delivers some additional benefits while doing its basic job of moisturising. So the short, annoying answer is: 'the one that suits your skin and your budget'. Bear with me.

There are thousands upon thousands of moisturisers to choose from. Finding the perfect one for you will be a question of trial and error. The following sections show you some of my favourites to help steer your choices.

MOISTURISERS FOR DRY SKIN

Here are three moisturisers from widely available brands that can help with dry skin:

- **Superdrug Vitamin E Radiance Face Cream**, £4.49, superdrug.com. This cream is as basic as they come, but I still love it. Plus, it has SPF15.

- **CeraVe Moisturising Cream for Dry to Very Dry Skin**, £9, boots.com. Really nice and unthreatening for skin that verges on irritable, with ceramides to help barrier-building.

- **Embyrolisse Lait-Crème Concentré Nourishing Moisturiser**, £13, boots.com. This cult classic is old-fashioned (it contains a lot of liquid paraffin, so it's not one for the 'natural' brigade) but does a brilliant job.

Here are four moisturisers from specialist brands that can help with dry skin:

- **NeoStrata Problem Dry Skin Cream**, £32, thetweakmentsguide.com. You might not immediately see why a cream full of alpha hydroxy acids (there's glycolic, mandelic, and lactic acid in here) would be the answer to dry skin, and it's not one for sensitive skin; but by exfoliating the surface a little and improving the skin's ability to hold water, it works a treat. It's good on the body (for keratosis pilaris, the bumpy 'chicken skin' that can plague the upper arms) as well as the face.

- **Paula's Choice Resist Anti-Aging Barrier Repair Moisturiser**, £33, thetweakmentsguide.com. Great moisturiser which does a great job thanks to ingredients like glycerin, shea butter and squalane, with a soupçon of retinol to boost skin regeneration into the bargain.

- **SkinCeuticals Triple Lipid Restore 2:4:2**, £135, skinceuticals.co.uk. A fabulous product for the 45+ face, this offers older, drier skin the essential lipids that it needs (ceramides, cholesterol, and essential fatty acids) in the right proportions to significantly improve skin quality.

MOISTURISERS FOR NORMAL SKIN OR COMBINATION SKIN

Here are three moisturisers from widely available brands that are good for normal skin or combination skin:

- **Philosophy Renewed Hope in a Jar Gel Cream**, £35.50, philosophyskincare.co.uk. Oil-free version of this classic and much-loved moisturiser. Lightweight and easily absorbed, so it's a pleasure to use.

- **Elemis Pro-Collagen Marine Cream**, £87, elemis.com. Lightweight, nourishing moisturiser which has now become a modern classic, and is clinically proven to reduce wrinkle depth.

- **Augustinius Bader The Cream**, £205, cultbeauty.co.uk. Phenomenally expensive all-in-one moisturising and rejuvenating cream with a growing reputation for working wonders. I didn't quite get what the fuss was when I tried it, and passed it on to my mother, who says it is the best product she has ever used. Would it work wonders for you? You'd have to try it to see. There's a 'rich' version for drier skin.

Here are three moisturisers from specialist brands that are good for normal skin or combination skin:

- **Profhilo Haenkenium Cream**, £60, thetweakmentsguide.com. The name may be unpronounceable (it comes from the salvia haenkei extract used as an antioxidant in the formula), but this is a lovely, light lotion of a cream, packed with hyaluronic acid as well as that antioxidant, so it helps hold onto moisture and build the skin barrier.

- **iS Clinical Reparative Moisture Emulsion**, £78, isclinical.co.uk. Along with hydrating hyaluronic acid, this 'emulsion' includes 'extremosomes' – ingredients which help limit DNA damage to skin cells. This product also includes a collagen-boosting copper peptide growth factor for further skin-boosting.

- **Epionce Renewal Facial Lotion**, £81.50, epionce.co.uk. This soothing lotion calms inflammation, improves the strength of the skin barrier, and delivers active ingredients that soften wrinkles and give back elasticity to older skin.

MOISTURISERS FOR OILY SKIN

If you have oily skin, look for moisturisers that will hydrate your skin and boost its moisture levels without adding oil. Consider the hydrating serums I mentioned in Rule Three of Part 2 (see page 71), or try one of these.

Here are three oil-free hydrating products from widely available brands, that suit oily skin:

- **Neutrogena Hydro Boost Water Gel Moisturiser**, £12.99, boots.com. An oil-free hydrating gel which delivers and traps moisture in the skin.

- **Vichy Normaderm Phytosolution Double Correction Daily Care Moisturiser**, £18, boots.com. A great choice for spot-prone skin, this lightweight cream contains 2% salicylic acid, so it is really a hydrating, pore-clearing acne serum.

- **Chanel Hydra Beauty Micro Serum**, £70, chanel.com. Luxury serum that delivers an intense dose of moisture without any of the 'heaviness' of a cream that might upset oily skin.

Here are three oil-free hydrating products from specialist brands, that suit oily skin:

- **Paula's Choice Water-Infusing Electrolyte Moisturiser**, £32, paulaschoice.co.uk. This product describes itself as a cream, but it is more of a mega-dose of hydration for the skin, with added electrolytes – minerals – that help improve the skin barrier by transporting ceramides and glycerin to where they're needed.

- **PCA Clearskin**, £42, pcaskin.co.uk. A great choice for blemish-prone skin, this oil-free hydrator has niacinamide to calm oilier patches of skin and a touch of vitamin A to help improve skin-cell turnover.

- **Skin Medica Ultra Sheer Moisturizer**, £60, amazon.co.uk. More lightweight moisture, in the form of hyaluronic acid, with added vitamin C for antioxidant support and vitamin E to help skin suppleness.

MOISTURISERS FOR SENSITIVE SKIN

If you have sensitive, reactive skin, you need to make sure that you avoid products with potential irritants such as fragrance (the worst culprit, listed as 'parfum' on the ingredients list). The key thing you need to do for sensitive skin is hydrate it and strengthen its barrier. Once the skin barrier is working properly, your skin won't be so sensitive.

Here are three moisturisers suitable for sensitive skin from widely available brands:

- **Neutral 0% Intensive Repair Cream**, £6.99, neutralsensitiveskin.com. If you don't know the Neutral range, it's brilliant, as it is properly free from all fragrance elements (many 'sensitive' ranges aren't). This cream will moisturise without causing any untoward reactions.

- **Emulsion Face Cream base**, £22, emulsion.co.uk. Emulsion is a clever range where you can buy the base product and add a fragranced blend of essential oils of your choice to it. If you're a fragrance-avoider, it's a nice oil-based cream containing sunflower, coconut, jojoba, and grapeseed oils, to use on its own.

- **Kate Somerville Goat Milk Moisturising Cream**, £55, katesomerville.co.uk. A comfort-blanket of a modern classic, this sinks softly into the skin. Its jojoba and avocado oils, milk proteins, and aloe extract all feel really soothing for anxious skin.

Here are three moisturisers suitable for sensitive skin from specialist brands:

- **Hydropeptide Soothing Balm**, £35, skincity.co.uk. A three-in-one balm with plant oils for soothing and smoothing, allantoin for calming the skin, and antioxidants to reduce environmental damage.

- **Epionce Renewal Facial Cream**, £84, epionce.co.uk. Soothing and gentle, this calms inflammation, improves the strength of the skin barrier, and is really good for giving back elasticity to older skin. Seriously skin re-conditioning, and it feels indulgent, too.

- **Perricone Hypoallergenic Nourishing Moisturiser**, £59, perriconemd.co.uk. With squalane and olive polyphenols, this velvety cream gives gentle hydration and protection to dry, sensitive skin.

ALL-IN-ONE TINTED MOISTURISING CREAMS

If you're in a hurry, or can't be bothered with endless layering of products, choose one of these lightweight, tinted, hydrating moisturisers with SPF. They're wonder-workers that moisturise, protect and give you a more even skin tone, all at the same time.

- **Garnier BB Cream**, £9.99, superdrug.com. It's not new, and it's not expensive, but it does a creditable job to hydrate and make skin look smoother and more even toned. Its only drawback? Even though there are many variations (for oilier skin, for older skin, for sensitive skin), this cream still only comes in light and medium shades.

- **Bareminerals Complexion Rescue Tinted Hydrating Gel Cream SPF30**, £30, bareminerals.co.uk. In a now-crowded market of tinted moisturisers, this one still stands out. It's available in 20 shades, gives a lovely, hydrating finish, and works on oilier skins as well as drier ones.

- **Trinny London BFF Cream SPF30**, £35, trinnylondon.com/uk. A clever and addictively useful product from the Trinny London make-up range, with bursting pigments of colour that develop on the face. It comes in five shades which will work for skin tones from super-pale through to deep brown. Hydrating and protective into the bargain.

How to Use Moisturisers

Use your chosen moisturiser as much as you feel your skin needs it. When you apply the moisturiser, do so gently. Watching other people put their moisturiser on, I'm often amazed by how many people slap it on and rub it around enthusiastically. There's a time for using firm pressure on the skin – when massaging it – but applying skincare products is better done with a light touch. Dragging and stretching the skin really isn't helpful.

Put your chosen product onto the three middle fingertips, rub these against the fingertips on your other hand so that you have some product on each side, then pat and slide the product gradually round your face. Or put dots of product onto your face – easier with a cream, trickier with a slippery serum – and gently pat and massage it in.

The time-honoured way of applying face cream is to start at the neck and apply with sweeping upward and outward motions. I think the thinking behind this is that it is somehow a 'beautifying' motion that will have an uplifting effect on the whole face. News-flash: it won't. (Think about it. If this move worked, we'd all be doing it the whole time, and we'd all look about 25.) Light patting movements, in any direction you like, are just fine.

WHY OILY SKIN NEEDS HYDRATION TOO

If you have oily skin, you may think you are better off without mois-turiser. But it may be that your skin would love a dose of hydration, just without the oiliness that a creamier sort of face cream would give it. So you could use a hydrating serum (see 'To Soften Dry Skin: Hydrating Serums' on page 71) or try an oil-free moisturiser.

Keep in mind that water and oil are separate things, and even if your skin gets oily, it may be lacking in water. It's quite possible to have oily, dehydrated skin, particularly if you use foaming face washes to get rid of the oil, as the skin gets all stressy and realizes it is being dried out, and starts to produce even more oil to make up for it. Giving the skin a dose of hydrating moisture will help bring it back into balance.

Do I Need a Special Eye Cream?

You might need a special eye cream. You could just use the same moisturiser all the way from your hairline to your breastbone (yes, you should take it down your neck and over your décolletage, see the section 'Do I Need a Special Neck Cream?' on page 134) on the grounds that skin is skin and it all needs looking after.

I don't usually bother with an eye cream, because I put the treatment serums that I use on the rest of my face up to and around my eyes – antioxidants, retinoids, the lot. That might make some-one with sensitive skin flinch, but it works for me.

But there are reasons why you might want to use a special eye cream. Let's look at them quickly.

WHAT'S DIFFERENT ABOUT THE SKIN AROUND THE EYE?

The skin around the eye is thinner and more fragile than the skin on the rest of your face. It has fewer oil glands, so it dries out more easily; and because our eyes help us express ourselves, the skin around them gets more than its fair share of being pulled and stretched and scrunched up.

Put together, that all means the eye area is the first to develop wrinkles. Loading on a cream that is too heavy can make it become puffy, too; this is why most eye creams are lightweight serums or gel-cream formulations which won't cause any puffiness. Then there's the way that, because the skin is thin, blood vessels beneath the eyes can show through as dark circles...

CAN EYE CREAMS HELP WITH DARK CIRCLES AND EYE BAGS?

If you suffer with dark circles or bags under your eyes, the first thing to blame is your genes, though a lack of sleep and an unhealthy lifestyle will only make dark circles or bags under the eyes look worse.

Unfortunately, there are very few eye creams that have any sort of impact on eye bags or dark circles, no matter what the manufacturers claim. But if you want to try an eye cream that will help you minimize puffy or baggy eyes, look for one that is light and hydrating and that contains active ingredients such as peptides that may help to soothe and smooth the eye area.

Eye creams often contain caffeine. Rather than 'waking up' the skin in the way that drinking coffee jump-starts the nervous system, caffeine in eye creams has an anti-inflammatory effect, so it calms redness and constricts blood vessels, which may make dark circles and puffiness less obvious. I say 'may' because there is little evidence that caffeine actually gets into the skin to do this.

Many eye creams are tinted, which is helpful for covering up dark shadows if you can find a cream the right colour for your skin tone. Eye creams may also contain optical brightening ingredients which help to bounce back the light in a way that blurs wrinkles and reduces the look of dark circles, though you will get a better cover-up effect if you use concealer designed for the purpose.

MAKE SURE YOUR EYE CREAM IS FRAGRANCE FREE

Most eye creams are unfragranced. This is because fragrance is irritating to the skin, and putting it around your eyes is asking for trouble, particularly if your eyes are sensitive.

HOW TO USE AN EYE CREAM

Apply the eye cream sparingly, using your ring fingers. Why the ring fingers? Because they're less powerful than your first and second fingers and a bit less dexterous, so you will use them thoughtfully and lightly.

Rather than smushing the product into your skin, tap it on lightly to distribute it beneath the eye and up around the browbone. Most skin experts advise not putting product onto the upper eyelid itself, pointing out that some product will probably transfer itself from your browbone.

During the day, don't forget to use an SPF over your eye cream, to protect the delicate eye area from UV damage.

GREAT EYE CREAMS TO TRY

These eye creams have a particularly good reputation for being effective. Here are three from widely available brands:

- **Olay Eyes Pro-Retinol Eye Treatment Moisturiser**, £29.99, boots.com. The word 'retinol' might make you flinch, but this is designed for use around the eye – the 'pro-retinol' bit is retinyl propionate, a gentler ester of retinol. The product also contains palmitoyl pentapeptide to boost collagen production.

- **Estée Lauder Advanced Night Repair Eye Supercharged Complex**, £46, esteelauder.co.uk. A lightweight gel-cream, with a patented ingredient that aims to work on dark circles and puffiness as well as hydrate and support the delicate eye area.

- **Murad Retinol Youth Renewal Eye Serum**, £70, murad.co.uk. Yes, I like this range (and yes, this is expensive). This serum contains retinyl propionate and can give results within four weeks.

  Here are three great eye creams from specialist brands:

- **Elequra Eye Architecture**, £48, thetweakmentsguide.com. A potent mix of hydrating ingredients and peptides, this gets rave reviews from testers for its ability to depuff the eye area and smooth away lines.

- **iS Clinical Youth Eye Complex**, £85, thetweakmentsguide.com. This has a raft of high-tech ingredients, including peptides and growth factors, to help regenerate skin.

- **Medik8 r-Retinoate Day & Night Eye Serum**, £90, thetweakmentsguide.com. This is the eye area–compatible partner to Medik8's other skin-regenerating products powered by the gentle-but-powerful retinoid called r-Retinoate. A serious de-wrinkler that's ultralight on the skin.

Do I Need a Special Night Cream?

A traditional beauty routine would always include a special night cream, probably something 'rich' and heavyweight, to nurture your skin and deliver extra moisturisation while you slept.

But with skincare's current fixation with lightweight serums and active ingredients, the whole idea of a night cream now seems old-fashioned. At least, it does to me, and I don't use a night cream, as I prefer to load up on ingredients like retinoids and glycolics overnight.

Yet the concept of a night cream is still deeply rooted in our idea of skincare. Moreover, there is plenty of skincare research showing that our skin functions differently at night, when it is busy repairing itself in a way it can't during the day, when all its energies are going into defending itself against the environment.

So in the interests of anyone who's looking for a night-time product, here are a few beauties.

OVERNIGHT SKIN REVIVERS

Here are three great night-time products from widely available brands:

- **Sarah Chapman Overnight Facial**, £54, sarahchapman.com. Terrific skin-reviving serum which gives the skin a lovely, well-rested glow; from one of London's best facialists. Be warned that her USP, along with cosmeceutical ingredients, is a strong fragrance blend of essential oils, so this product may not suit sensitive skins.

- **Filorga Sleep & Peel Resurfacing Night Cream**, £57, marksandspencer.com. This effective night cream delivers a decent dose of glycolic acid to help exfoliate, brighten, and hydrate the skin. Test it on a small patch of skin before plastering it on everywhere.

- **Estée Lauder Advanced Night Repair Synchronized Multi-Recovery Complex**, £60, esteelauder.co.uk. A hugely popular classic which hydrates, strengthens, and repairs the skin and whose formula is constantly evolving to take advantage of the latest skincare research.

Here are three great night-time products from specialist brands:

- **Medik8 Crystal Retinal**, £39, thetweakmentsguide.com. We're back to retinoids for this one: it contains retinaldehyde (in the family tree of retinoids, this is a step up from retinol, and a step closer to retinoic acid – so yes, its strong stuff). A lovely peachy cream that's easy to use. I'd suggest starting with level 1 and seeing how you go with that before trying the stronger levels.

- **Exuviance Age Reverse Night Lift**, £63, skincity.co.uk. It's got peptides, it's got antioxidants, it's got polyhydroxy acids – so it will smooth, strengthen, and repair your skin.

- **SkinCeuticals Glycolic 10 Renew Overnight**, £80, skinceuticals.co.uk. Start gradually with this one, too; there's 10% glycolic acid in here, and also some phytic acid, to gradually resurface the skin and boost its hydration levels.

Not all the experts believe that we should put products on our faces at night. Some skincare brands believe that skin is best left bare at night so that it can 'breathe'. That's a decision for the individual. I'll just mention that the skin does not respire, and leaving it bare at night may simply make it dry, particularly as most of us sleep with our faces pressed into cotton pillowcases. which both pushes the skin into creases and dehydrates it. (Yes, I'm serious – skin experts say they can tell which side a person sleeps on just by looking at the patterning of their wrinkles.)

Do I Need a Special Lip Serum?

Well, that's a good question, I almost forgot lips. We all tend to forget our lips when it comes to skincare, then worry when they get chapped and dry, and smother them with lip balm to try to make them better. After which we forget about them for the time being. But your lips will benefit from a bit of care and treatment with products that do more than simply cover them with a protective barrier.

WHY LIPS NEED HELP

Our lips get worked hard. Quite apart from all the movement they go through when we're talking and smiling, eating and drinking, we are always rubbing our lips together, licking them, and wetting them with all the things we're drinking, many of which are hot beverages.

All of this means the surface skin on the lip is constantly being eroded; and as a result, it is easy for the lip skin to become dry – it's barrier damage again, in lip form. There are few oil glands in the lips, so they don't just recondition themselves automatically like, say, the nose – which is well supplied with oil glands – does.

THE TROUBLE WITH LIP BALM

When our lips get dry, what do we do? Reach for the lip balm. There are thousands of different types of lip balm, most of which are based on waxes and emollients, ingredients that smooth over the surface of the lip and stop moisture from within the skin tissues escaping into the air. That works, but it doesn't do anything to improve the health or function of the lip tissues. Worse, it creates a dependency on the balm.

Our lips ought to be able to adjust to their environment, but if we keep smothering them with occlusive ingredients like heavy lip balms, they lose the plot.

It doesn't help that many lip balms contain ingredients which irritate the lips. Peppermint oil, menthol, and camphor give lip products a 'fresh' feel but also make the lips sting a bit. That might plump up the lips fractionally, but it's the sort of swelling, resulting from uncomfortable irritation, which really isn't good for the lip tissue (you wouldn't want this sort of irritation and swelling happening on your eyelids, would you?)

HOW TO TREAT YOUR LIPS MORE KINDLY

What can you do? Treat your lips to a spot of barrier repair with hydrating ingredients which will help restore that fragile lip-skin barrier. If I'm using hyaluronic acid serum on my face, I usually put it on my lips, too; ditto ceramide-rich creams. I also sometimes stick a bit of retinol on my lips at night, which I'm not sure the brands who make the serums would recommend.

You could try one of the lip products I've mentioned below, many of which have ingredients that hydrate as well as protecting the lips. If you lick your lips a lot, try to stop.

While I'm talking of protection, do add a lip balm with SPF to your daily essentials. Lips need protection from UV rays, too.

Here are three great lip-conditioning products from widely available brands:

- **Nuxe Reve de Miel Lip Balm**, £11, uk.nuxe.com. This stuff is glorious. It's all beeswax and shea butter and almond oil, so it smooths and comforts chapped skin. It comes either in a little pot or in a stick version, and it's many a make-up-artist's secret weapon for softening up dry lips before a photo-shoot. The stick has a lighter texture; the one in the pot is thicker; either way, it is fabulous.

- **Balmkind Alpine Rose & Lysine Lip Balm**, £13, balmkind.co.uk. A lightweight balm based on castor oil that delivers much more soothing hydration than you'd expect, thanks to the oat-derived lipids that help repair the skin barrier.

- **Clarins Hydra-Essentiel Moisture Replenishing Lip Balm**, £20, clarins.co.uk. Another lovely lightweight gel-cream which melts into the skin and feels really, really nice. That doesn't sound very compelling, yet everyone I've introduced to this product simply loves it, too.

Here are three great lip-conditioning products from specialist brands:

- **Medik8 Mutiny Lip Balm**, £19, thetweakmentsguide.com. More of a gel than a balm, this somehow melts into the lips to hydrate them with hyaluronic acid and squalane, and makes lips feel amazing. Why is it called Mutiny? Because the company wants to take a stand against the sort of petroleum-based lip balms that simply cover over the lips to stop moisture getting out, without actually improving the skin barrier on the lips or hydrating their lower layers.

- **PCA Skin Peptide Lip Therapy**, £24, pcaskin.co.uk. As well as regular conditioning and soothing ingredients such as shea butter, squalane, bisabolol, and aloe vera, this gel contains peptides to stimulate collagen production. It feels lovely to use, too.

- **Teoxane 3D Lip Serum**, £35, thetweakmentsguide.com. This lip-saver contains the same high-grade hyaluronic acid as you find in the injectable dermal fillers made by its parent brand, to help the lips hold more moisture and plump them up a little. Non-sticky and good under lipstick, too.

Do I Need a Special Neck Cream?

You absolutely don't have to use a special neck cream. I don't. I just use the same products from my hairline down to my breastbone. But if you are not already exhausted at the thought of applying different creams to different zones of your face and neck – then, yes, sure, you could use a separate neck cream if you wanted to.

WHY USE A SPECIAL NECK CREAM?

As with the skin around the eye, the skin on the neck is thin and not well supplied with oil glands; and it gets twisted and stretched a good deal. This all conspires to make neck skin show its age sooner than most of us would like.

THE MOST IMPORTANT PRODUCT TO USE ON YOUR NECK AND DÉCOLLETAGE

As well as some kind of supportive, hydrating, restoring treatment, what this whole neck-and-dec zone really does need is protection from the sun. I'll talk about this in detail in 'Rule Five: Protect Your Skin' (see page 140).

The way our décolletage is angled makes it like our very own solar panel – it's great at catching the sun, which of course is very bad for it in terms of skin health. So the one thing you really must use on your neck every day is sunscreen, whether or not you are using a special neck cream.

WHAT TO LOOK FOR IN A NECK CREAM

You want plenty of hydration from a neck cream, and possibly some skin-reviving ingredients such as retinol, peptides, or glycolic acid. I'd argue that you could get those from treatment serums like the many I've listed in 'Rule Three: Treat Your Skin' (see page 65). But if you still fancy a separate neck cream, here are some that will do you proud.

GREAT NECK CREAMS

Here are three great neck creams from widely available brands that you could try:

- **Prai Ageless Throat and Décolletage Night Crème with Retinol**, £35, marksandspencer.com. I became a fan of Prai's original neck cream when I found – much to my surprise – that this bouncy gel cream really did make my neck look better after a week's use (there's a video about this on my YouTube channel). Now that they've beefed up the formula with retinol, it's even better.

- **Stellar Décolletage Velvet Restore Sleep Complex**, £78, stellardecolletage.com. Made with facial-grade active ingredients including a peptide complex and hydrating hyaluronic acids, this is a seriously good overnight treat to plump the skin and reduce wrinkles on the neck and dec.
- **Dr Levy Décolletage Regenerating Silk**, £290, cultbeauty.co.uk. Ok, you need money to burn to even contemplate using this product, but should you be feeling flush, it's a cracker. It includes trademarked ingredient complexes to repair and rejuvenate the skin.

Here are three great neck creams from specialist brands that you could try:

- **NeoStrata Triple Firming Neck Cream**, £46, thetweakmentsguide.com. This product has something of a cult following in the aesthetics world for its dedicated formula that lifts the skin, smooths out creases, and tones down pigmentation.
- **Jan Marini Marini Juveneck**, £65, skincity.co.uk. The ingredients in Juveneck are mostly all about soothing and smoothing rather than regenerating, but it claims clinical proof to soften wrinkles and re-define the jawline, which is a big inducement to give it a go.
- **iS Clinical Neckperfect Complex**, £86, thetweakmentsguide.com. A dedicated thick cream for neck rejuvenation, with exfoliating acids to tighten and smooth the skin, and hydrating hyaluronic acid for stronger, smoother, sprightlier skin.

Does Everyone Agree That Using Moisturiser Is a Good Thing?

No – but then, is there any subject where all the experts agree?

There's a science-based school of thought that points out that the natural moisturising factors in our skin should attract water into the skin and hold it there – if they're doing their job properly. If we persistently use moisturiser, our NMFs will get lazy and stop doing their job properly, creating what you might call a vicious circle of moisturiser-dependency.

This is how most of us get by, without much harm being done. But if you are intent on pursuing the path of optimum skin function, you need to wean yourself off moisturiser and kick-start your natural moisturising factors back into action. This is tricky, but you *can* do it.

Why Your Skin Gets Hooked on Moisturiser: Could You Do Without It?

Most of us who use moisturiser are dependent on the stuff. We, and our dry skin, would miss it if we didn't use it, since our natural moisturising factors just don't seem to be up to doing the job by themselves. Is this a bad thing?

It depends who you talk to. Some skincare experts feel that if you use moisturiser, the skin forgets how to do the job itself. Children, they point out, don't need moisturiser, and their skin looks lovely because the skin is healthy and can look after itself.

Normal, well-functioning skin keeps itself moist by producing natural moisturising factors. How much of these it produces depends on the environment it finds itself in. If you go somewhere dry, your natural moisturising factors will work harder to keep your skin comfortable. But if you cover your skin in moisturiser, they become idle, presume that everything is just fine and that no moisture is needed, and stop doing their job.

Moisturiser provides a cling-film-type barrier to your skin, which makes your skin feel soft and comfortable by stopping moisture escaping from its lower layers. But it does shut off the skin's natural repair mechanism, so that if you then stop using moisturiser, your skin feels terribly dry.

Using moisturiser, in other words, traps your skin into a vicious cycle of need. How to break out of this? By using products that encourage the skin to re-learn to regulate itself better, so that it can look after itself. It can do this, but breaking away from moisturiser dependency will mean putting up with very dry skin for a while as the skin adjusts – and like most things to do with the skin, this ad-justment becomes slower with age.

A specialist skincare practitioner can help you kickstart your natural moisturising factors back into action with a course of treatment that might involve skin peels with glycolic acid, which stimulate skin cells to turn over more quickly and produce more of their own moisture, along with treatment skincare products that include a hydrating gel that sinks into the skin and supplies moisture – and a sunscreen, but not a moisturiser as such.

The Obagi Nu-Derm skin protocol – where you use specialised products prescribed to you by a practitioner who supplies them and who supervises your journey through the process – will also take you through this transformation, though it is famously not easy and may mean reddened, peeling skin along the way.

Is it bad to be hooked on moisturiser? That depends on how tough a line you fancy taking with your skin. From the specialists' point of view, skin will function better and more efficiently if its natural moisturising factors are prodded back into action. But for the rest of us? Being hooked on moisturiser is not so bad.

Where Do Facial Oils Fit into the Picture?

Whole books have been written on using facial oils for skincare, though it is still a topic that divides people quite sharply. Oil aficionados praise their benefits, but anyone who suffered with oily, acnefied skin when younger – or who still suffers – may find it hard to get their head round the idea of voluntarily rubbing more oil into their faces.

I'm not a massive fan of facial oils, but not because I hate them. I can see they have benefits. It's just that most of the time, I'd rather use serums packed with active ingredients. Do I have facial oils on my bathroom shelf? Yes, absolutely. I just don't use them very often.

WHY USE A FACIAL OIL?

Facial oils are brilliant for softening and reviving the skin, because they contain fatty acids that keep the skin barrier in good shape, while holding moisture in the skin. They make effective cleansers (see page 40 in Rule 1) as well as moisturisers, and they are often made from pure plant oils, so they tick the organic-and-natural boxes – though bear in mind that extracts of essential oils, especially citrus ones, can be allergenic.

HOW TO USE FACIAL OILS

The trick to using oil as a moisturiser is just to use a little, to warm it up in your hands, and then to press it onto the skin. You don't have to rub the oil in, or put on so much that you shine. I find it hard to get this balance right, so if I'm going to use an oil, I prefer to use it at night, because then it doesn't matter if I've overdone it and my face looks like an oil slick.

> Many natural-skin aficionados swear by olive oil as a skin conditioner, but I'd go easy on it. Studies have shown that oleic acid, one of its key components, has a thinning effect on the skin over time.

MY FAVOURITE FACIAL OILS

Rather than wading through the pros and cons of all the ingredients of facial oils, I thought it would be easier just to mention some of my favourites. These oils are all available online.

- **The Ordinary Plant-Derived Squalane Oil**, £5.50, theordinary.deciem.com. Plain, unfragranced, soothing, hydrating... and really good for skin that is feeling too frazzled to cope with anything else.

- **Trilogy Certified Organic Rosehip Oil**, £19.50, trilogyproducts.co.uk. Packed with essential fatty acids and antioxidants, with a great reputation for softening scarring and wrinkles, this oil gives skin an overnight, freshening boost.

- **MV Skincare Pure Jojoba Oil**, £32, cultbeauty.co.uk. Jojoba oil is very similar in composition to the sebum in our skin, so it is very gentle and user-friendly on the face. It will hydrate the skin and won't block pores; it contains vitamins A, D, and E; and it is good on oily, break-out prone complexions, too.

- **Votary Super Seed Facial Oil**, £70, votary.co.uk. A great one for sensitive, reactive skin. It's made from 22 seed-oils and is fragrance free.

- **Dr Michael Prager Urban Protect Night Oil with Retinol**, £149, pragerskincare.com. Sophisticated oil with a decent dose of retinol to revive skin over time while keeping it soft and supple.

The Bottom Line: Moisturising Your Skin

Using moisturiser keeps your skin soft and smooth by holding water in the skin, which plumps up the skin cells and makes them look and feel better.

There are many, many types of moisturiser available, from rich, creamy ones to light, gel-based ones.

But using moisturiser is not the law. How much you need it depends on your skin type, the time of year, and where you live. You can get by without moisturiser, particularly if you are using a serum or a sunscreen that gives your skin a bit of moisture.

And you can get by without it altogether if you commit to a regime to kickstart your skin's own natural moisturising factors back into action.

RULE FIVE: PROTECT YOUR SKIN

Now your skin is clean and treated and moisturised, the final step in your morning skincare routine is to apply something to protect your skin. That something is sunscreen. Well, it doesn't have to be sunscreen; it could be a moisturiser with UV protection. But you need one or the other.

Even if you use no other skincare, I urge you – I beg you – to use sun protection.

You might think that moisturiser is all your skin needs by way of protection. I used to think that too. It's true that moisturiser will protect your skin from the drying effects of wind and cold, central heating and air-conditioning, but it won't guard against the damaging effects of daylight.

Yes, not sunshine; just daylight. Is that such a problem, I hear you wondering, particularly if you live somewhere where it is not even that sunny most of the time? Again, I thought that too; but having spent years learning about skincare from dermatologists and doctors, I've come over to their way of thinking. Here's why.

Does My Skin Need Protection?

Here's a statistic. It's much used, but it's still a cracker: up to 90 per cent of what we think of as the 'signs of ageing' – all the wrinkles, the age spots, the rough texture – are all due to exposure to UV light.

If you're wondering whether 'exposure to UV light' means 'being outside in the sun', the answer is yes. Being outside in the sun is the most direct and obvious way of exposing yourself to ultraviolet light – but it's not just sunshine that delivers UV light.

There are two key kinds of ultraviolet rays, UVA and UVB. UVB is the kind which will burn the surface of our skin if we give it a chance. UVA is the longer-wavelength ultraviolet rays which reach deeper into the skin and help to break down the collagen and elastin that keep the skin firm and springy. UVA and UVB rays work together to produce a tan. UVA darkens existing pigment in the skin, while UVB prompts the melanocytes to produce more pigment. Both reactions are trying to protect the DNA in the skin from the damage that those UV rays are causing.

In the UK, we get decent amounts of UVB only in the summer – mostly in the sunshine, though it also finds its way through clouds. But UVA reaches us all day every day, not just in the summer or when it's sunny, but in boring old grey daylight, all year round. UVA rays also pass through glass, so if you are in the car a lot, or have a desk by the window, those damaging rays will reach you there, too, though you won't get a tan through glass.

It is the everyday, incidental exposure to UVA which slowly, gradually stacks up over a lifetime and which results in clusters of melanin (age spots), broken-down collagen and elastin (wrinkles), and a damaged skin barrier (rough texture). Nothing dramatic or sexy about it, just life, slowly eroding the structure of the skin. This accumulated damage can also, over time, provoke skin cancer.

That is why dermatologists and skincare experts and beauty editors all bang on about wearing high-factor sunscreen the whole time, and why UV protection is fundamental to looking after your skin.

Sunscreens – SPF/UVA and 'Broad-Spectrum' Protection

Sunscreens are usually described by how much SPF they contain. Now, the SPF rating for a product tells us how much UVB light it can block, or absorb. For preventing UV-related damage, you also need the sunscreen to block UVA rays. Most sunscreen products are formulated to offer 'broad spectrum' protection, with a certain proportion of UVA blockers. In general, the higher the SPF, the higher the UVA protection, too.

See the section 'How High a Factor Should I Use?' on page 148 for an explanation of SPF and how SPF ratings work.

SUNSCREENS: ONES THAT ABSORB THE RAYS, ONES THAT REFLECT THE RAYS

Apart from picking a high enough SPF, the main choice with sunscreens is between physical sunscreens and UV-absorbing sunscreens. Physical, reflective sunscreens literally shield the skin with a physical barrier of product, absorb some of the light energy, and bounce back the rest of the UV rays away from the skin. UV-absorbing sunscreens work by absorbing the UV light and preventing it affecting the skin.

Physical sunscreens are the type that used to be called 'sunblock' or 'mineral' sunscreens. They contain finely milled titanium dioxide or zinc oxide. If you have tried physical sunscreens in the past and rejected them because they come up a bit chalky, it's worth taking another look at them, because every year the formulations get better, and the finish that the product gives improves.

UV-absorbing sunscreens are sometimes called 'chemical' sunscreens – an unfortunate term given the huge numbers of people who see the word 'chemical' as equivalent to 'evil'. These 'absorbing' sunscreens contain ingredients like oxybenzone (for UVB and some UVA), avobenzone (UVA), octisalate (UVB), or homosalate (UVB), which absorb the energy from UV rays and turn it into heat.

There are also newer sun-screening ingredients, such as Tinosorb M and Tinosorb S. Tinosorb M is halfway between a physical sunscreen and a chemical sunscreen; gives UVA and UVB protection; and is stable, unlike some of its predecessors. Tinosorb S is a chemical sunscreen which protects against the whole spectrum of UV light.

Most skins can tolerate these absorbing sunscreens well, but anyone who prefers to keep their skincare natural will have an instinctive aversion to this second group of ingredients. I'm big on using sunscreen of any sort, but I can see that the older types of absorbing sunscreens and their synthetic ingredients have their problems. Hawaii has banned the use of sunscreens containing oxybenzone and octisalate from use on its beaches, because these ingredients have been found to kill developing coral, bleach existing coral, and inflict genetic damage on coral. They also appear to have gender-bending effects on fish, feminising male fish.

That might make you think these chemical, absorbing sunscreens are all bad, and best avoided; but because they bind into the surface of the skin, they provide more effective protection than physical sunscreens, which simply sit atop the skin's surface and are more easily wiped or sweated off.

AMERICAN SUNSCREENS VS SUNSCREENS IN THE REST OF THE WORLD

If you have read online that in the USA, there are only two sunscreen ingredients that are regarded as safe, and that chemical sunscreen ingredients are 'under investigation', it may have worried you.

Briefly, you needn't worry; the Food and Drug Administration (FDA), regards sunscreens as over-the-counter medicines, rather than cosmetics, and its approvals process is very slow.

Fewer sunscreen ingredients – and none of the newer ones, like those Tinosorb ones I mentioned – have been approved for use, so US sunscreens tend to be more old-fashioned formulae that are less pleasant to use than those found elsewhere in the world.

Skin Cancer – What Are the Risks?

Sorry, it's a bit of a downer to introduce skin cancer, but I have to mention it.

The more exposure your skin has to UV light, whether that is the normal sort of exposure that you get in everyday life, or lying in the sun tanning your skin, the greater the chances are that you could develop skin cancer. I know that lying out in the sun feels fabulous, and most of us, me included, still think we look better with a tan than without. But tanned skin is damaged skin, and tanning has consequences in the form of wrinkles, pigmentation marks, rough skin texture, and, possibly, skin cancer.

I know that sounds like a crude scare tactic, but look at the figures. According to the latest statistics from Cancer Research UK, over 16,000 people in the UK are diagnosed each year with melanoma, the more rare but more dangerous type of skin cancer that kills around 2,400 people each year there. And over 150,000 people are diagnosed with non-melanoma skin cancers every year. That's a lot of people, enough to fill Wembley Stadium one and a half times.

How likely are you to get skin cancer? Well, it all depends. If you have pale skin, you are more susceptible to sun damage. The Cancer Research website (cancerresearchuk.org) is good and matter-of-fact on this, if you want to look further.

You might have genes that deal well with skin-related environmental stress like UV exposure, or you might not. How to tell? You can't. Dr Mark Birch-Machin is Professor in Molecular Dermatology at the Newcastle University Institute of Cellular Medicine and a great expert in the damage that UV light does to our skin. The way he puts it is that the damage UV light creates in your skin stacks up over time. It is akin to building a Jenga-style tower of damaged DNA in your skin cells.

At what point does that DNA damage tip over into the sort of cellular mutations that can lead to skin cancer? It's hard to say. Think of it like throwing a pair of dice, says Prof Birch-Machin. When you get the double six, that's skin cancer. It might take a lifetime. But what you don't know is whether your genes have already thrown one of those sixes for you, in which case it may happen a lot faster.

It's hearing that sort of stuff repeatedly over the years that keeps me reapplying sunscreen and keeps me off the sun-lounger on holiday – or at least makes me drag the sun-lounger into the shade and bump up my skin colour with self-tan.

But Don't We Need Sunshine for the Vitamin D?

One big argument for lounging around in the sun – apart from the fact that it feels great – is that we all need more vitamin D.

It's a fair point, particularly if you live somewhere like northern Europe, where we have such a miserably small quota of sunshine that most of us are short of vitamin D by mid-winter, which is a serious issue. Wearing sunscreen, as you might suspect, blocks most of the production of vitamin D.

Vitamin D is a hormone rather than a vitamin. It has a role in regulating our immune system, and it helps keep bones strong because it is needed to help absorb calcium from the gut into the bloodstream; that's also why, if you have too little vitamin D, bone growth suffers. Oily fish, cow's milk, and dairy products are all good sources of vitamin D, but it is quite hard to pack in enough vitamin D just from your diet.

As with other vitamins, you can take supplements to increase the amount of vitamin D in the body. The latest government advice is that we should all take supplements; aim for 1,000–2,000 iU a day.

But the swiftest way for the body to acquire vitamin D is though exposure to UVB rays in sunshine. If you live anywhere north of 40 degrees latitude (that's anywhere north of Majorca, so most of Europe), the sun only delivers enough UVB light to create vitamin D in the skin between April and September. You don't need to spend much time in the sun for the skin to start generating vitamin D. Around 20 minutes, two or three times a week, is enough for pale skin, depending on how much skin you expose – in darker skin types, the process takes longer – and because vitamin D is a fat-soluble vitamin, the body can store it.

The easiest parts of your body to expose to the sun are your face, neck, and hands, though of course they're also the ones most prone to wrinkling. So think laterally. When the sun is hot enough, bare your legs, or your back, or your arms for a few minutes to boost your vitamin D supplies before you slap on the sunscreen – but keep your face protected. I understand that doing this won't be an option if you need to stay covered up for cultural or religious reasons – in which case, you may need to consider supplementation. Also, bear in mind that wearing sunscreen will reduce the rate at which the body makes vitamin D from sunshine, but it doesn't prevent the process from happening, largely because we rarely wear as much sunscreen as we should.

How can you tell if you are short on vitamin D? You can ask your GP for a blood test to see whether you need to be concerned about your vitamin D levels or not. I follow all the advice above, yet every time I have my vitamin D levels tested, I am told that they are low, even when I have been on holiday and have diligently stuck my legs and back in the sun for 20 minutes every day without sunscreen.

Is It an Age Spot or Is It Skin Cancer?

If you're worried about particular marks, moles, or age spots, and are wondering whether they are ordinary pigmentation or potentially cancerous, glance over this list of warning signs from skincancer.org:

A – Asymmetric. Is it a lopsided mark? That's a red flag.

B – Borders. Are these smooth (which is fine) or ragged (which is not)?

C – Colour. Is the mark all the same colour, which probably means it is harmless, or are there different colours within it?

D – Diameter. Is the mark small? That usually, but not always, means it is less of a problem. Or is it bigger than the diameter of the end of a pencil?

E – Evolving. Is the mark changing in shape and growing? If so, that is a warning sign.

There are a number of 'mole clinics' that offer to check over your body for abnormal pigmentation, but the best person to assess whether a mark or mole is problematic is a trained dermatologist who will know exactly what they are looking for, and what may be a problem and why. GPs don't usually know very much about pigmentation and moles, but they can refer you to a dermatologist.

Dermatologists advise that you should get to know your own moles, and check over them every few months. You can take pictures of them on your phone, alongside a ruler, to measure their size. That way, you can assess if anything about them is changing over time.

IS SUNSCREEN ENOUGH TO SAVE OUR SKIN?

I have felt strongly about the need to use sunscreen ever since I began writing about beauty and skincare. It always seemed to me that most of the hot debates in the beauty world – which is the best foundation; should you exfoliate before you cleanse or afterwards; should your nails be squared off or oval-shaped – are ultimately a matter of personal opinion.

But this knowledge about the effects of ultraviolet light is a matter of scientific fact. Over the past 20 years, many scientific studies have shown the damaging effects of UV light on the skin. So not using sunscreen and then complaining about wrinkles is just crazy.

It seems to me to be like knowing that brushing your teeth is a good and necessary thing to do, because it keeps down levels of plaque and stops your teeth from decaying – but not doing it because you think it doesn't really matter, then complaining when your teeth begin to rot and the damage is done.

I wear sunscreen every day, all year round, and would encourage you to do the same.

And yet, not everyone agrees with this approach, even the experts. Dr Natalia Spierings is a dermatologist based in London and someone whose opinion I rate highly. So when I was interviewing her and asked whether we all need to use sunscreen religiously, even in winter, and she shook her head, I was amazed. She pointed out that when it is grey and cold in the UK, we are rarely outside for long enough to make wearing sunscreen an essential part of a daily routine. She says that, even when it is bright and sunny, our first line of defence against sun damage should be avoidance, then physically covering up (with wide brimmed hats, for example) and finally sunscreen. 'Most people do not use nearly enough sunscreen to achieve the stated SPF, so it is not protecting us as much as we think it is,' she says. 'You need about 2.5 ml (half a teaspoon of sunscreen) for the entire face. Many studies have shown that this does not happen in real life, and people only apply half that much.'

(continues)

> **SUNSCREEN – WEIGHING UP FACT AND OPINIONS** *(continued)*
>
> Should you give up on the sunscreen? No. I would keep wearing it. I just mention this, above, to show there's always more detail to consider, even when an issue looks clear-cut.

If you are at all worried, get an expert opinion as soon as you can. Rates of incidence of skin cancer have more than doubled since the 1990s. As I mentioned, there are over 136,000 new cases of skin cancer in the UK every year, and the number is rising, even though we are theoretically much more sun- and skin-aware than in decades past. So it's not something we can ignore.

How High a Factor Should I Use?

Would you be shocked to hear that I'd be happy if you're wearing SPF15 (as long as you reapplied it later in the day)? That's because the protection offered by sunscreen depends partly, but not entirely, on the UV filters or blocks that it contains.

SPF – sun protection factor – refers to the ingredients that block UVB, the 'burning' rays. SPF15 blocks 94% of UVB, SPF30 blocks 96%, and SPF50 blocks 98%. So you can see that SPF15 is able to block the vast majority of UVB rays. The ingredients that shield against UVA are included in proportion to the amount of SPF; as long as the product offers 'broad spectrum' protection, that will be enough. A product doesn't have to say 'five star UVA; that's just a description used by one of the major retailers. A logo of UVA in a circle, or merely the words 'broad spectrum protection' will tell you that it's there.

So although SPF15 might not sound like much (these days; I remember when the idea of wearing factor 6 seemed like a lot, but that was back in the 1970s), it will actually provide good protection from UVB rays.

Why I said, above, that protection from sunscreen depends only 'partly' on the UV filters is because the main issue with sunscreen is generally that we don't apply enough of it, we don't apply it thoroughly enough, and we don't reapply it as frequently as needed to gain the protection offered on the label.

Dermatologists always like to point out that products with SPF50 can give us a false sense of security about staying out in the sun. They would like us to remember all the other sensible sun strategies – like seeking shade, wearing a hat and sunglasses, and covering up with clothing.

Which Sunscreen Should I Use?

Any, any you like, because if you like the formulation, you are more likely to use it. If you prefer to wear a physical sunscreen, fine, and they may be a better choice for sensitive skins; but be aware that purely physical sunscreens shift off the skin more easily, and don't provide as thorough protection as combined, or chemical sunscreens. The following sections tell you some of my favourites.

Physical Sunscreens

Here are three physical sunscreens, ones that shield your skin with a physical barrier of product, from widely available brands:

- **Avene Mineral Fluid**, SPF50, £18.50, boots.com. This sunscreen is runny enough to spread easily, and settles down to a matt finish. It's a good choice for sensitive skins.

- **Clinique Mineral Sunscreen Fluid for Face**, £22, clinique.co.uk. This sunscreen looks alarmingly white when you first apply it – but as you rub it in, it blends properly into the skin.

- **Murad City Skin Age Defense Broad Spectrum SPF 50**, £60, murad.co.uk. This sunscreen is expensive, but it manages to be broad-spectrum-protective, and all-mineral, yet pleasant to wear without looking chalky on pale skins or ashy on darker ones.

Here are three physical sunscreens from specialist brands:

- **Heliocare 360 Mineral Tolerance Fluid**, £27, thetweakmentsguide.com. This broad-spectrum sunscreen is really runny and spreads well. Though there is a suspicion of chalkiness when you first rub it into the skin, it dries down properly clear so it suits all skin tones. The formula contains Heliocare's special antioxidant, Fernblock, which adds an extra level of environmental protection, too.

- **NeoStrata Sheer Physical Protection SPF50**, £30, thetweakmentsguide.com. Great sunscreen that looks and feels more like a make-up primer. It has a beige tint, too, so it gives a bit of coverage on pale and medium skin tones.
- **Alumier Clearshield Broad Spectrum Sunscreen SPF42**, about £38, alumiermd.co.uk. Lightweight, broad-spectrum protection, with added niacinamide which is soothing and calms blemishes, so it's a good choice for acne-prone skin. You need to go via the website to find a clinic that supplies this range in order to buy it.

Absorbing Sunscreens

Here are six absorbing sunscreens, ones that use chemical filters to absorb the UV light and prevent it affecting your skin.

These first three absorbing sunscreens are from widely available brands.

- **Altruist Sunscreen SPF50**, £8 for two, amazon.co.uk. Created by a skin-cancer specialist using his industry contacts to make a product that is effective but also a total bargain so that everyone can afford it, this is a product that everyone should have to hand. Lightweight, well-absorbed, fragrance free... you can buy the SPF30 version of it by the litre, so there's no excuse for not wearing the stuff.
- **La Roche-Posay Anthelios Ultra-Light Invisible Fluid Sun Cream SPF50**, £17.50, boots.com. Lightweight, moisturising, runny so that it spreads easily, yet gives decent coverage, this is a brilliant all-round product and works well on darker skin tones, too.
- **EVY Daily UV Face Mousse SPF30**, £25, evy.uk.com. Fabulous mousse-textured sunscreen with a special type of patented medical technology in its mix which means the sunscreen binds itself right into the outer layers of the skin and, the brand says, isn't shifted by sweating or rubbing, for six hours. Good for sensitive skin.

Here are three great absorbing sunscreens from specialist brands:

- **Paula's Choice Clear Ultra-Light Daily Hydrating Fluid SPF30**, £34, paulaschoice.co.uk. Paula's Choice has so many fab sunscreens it's really hard to pick out just one. I've flagged up this one because it really is ultra-lightweight, so all you people who say you can't stand the feel of sunscreen on your skin, please try this one before giving up on the stuff.

- **SkinCeuticals Advanced Brightening UV Defence SPF50**, £45, skinceuticals.co.uk. This sunscreen is getting a lot of interest because it contains tranexamic acid, an ingredient which can help reduce pigmentation, and niacinamide. Technically, its sunscreen component is a new hybrid which has physical protective aspects as well as absorbing ones.

- **Medik8 Advanced Day Total Protect SPF30**, £48, thetweakmentsguide.com. With broad-spectrum filters to guard against UVA and UVB, hyaluronic acid to keep skin comfortable, and antioxidants including superoxide dismutase, this is a multi-tasking moisturiser with SPF 30.

Physical and Absorbing Combined Sunscreens

Here are three absorbing sunscreens, from widely available brands, that also include physical protection:

- **Bioderma Photoderm M**, £13.20, boots.com. Thorough UV protection, in a formulation including an ingredient called glabridin, which helps rein in the activity of tyrosinase, an enzyme involved in creating pigment in the skin, so the product really can help reduce the formation of pigmentation.

- **Eucerin Sun Face Pigment Control SPF50**, £16.99, boots.com. New offering from this reliable brand, with extra protection against high-energy visible light (which is an added stress on the skin). Nice to use, too.

- **Ultrasun Face SPF30**, £20, victoriahealth.com. Particularly nice product from this excellent range of sunscreens, with no fragrance or oil, but with added antioxidants to help protect the skin.

Here are four absorbing sunscreens, from specialist brands, that also include physical protection:

- **Heliocare 360 Fluid Cream SPF50**, £27, thetweakmentsguide.com. Great sunscreen for converting people who say 'but sunscreen is so icky and sticky' – it sinks in well, has a matte finish, and gives reliable protection.

- **Epionce Ultra Shield SPF50**, £31, epionce.co.uk. Great, effective, gentle, hydrating sunscreen. Very good for sensitive skin, too.

- **Teoxane Advanced Perfecting Shield SPF30**, £52, thetweakmentsguide.com. Lovely light cream which feels more like a sophisticated moisturiser than a sunscreen. It's pricey, but I love this because it has hyaluronic acid and antioxidants in it, too, and sits beautifully both on its own and under make-up.

- **iS Clinical Extreme Protect SPF30**, £66, thetweakmentsguide.com. A thick and creamy sunscreen you just know is doing a solid job of protecting your skin. It's one I reach for when I know I'm going to be outside for longer than I ought to be on a summer's day.

How Much Sunscreen Should I Use on My Face?

You probably need to use more sunscreen than you'd expect.

When sunscreen is being tested in the lab – by the stringent regulations of EU law, they have to be put through consistent tests on standardized equipment) – it is applied quite thickly. The testers use 2mg of product per square centimetre of skin. That works out at the equivalent of using 3ml, or half a teaspoon of sunscreen, to cover your face and neck. Do you use that much? If you're spreading the stuff more thinly, you won't be getting the protection suggested on the product.

That's one of the big arguments for using products with a higher SPF. At least, if you spread SPF50 a bit thinly, you'll be better protected than if you spread SPF15 a bit thinly.

Do I Need to Wear SPF If My Skin Is Brown or Black?

Yes. Darker skin has more melanin in it, which provides greater defence from burning from UVB rays, but it is still susceptible to the pigmentation changes that UV light provokes. Applying sunscreen carefully will reduce this. (See the section 'How Skincare Can Help with Everyday Pigmentation and Post-Inflammatory Hyperpigmentation' on page 193 for more about managing pigmentation.)

Here are some sunscreens, recommended by my brown- and black-skinned beauty expert friends, which absolutely won't look ashy on darker skin.

- **La Roche-Posay Anthelios Ultra-Light Invisible Fluid Sun Cream SPF50**, £17.50, boots.com. Lightweight, moisturising, runny so that it spreads easily, yet gives decent coverage, this is a brilliant all-round product.

- **Beauty Pie Ultralight UVA/UVB SPF25,** £35, beautypie.com. Creamy, yet as light as it promises, this leaves skin feeling hydrated and velvety, so it works well as a primer for make-up.

- **Glossier Invisible Shield Daily Sunscreen SPF30**, £20, glossier.com. This is more like a serum-gel in texture, and clear, too, so there's absolutely no white cast to it. It sinks into the skin easily and makes a great make-up base.

- **Ecooking Sunscreen SPF30**, £16.50, feelunique.com. Light and moisturising sunscreen from this Danish naturals brand, which gives good coverage and a glowy finish.

- **Heliocare 360 Mineral Tolerance Fluid** SPF50, £27, thetweakmentsguide.com. You wouldn't expect this to be a good choice for skin of colour, seeing as it comes out of the bottle as a white liquid and is made with mineral-only filters, but it absorbs well into the skin and dries down clear and invisible. A good choice for sensitive skin.

- **Supergoop Unseen Sunscreen**, £30, cultbeauty.co.uk. Clear and undetectable, this is fragrance-free and super-lightweight, too. Another one that's good under make-up.

- **Murad Invisiblur Perfecting Shield Broad Spectrum SPF 30,** £65, murad.co.uk. It's really a primer, this lovely smoothing, line-and-pore-blurring product, but it's also a broad-spectrum sunscreen. It's a thick-ish gel that spreads well on the skin; because it's clear, it works on all skin tones.

Sunscreens for Sunscreen-Haters

If you have avoided sunscreens because you hate the feel of them, here are six oil-free sunscreens that might just make you change your mind – and they're great for oily or acne-prone skin.

- **La Roche-Posay Anthelios Sun Protection Face Mist SPF 50,** £14, boots.com. The normal Anthelios XL formulation, which I've mentioned before, is light and good on oily skin (the XL stands for Extra Light). But if you want something even lighter – this mist was designed for people with oily skin, and it's also a blessing for anyone who really objects to the feel of a cream or lotion. Just make sure you spray on enough to get full protection. Also great for topping up sunscreen during the day.

- **Avène Cleanance Tinted Suncare for Oily and Blemish-Prone Skin SPF50+,** £18.50, boots.com. Avène's whole Cleanance range is geared towards oily skin types, and this is non-greasy and non-irritating, so it's great for skin that's prone to breakouts.

- **Heliocare 360 Oil-Free Gel SPF50,** £27, thetweakmentsguide.com. This is a lightweight gel which dries down to an invisible, matte finish, with ingredients that help protect your skin's DNA. The '360' in the name refers to the fact that it protects against visible light and infra-red light, as well as providing broad-spectrum UVA and UVB protection.

- **Clarins UV Plus Anti-Pollution Sunscreen,** £32.50, clarins.co.uk. This is super-light and oil-free, with an extra layer of pollution-shielding technology, so a great one for anyone still working in a busy city.

- **Paula's Choice Resist Anti-Aging Moisturiser SPF 50**, £34, paulaschoice.co.uk. So lightweight and luxe-feeling you won't even know this is a sunscreen. You also won't even notice it's there once it has vanished into your skin, leaving it hydrated and matte.
- **PCA Skin Weightless Protection Broad Spectrum SPF45**, £40, pcaskin.co.uk. Another sunscreen that you simply won't know is there. Ultra-light, highly protective, and with a formula enhanced with skin-supporting antioxidants.

Do I Have to Reapply Sunscreen During the Day?

I'm sure you know that on holiday, you need to reapply sunscreen every few hours, or after swimming, or after sweating it off. But what about facial sunscreen, when you're going about your everyday business at home?

If we wear sunscreen on an everyday basis, we tend to put it on first thing in the morning, then never top it up – either because we're not in the habit of doing it, or because it would mean taking off our make-up and doing it all over again, and who can be bothered, particularly if you're not spending the day outside?

You may well feel that, unless it's the summer, and you're out and about, you don't really need to reapply sunscreen.

That's fair enough – but if you don't top it up, you won't be getting the protection that the product claims it is offering. How to top up your sunscreen without messing up your make-up? Try a spray-on product, a wipe-on product from a make-up-style compact, or a brush-on mineral powder. The brush-on powders are really helpful for topping up sunscreen, and I love them because they're especially useful for faces like mine which always go shiny during the day, but I wouldn't want to rely on them on their own without a liquid sunscreen underneath.

Here are two great spray-on sunscreens:

- **Vichy Capital Soleil Solar Protective Water SPF50**, £19, vichy.co.uk. This is a proper sunscreen – but in a light enough formulation that you can spritz it on over make-up.

- **Kate Somerville UncompliKated SPF50**, £32, katesomerville.co.uk. It's a soft-focus make-up setting spray... and it's also SPF50 and has a light-as-air feel on the skin.

Here are two great sunscreens that come in make-up-style compacts:

- **Heliocare 360 Colour Compact SPF50**, £34.99, heliocare.co.uk. Another great sun-protecting compact – but this one is a liquid formulation in a spongy compact, to pat on where it's needed. This has mineral and chemical/ absorbing sunscreens and comes in two colours – beige, which suits pale-Caucasian skin like mine, and bronze which is a couple of shades warmer. Easy to use and easy to carry about.

- **Skinbetter+ Science Sunbetter**, £55, thetweakmentsguide.com. This is a really clever, easy-to-apply mineral sunscreen which, thanks to its colour-adapting pigments, works on a wide range of skin tones. It looks like a solid-cream foundation compact, in a click-shut case, goes on easily and gives a fabulous smooth, pore-blurring finish that's as good as make-up.

Here are two great brush-on sunscreens:

- **Brush on Block SPF30**, £34, brushonblocksunscreen.co.uk. A lightweight powder sunscreen, delivered through a brush. It's a great product, and easy to stash in a pocket or handbag.

- **ZO Skincare Sunscreen + Powder Broad Spectrum SPF30**, about £54, zo-skinhealth.co.uk (see the website for stockists; you need a consultation with a skincare advisor before you can buy from this brand). This has a big brush and a powder-capsule which screws into its base. The product comes in different colours, and gives out a fine, even cover of powder.

What About Moisturisers-with-Sunscreen?

Yes, absolutely, you could use a moisturiser that includes sunscreen. These products have been tested the same way as sunscreens, so the SPF rating is accurate. Just check they contain UVA protection too, and be sure to apply them liberally – a few dabs on your dry patches won't give you the protection you need.

What About Make-Up with SPF Protection?

Wearing foundation with SPF seems like an easy way of killing two birds with one stone. It's great that cosmetics companies are beginning to add sun protection filters into their make-up, but think of these as an additional layer of protection, rather than something that you wear instead of sunscreen. Why? Because you'll need to wear half a teaspoon of make-up on your face and neck in order to get that protection promised on your tube of foundation. None of us is going to wear that much makeup. So don't rely on the SPF in make-up alone.

If you *are* relying on the SPF in your makeup, check whether the product offers UVA protection, too (it will say on the packaging). Some do, some don't, so it's worth checking.

And What About Edible Sunscreen?

I promise, I'm not pulling your leg. There is a skincare supplement called Fernblock, found in Heliocare Ultra Capsules, which you can take to bolster your skin's defences against UV light.

I had presumed that this edible sunscreen was random marketing hype until, attending a cosmetic-doctors' conference last year, I found the subject being discussed in serious depth in one of the sessions. Yes, these doctors often recommend it for patients who can't or won't use sunscreen; and yes, it seems to work, increasing skin's resistance to sunburn by 300 per cent. How? Fernblock is a natural antioxidant extract which prevents ultraviolet light damaging the skin's DNA. You can buy it online at around £28 for 60 capsules, though Heliocare and any website selling the product will emphasise that this is not designed to replace sunscreen, but to be used in conjunction with sunscreen. Just in case you were thinking of trying it.

How to Apply Sunscreen

Put sunscreen on last, on top of any other skincare that you are using, as a shield for your face and neck.

Blue HEV Light, Infra-Red Light...

Apart from UVA and UVB, various other types of light reach our faces – and skincare science is showing some of these to be bad for the skin.

The first of these types of light is *high energy visible light*, or *HEV light*. This is part of the spectrum of daylight, and is also the blue light from our beloved phones and tablets, and from our computer screens. HEV light is bad for the skin because it has a longer wavelength than UVA rays, which means it can reach further into the skin and damage it.

Next is infra-red light (IR light), which reaches further still into the dermis. IR light can be very beneficial for the skin. I'm a big fan of skin treatments that combine red light and near–infra-red light, which have been shown to stimulate genuine repair deep within the skin. That only takes a small dose of IR light a few times a week. Clinical studies on IR light have found it to be harmful, but that is usually looking at doses of IR light many, many times more than most of us would experience in a week of exposure.

Health researchers have been publishing more about the effects of HEV light and IR light recently. As a result, skincare companies are flagging up the dangers of these types of light as a way to sell more products.

Just how much of a problem HEV and IR light pose depends on whom you talk to. Most dermatologists will say that wearing a good sunscreen during the day is as much you can do to keep blue light and IR light at bay, and will add that using an antioxidant rich serum will help the skin defend itself against light-induced ageing.

If you're habitually on your laptop late at night, you could invest in a pair of yellow tinted computer-glasses, which don't cost much and which block the blue light from the screen. I don't know how much wearing them is protecting my eyes, but I find that if I'm working late, wearing these glasses reduces the glare from the screen, and that's a really good thing for tired eyes. Reducing exposure to blue light should also help limit the disruption that blue light can cause to your body clock.

Pollution and Skin Protection

The issue of air pollution and what this does to our skin is one that has come to the fore in the past few years. In short, it's not good news.

WHY IS POLLUTION BAD FOR THE SKIN?

In a nutshell, pollution accelerates ageing processes in the skin. It is particularly bad news for the skin because pollution particles are so very small, up to 20 times smaller than our pores, that they slip straight into the skin where they cause inflammation. That's bad enough in itself, as low-level inflammation is the root of all ageing in cells; but pollution particles also dehydrate the skin and speed up the breakdown of collagen and elastin, the proteins that keep the skin firm and stretchy.

ARE THERE SPECIAL ANTI-POLLUTION SKINCARE PRODUCTS?

Skincare companies have woken up to the need to tackle pollution and responded with a range of products including anti-pollution cleansers, protective serums packed with extra antioxidants to fight the free radical molecules that pollution produces in the skin, and special sunscreens to help shield the skin. There are also new anti-pollution active ingredients which form a sticky film on the skin and help trap pollution molecules, which work well.

DO I NEED SPECIAL ANTI-POLLUTION SKINCARE PRODUCTS?

All these products are useful for the skin, and it's good to get the skin as clean and keep it as well protected as possible – but here's the thing. Those microscopic scraps of PM2.5 'particulate matter' will weasel their way deep into your skin regardless of the sunscreen you use, or the cleanser with which you try to extract them.

You can do yourself a favour by cleansing thoroughly, loading on the antioxidants, and using sunscreen. These actions will help keep your skin in good shape, which will help it resist the effects of pollution to the best of its ability.

So do you need special anti-pollution skincare products? No – unless you find properly specialised products with active ingredients that trap pollution before it gets into the skin. Here are two to consider:

- **Ren Flash Defence Anti-Pollution Mist**, £24, spacenk.com. A super-light spray containing biosaccharide gum which provides a fine, non-sticky invisible shield to trap pollution.
- **Ultrasun Anti Pollution Daily Face Fluid**, SP50, £28, marksandspencer.com. This contains an ingredient called Pollustop which creates a protective film over the skin to keep out pollution particles. And it's a great sunscreen, too.

The Bottom Line: Protecting Your Skin

You need to wear a broad-spectrum sunscreen all year round to protect your skin from the damage that ultraviolet rays will do to it. Which type of sunscreen – physical, chemical, natural-and-organic – and whether you apply it straight to clean skin in the morning or on top of your other products is entirely up to you. But just do yourself a favour and wear it.

RULE SIX: SUPPORT YOUR SKIN

What else can you do to support your skin and to improve the way it looks, apart from using skincare? This is where lifestyle factors come into play, and there's a lot you can do to help yourself. All these factors have an impact.

Food and Drink

We're all familiar with the idea that what we eat affects the way we look. There is a good case to be made for the 'beauty from the inside out' argument. What we eat certainly affects the way our skin looks. But we get a bit hazy about exactly how what we are eating or drinking might improve or damage our skin.

I'm sure you don't need me to labour the point about a healthy diet, but in general, eating more vegetables, lean protein, and healthy fats, and cutting back on sugar, refined carbohydrates, and alcohol will benefit your skin no end. Here's a quick recap on the detail of how to eat your way to smoother skin.

WHAT TO EAT

This is the good stuff. I know you know this already. This is just a reminder. Base your diet around these, and you won't go far wrong.

- **Vegetables.** Not just an add-on-extra at mealtimes, these should make up the bulk of our diet. Colourful vegetables provide a range of antioxidants (carotene in carrots, lycopene in tomatoes, anthocyanins in blueberries) which help neutralise free radicals, the unstable molecules that accelerate the ageing process within all cells of the body, skin included. So 'eating the rainbow', as nutritionists urge, is really good for our skin. All the fibre in vegetables is good for gut health, too.

- **Protein.** Eggs, tofu, fish, meat, cheese, nuts, and pulses are all good sources of protein. Our bodies use protein as the building blocks of the skin as well as of muscles, bones, and hair.

- **Fats.** Lipids, aka fats, are a vital component of the membrane that surrounds every cell in the body; having your cell membranes in good nick improves everything from the general health to better cell-to-cell communication). In the skin, healthy cell membranes help keep water inside the cells, and help the skin to form a better defensive barrier to the world, through which water does not escape so easily, and through which bacteria, dirt, and pollution cannot so easily penetrate. What we particularly need are omega-3 fatty acids, because our bodies do not make these and because very few of us eat enough of them. Find them in oily fish – see the section 'Essential Fatty Acids (EFAs)' on page 164 for more detail on this – and supplements.

- **Wholegrains.** Wholegrains such as brown rice and porridge oats are well known as some of the dietary 'good guys'. They are rich in fibre and nutrients; they're unprocessed; and they help to improve the balance of 'good' bacteria in our gut, which has a knock-on effect for skin health.

- **Fermented foods**. Kimchi and kefir are not foodstuffs that many of us would have considered with interest 10 years ago. But there is now such overwhelming evidence of the benefits of foods like these for the health of our guts, and such a close connection between the health of the gut and the health of the skin, that for many of us they've become staples in our grocery baskets.

WHAT TO AVOID EATING

Again, this won't be news to you. But in case you need a reminder, these are the worst of the bad stuff, as far as your skin is concerned.

- **Sugar.** Eating sugar will age your skin faster than anything except smoking or sunbathing, thanks to a process called glycation, which basically results in a hardening – a crystallising, if you like – of the collagen fibres that help keep your skin strong. And, yes, 'sugar' means sugar in all its forms. As well as the sugar you might spoon into tea or coffee, it means sweet things, such as cakes, biscuits, jam, sweetened yoghurts (they may be low-fat, but their sugar content is often high), sweetened savoury cooking sauces (teriyaki sauce is almost 40 per cent sugar) and, depending on how far you want to take it, higher-sugar fruit such as dates or tropical fruit. Some people think 'natural' sugar, such as agave syrup or honey, is a better choice than refined sugar. Here's the bad news: as far as your body is concerned, it is still sugar, and still bad for your skin.

- **Processed food.** This offers fewer nutrients and more added extras with names your grandmother wouldn't have recognised. Freshly prepared meals are much better for our bodies and for our skin.

WHAT TO DRINK

Water is a good starting point. Boring? Yes. Obvious? Of course. But it is still very true that water is the best thing for your body and hence, for your skin.

WHY IS DRINKING WATER GOOD FOR THE SKIN?

I mentioned earlier (in the sidebar 'How Drinking Water Affects Skin Moisture Levels' on page 75) that, from a physiological point of view, there is no direct connection between internal hydration – how much water you have consumed – and your skin's hydration. You don't 'hydrate your skin' by guzzling gallons of water; that's just not the way your body works. So why is it that people who drink more water look brighter-eyed and clearer skinned than those who don't?

When your body is well-hydrated, all its systems function better. The gut works better, the immune system kicks into a higher gear, and your skin tends to look better, too. Many experts say this is not simply due to drinking water, but because people who drink lots of plain water probably have a bunch of other healthy habits, too. They probably eat plenty of vegetables, drink modest amounts of tea, coffee and alcohol, avoid sugary soft drinks, take regular exercise, avoid smoking, and get enough sleep, too. And put together, all of these things impact the look of your skin.

WHAT TO AVOID DRINKING

Ideally, you should avoid drinking all the usual suspects:

- **Alcohol.** Apart from the fact that it is such a pleasure to drink, alcohol has little to recommend it, particularly where the skin is concerned. Alcohol dilates the blood vessels, and repeated dilation stretches the capillaries and can make them show up permanently as red veins on the skin, leaving the complexion looking weathered. Persistent regular drinking leads to bloating of the face, too. If you're hanging onto the fact that red wine contains the powerful antioxidant resveratrol – sorry, but you'd need to drink 500 litres of it to achieve a therapeutic dose.

- **Caffeinated drinks.** Yes, we love them, but they rev up our nervous systems and can cause flushing in anyone prone to rosacea.

- **Fizzy drinks.** These are packed with sugar – there's eight or nine teaspoons of sugar in the average cola drink.

- **Fruit juice.** I'm not a fan, as this is also packed with sugar and lacks the useful fibre that you get if you eat whole fruit.

- **Smoothies.** Great if they're full of vegetables, less great if they're mostly fruit juice.

- **Milk.** Some studies in the USA have identified a link between drinking a lot of milk – say, a litre a day – and acne. It is thought that the hormones in the milk, produced by the cows that are stimulated continually to lactate, provokes hormonal imbalance which is what is causing spots in the first place (see the website of the American Academy of Dermatology, aad.org, for more on this – it's a 'maybe', not a definite thing). And, anecdotally, you can always find a friend or two who claims their skin improved when they gave up their latte habit. But I'm reluctant to condemn milk, as it's a good thing, nutritionally, and a good source of calcium, and most of us need more calcium to shore up our bones.

WHAT ABOUT DIETARY SUPPLEMENTS AND 'BEAUTY SUPPLEMENTS'?

Beyond those general guidelines for what to eat, here are some specific supplements which I have found helpful.

Essential Fatty Acids (EFAs)

Although their reputation for improving heart health has been called into question, omega-3 essential fatty acids are vital for the health and good functioning of the skin, because they're a crucial part of the lipid (fatty) membrane that surrounds every cell in the body. When the skin-cell membranes are in good shape, they hold onto moisture more effectively, and so keep the skin softer. Can you make your skin softer and better hydrated simply by loading up on essential fatty acids? You probably can.

The quickest way to pack in the omega-3s is to eat oily fish (salmon, mackerel, sardines, fresh tuna) but without overdoing it, because although this fish is really good for us, it tends to contain low levels of pollutants like mercury, which can then build up in the body (unless you're buying wild Alaskan salmon, but that is super-expensive). Two portions a week is the usual amount suggested as the maximum by health experts, though I tend to think that, being well past child-bearing age, and less bothered about heavy-metal accumulation, I may as well eat as much oily fish as I can, because of the benefits.

What oily fish gives you is two particular omega-3 fatty acids called docosahexaenoic acid (DHA) and eicosapentaenoic acid (EPA). There is a third, plant-based omega-3 fatty acid called alpha-linolenic acid (ALA), which is found in foods like walnuts, flaxseed oil, and chia seeds; such foods are worth adding into your diet for omega-3 backup, as it were, but fish is a better source, unless you're vegan. That's because once you've eaten ALA, your body has to convert it to DHA and EPA, so it ends up being only about 10% as effective as the marine-based omega-3s. This is why nutritionists are always going on about eating oily fish, and why omega-3 supplements are such a good idea if you're not a great fish-eater.

Vitamin C Supplements

We have all grown up with the idea that vitamin C is good for our body and, by extension, for the skin – and that we need to get vitamin C from our diet because, along with monkeys and guinea pigs, humans are the only mammals whose bodies can't make their own supplies of vitamin C.

Lots of us scoff vitamin C supplements, particularly if we are feeling under the weather, with a view to boosting our immune systems and warding off coughs, colds, and viruses. And I can't be the only person to be disappointed often to read in the papers about new studies showing that vitamin C has no special powers in this area, and that because it is a water-soluble vitamin and our bodies cannot store it, if we ingest large amounts of it, we will simply excrete it, thus creating expensive urine but no great benefit to our bodies.

I had given up on vitamin C as a supplement until three years ago, when I heard that a special sort of vitamin C, called Altrient C, had just completed clinical trials – proper double-blind, placebo-controlled, medical-grade clinical trials. These trials showed that if you took enough of their product – three 1,000mg doses a day – for three months, it could achieve impressive improvements in skin elasticity and hydration, as well as boosting collagen levels in the skin.

Would I like to be the first writer to try it out? the company asked. You bet. So I stopped all the 'active' skincare that I usually use (the retinoids, the glycolic acid, and the vitamin C serums), stopped having any of the tweakments that I have to keep my skin in good shape, and stopped taking collagen supplements which I also take for the same reason (yes, they work, too, see below). Then I had detailed measurements taken of my skin elasticity, hydration levels, and collagen density with the most sophisticated machines available in London, and started taking the vitamins.

What's different about Altrient C is that the active part of it, sodium ascorbate, is encapsulated in tiny fatty particles called *liposomes* which make a great delivery system (if liposomes sound familiar – yes, they are the same things used to transport active ingredients into the skin in face creams). In a liposomal vitamin C supplement, the liposomes enable the vitamin C to get through the stomach, without being broken up by the stomach acids, into the gut, where it is absorbed into the blood stream. The advantage of this is that your body gets the benefit of around 98% of each dose of vitamin C, whereas from normal high-street supplements of the stuff, you can absorb as little as 10–15 per cent – and if you have ever tried taking more than 2,000mg of those a day, you will know how much normal vitamin C upsets the stomach and irritates the gut.

Altrient doesn't taste great, but it's not revolting. Each individual dose comes in a sachet that you squeeze out into a small amount of water, swill around, and gulp down. Really not too difficult, even if it has the consistency of orange snot.

I really didn't think Altrient would make a difference to my skin. I thought my skin would get a lot worse before it showed any improvement – if there was any. But guess what? It worked. My hydration levels were picking up before the end of the first month, and after three months I had notched up 22.8 per cent more collagen, a 30 per cent rise in hydration, and a whopping 64.3 per cent improvement in elasticity.

Altrient C isn't cheap, at around £1 a sachet, but two years on from that trial, I am still buying it in bulk, I was so impressed by those results, and I'm now stocking it in the shop on thetweakmentsguide.com. And of course it improves the skin all over your body, not just on your face, and gives your immune system a helping hand, too.

Another liposomal vitamin C that I have recently discovered is YourZooki. This also offers 1,000mg per sachet, costs around £1 per sachet, and tastes delicious.

Collagen Supplements

I used to be hugely sceptical about collagen supplements too, but became a convert a few years ago. Collagen drinks and collagen powders are one of those newish arrivals on the beauty scene that look like so much snake oil (Drink this potion! Look more lovely!). But the brands which contain enough of the right sort of collagen can make a measurable difference to your skin, and several brands have conducted clinical trials which demonstrate the improvements that their products can make.

The new collagen drinks contain 'hydrolysed' collagen – that is, collagen that has been broken up into tiny fragments. What I couldn't understand at first was why consuming collagen supplements would do you more good than eating lots of lean protein, which would be broken down into protein/collagen fragments in your stomach. But then I learned that providing the body with a ready supply of hydrolysed collagen has two effects. First, it encourages the body to use this collagen for repair where repair is needed. And second, by some curious internal alchemy, when our bodies detect a lot of these hydrolysed collagen fragments in the blood, it presumes there has been some trauma to the skin that is needing repair, so it starts to make more collagen of its own.

The hydrolysed collagen in these supplements is usually marine collagen, from, say, the skin of freshwater fish; sometimes it is bovine collagen, from cow hides.

In order to make a difference, trials have found that you need to consume somewhere between 3,000mg and 10,000mg a day of this hydrolysed collagen.

Lots of supplements offer this – including Totally Derma, Absolute Collagen, Pure Gold Collagen, Skinade, Pink Cloud Beauty, Rejuvenated Collagen Shots, LQ Liquid Health Hair,

Skin and Nails, and a newcomer called Aethern which is even more expensive than the others but has very impressive data from clinical trials. The other consideration, to get technical for a sec, is the molecular size of the hydrolysed collagen – because the smaller its molecules are, the better they will be absorbed by the body. Molecular size (or, more accurately, molecular weight) is measured in units called *daltons*, with larger molecules being measured in kilodaltons (kDa) – thousands of daltons.

Several of the supplements mentioned above have a molecular size of 2 or 3 kilodaltons, and some brands boast clinical studies showing how well their products work.

WHAT ABOUT IMEDEEN'S 'MARINE COMPLEX' SUPPLEMENT?

If you are familiar with the world of beauty supplements, you might be wondering whether Imedeen should be on this list. It's not, just because its key ingredient is a patented 'marine complex' that contains fish extract including collagen, but it isn't totally collagen-focussed like these other supplements. But Imedeen also improves the skin measurably; the company has a good deal of data on its website detailing all the studies they have conducted to prove this.

Imedeen also had 'Advanced Beauty Shots' which offer 2,500mg of hydrolysed porcine collagen – ie not as much collagen as the other supplements, though it should be enough to show some skin smoothing over time; and it is derived from pigs, which won't suit everyone.

I will happily consume any of the above. They're not cheap and, depending on which you choose, will add up to £100 a month to your skincare bill. If that's within your budget, they are worth considering, in order to firm up your beauty-from-the-inside-out strategy.

Don't go over the top and take more than the recommended dose of collagen supplements. While doses of up to 10,000mg a day have been shown to be effective, it is thought that taking too much collagen could have a negative effect on collagen building, though the researchers who are working on the studies for this can't yet say how much is too much. Just so you know.

Probiotics

Probiotics improve digestion and gut health. I have never taken probiotics consistently enough to note a difference in my skin, but other people often tell me how much probiotic supplements help their skin. So they might be something to try, particularly if you struggle with gut-related issues which may be having an impact on your skin.

Boost Your Skin with Smart Lifestyle Hacks

You can also support your skin by making lifestyle changes, such as getting proper sleep, taking exercise, finding the right balance between stress and relaxation, and practising being happy. I know those are all easier to say than to do – but here's the detail, to help your motivation.

GET ENOUGH SLEEP

Getting a proper night's rest is vital for the health of our skin, much more vital than we used to think. We all know how, after a bad night's sleep, or a week of bad nights, our skin seems to look greyish and drawn, with eyes that are both weary and puffy. If you've ever wondered whether lack of sleep is actually harming your skin and making you look tired, the bad news is that yes, it is.

There is now scientific backing to show the benefits of beauty sleep – and how a lack of sleep can accelerate signs of skin ageing.

A study conducted at the University Hospitals Case Medical Centre in Cleveland in 2013 showed that people who consistently slept badly – for five hours or less each night – had skin that was more dehydrated, had less elasticity, and was more irregular in tone than those who notched up seven hours or more. 'Sleep-deprived women show signs of premature skin ageing and a decrease in their skin's ability to recover after sun exposure,' said Dr Elma Baron, director of the skin study at UH Case Medical Center, at the time.

I know this from personal experience, too. Not just from going short on sleep and looking rough, but from a skin-and-lifestyle trial I did throughout 2014 with scientists at the University of Newcastle, who were funded by Procter & Gamble and Innovate

UK. Each month I adopted a different lifestyle behaviour – eating more vegetables, drinking more water, an extreme exercise regime, and so on, all the while sending swabs of skin cells to the labs at Newcastle so they could assess the state of the energy levels in my mitochondria. The mitochondria are the energy-producing power-houses of our cells, and the DNA within them faithfully records all the damage that is done to it, and this is what the scientists were measuring.

Why did I do this? Just for fun. And because I was curious to see what it showed, and because it made a cracking story, a year later.

But to get back to the point, few of these behaviours showed a great deal of difference. Drink more water? Not a jot of difference. Eating more veg? A bit of an improvement. But going short on sleep? I only did one week with less than five hours sleep each night, but that was enough for the scientists to record a massive 10 per cent increase in damage to those mitochondrial energy levels.

We all seem to be finding it more and more difficult to sleep, given our busy lifestyles and our addiction to our phones and tablets which overstimulate our poor brains. But getting more sleep is something we all need to work at – for our health as well as for the appearance of our skin.

TAKE SOME EXERCISE

Exercise is good for your heart, lungs, and body, and it's great for your skin, too. Taking regular aerobic exercise – the sort that raises your pulse – makes the heart pump blood more swiftly around the body; and as the body warms up, the blood flow through the tiny capillaries that run up towards the surface of the skin increases. As well as bringing a healthy glow to the face, this brings an increased supply of oxygen and nutrients to every cell in the skin, and carry away waste products such as free radicals. (It's not 'detoxing' the skin as such – detoxing is what the liver does – but it keeps cells healthier).

REDUCE YOUR STRESS LEVELS

There might not seem to be a direct connection between the stress that you suffer from in daily life and the way your skin looks, but scientific studies have shown that there is a very direct link. A little stress is good for us, to keep us on our toes and gee us up for the task in hand; but continuous, relentless stress certainly isn't good. Stress raises cortisol levels in the body, and this has a clear impact on skin. In that year-long study that I mentioned a moment ago, every time I recorded persistent high stress levels, the scientists noticed a leap in the damage to my mitochondrial DNA, even worse than the levels recorded from my lack-of-sleep week. Just saying.

MAKE TIME FOR RELAXATION

On the flip-side of stress lies relaxation. Not sleep, but just taking it easy, chilling, down-time. Taking some time out helps to put things in perspective, too. If your life is so busy that you need to schedule your relaxation, then schedule it. It's important for your wellbeing and your mental health – and for your looks.

> Another powerful tool for reducing stress and gaining perspective is to practice meditation or mindfulness. I can only manage meditation when guided by an online app, but I have persisted with practising it until it has more or less become an everyday habit, and I find it very helpful in all areas of life.

PRACTICE BEING HAPPY

I know that sounds mad. You might think you either *are* happy or you're not, that happiness is something that is given to you or taken away. But in fact happiness is very much more a way of looking at life than a fortunate state of being. We may not be able to control what happens to us in life, but we can control the way we respond to the things that do happen.

The point about happiness when it comes to skincare is that over the years, we develop habitual expressions which etch lines on our faces. If we are constantly frowning, looking anxious, or feeling down in the dumps, those expressions tend to show on our faces and become entrenched, even if the wind hasn't changed...

WHY YOUR LIFESTYLE MATTERS MORE THAN YOUR GENES

Whatever we used to think about genes having the upper hand in determining how our skin looks as we age, research (conducted on a large scale by Procter & Gamble in 2017) has shown that what really makes a difference is not genes but our lifestyle.

Eating a healthy diet, getting enough sleep and exercise, minimising your intake of sugar and alcohol, and, crucially, using decent skincare and being scrupulous with daily use of sunscreen, will have a far bigger impact on your looks, long-term, than your genetic make-up.

Explore Your Options for Hormonal Balancing

It is when our oestrogen levels take a nosedive – usually around the age of 50 – that women really notice the onset of ageing in the skin. If you look at a graph of how female hormone levels decline over time, the line for oestrogen, which has been on a slow downward trend, suddenly drops off the chart. Think of a car that is coasting along, slowly losing speed, which suddenly runs into a brick wall, and you get the idea.

Hormonal supplementation can help alleviate this change, and your GP or a doctor who specialises in the area may be able to help. Supplementation can use either HRT or compounded bioidentical hormones; the latter are not regulated in the UK, so the area can be a bit of a minefield.

I appreciate that hormonal supplementation is a no-go if you have had breast cancer or ovarian cancer, or have high blood pressure or liver problems, but if you don't fall into one of these categories, it might be something to consider. Start with your GP, to see what they can provide, before looking further afield.

The Bottom Line: Supporting Your Skin

Lifestyle matters. Reducing your stress levels, getting more sleep, and eating a healthy diet will have a huge impact on the appearance and quality of your skin, particularly if you wear moisturising sunscreen, too. Have a think about what you can do to improve your lifestyle.

RULE SEVEN: INDULGE YOUR SKIN

And finally, the fun bit. Alongside all the sensible, necessary cleansing and hydrating, your skin will benefit from a bit of indulgence, cossetting, and general TLC. As with the rest of life, there's a time to lighten up and enjoy things. Here are some ideas.

Massage Your Face

Getting into the habit of massaging your face is hugely beneficial for your skin. Gently manipulating the tissues of the face helps to improve the flow of blood to the skin, which means skin cells get more oxygen and nutrients; the skin looks a little healthier, too. Working on lymph drainage points will improve the flow of lymph, the clear plasma-like fluid that removes waste products from cells, and can take down puffiness around the eyes and the jaw.

Another benefit is that massage relaxes your muscles. We all tend to hold stress and tension in our faces, jawline, and necks. These patterns of tension work themselves into habitual expressions as we get older. Massaging these tight muscles encourages them to ease up and relax, which not only softens the look of the face but can help you feel less stressed and sleep better, too.

I know massage may feel the last thing you want to do when you are trying to get out of the bathroom and into bed as fast as you can. So maybe that's not the time to do it. Find a time when you can take a couple of minutes and not be in a hurry. Learn a short massage routine and do it every day for a couple of weeks – by which time you should see a difference, which may make you want to carry on. Heck, you might even find you enjoy it!

PICK A FAVOURITE PRODUCT FOR MASSAGE

Pick whatever product you prefer to use for the massage – this could be the sort of cleansing balm that melts in your hands, or a creamy cleansing lotion, or a face oil (or coconut oil, or almond oil) or a moisturiser – anything that will give your fingers enough 'slip' and which will feel good on the skin. I prefer to use something that isn't too runny, otherwise I find my fingers skate about without really getting a grip on the skin. Not that you need to grip the skin hard, but you'll know what I mean.

FACIAL MASSAGE TECHNIQUE

You could try the basic massage technique described in the section 'How to Do an Easy Face Massage' on page 50. Play with it and adapt it to what feels good for your face. One set of movements I particularly like is this jaw-relaxing massage from Beata Aleksandrowicz, queen of massage therapists, from her book *Quick & Easy Massage*.

1. Place the index, middle, and ring fingers of each hand on either side of your jaw (clench your jaw, then you'll know which muscles you're aiming at). Close your eyes.

2. Breathe in; then, as you breathe out, press into the muscle at its highest point, just below the cheek arch, close to the ear. Make five slow circles, pressing with your ring and middle fingers. Breathing regularly, work down along the muscle until you reach the corner of the jaw. Continue making circles as you come back up to the cheek arch. Repeat three times.

3. Place your thumbs on the corners of your jaw, with your fingers resting on your head. Taking a deep breath, open your mouth slightly. As you breathe out, press your thumbs gradually into your jaw and hold. Slowly release. Repeat three times, feeling the jaw relax each time.

4. Move to the next point, working with your thumbs from the top of your jaw down to the corners as in step 2, but this time just press and hold for five seconds in each place. Finish by resting your fingers softly along your jaw muscles and taking three deep breaths.

Treat Your Skin with a Pampering Face Mask

Face masks are not only good for your skin but also give you a licence to lie down and relax for 15 minutes – so what's not to like? Yes, you could still run around doing domestic tasks while you're wearing a mask, or sit at your laptop, but that rather spoils the fun.

If you're wondering whether using a mask will really make much difference – well, give it a try. A face mask can give your skin a big, blanket coating of a treatment, which delivers a bigger dose of active ingredients. Use a face mask regularly, and you will see the difference it makes.

WHAT KIND OF FACE MASK?

You have a vast choice of face masks, so start by choosing the style of mask you like.

Face masks used to be gloopy things that came in pots and tubes – and some still are. But what has completely taken over from these are sheet masks, made from paper or cellulose or gel, and soused in serums that can soothe, hydrate, or brighten the skin. Or 'purify' it, or peel it… the choice is endless. If you're going for a sheet mask, pick one that is biodegradable, and dispose of it sensibly.

The following sections tell you about some of my favourite masks.

MASKS IN TUBES AND POTS

The masks are gels and creams that you plaster onto your face in a thick layer, and leave on for as long as the instructions tell you.

- **Ren Glycol Lactic Radiance Renewal Mask**, £36, renskincare.com. A brightening mask to speed up the turn-over of skin cells and reveal a fresher, clearer complexion. Works well; be cautious with it if you have sensitive skin.

- **Aromatherapy Associates Hydrating Rose Face Mask**, £43, aromatherapyassociates.com. Comforting, hydrating, and smells gorgeous, too.

- **SkinCeuticals Phyto Corrective Masque**, £60, skinceuticals.co.uk. 'The green gloopy one' isn't the most flattering way to describe this – but that's what it looks like. There's a mass of soothing botanical extracts in there that will take the heat out of skin that's sunburnt, or simply calm skin that's irritated either after a procedure or just by life and stress levels.

EYE MASKS

A decade ago, these short, curved, stick-on patches that sit in an arc below the eye appeared outlandish and strange. Now, they're a shorthand for smart, targeted revival of the eye area.

- **Vichy LiftActiv Micro Hyalu Eye Patches**, £20, vichy.co.uk. Soothing, hydrating pick-me-up for tired or puffy eyes.
- **Skyn Iceland Hydro Cool Firming Eye Gels**, £25 for eight pairs, marksandspencer.com. Under-eye gel masks which soothe, hydrate, and depuff thanks to the hydrating serum they're in, which contains peptides and antioxidants.
- **Bioeffect EGF Eye Mask Treatment**, £75 for serum plus six pairs of eye patches, bioeffect.co.uk. With this treatment, you pat the serum around your eye first, then cover it with one of the little curvy patches and leave it to absorb. Always works a treat, and good for reducing puffiness, too.

SHEET MASKS

These sheet masks and gel concoctions can be fiddly to unfold and to get into place on your face, particularly as they will be all slippery with hydrating serum, so take your time to get them into place, then lie back and relax while they go to work.

Here are three great sheet masks from widely available brands:

- **Eucerin Hyaluron-Filler Mask**, £6, boots.com. Very hydrating and a good price – and it stays put firmly once it is in place.
- **Estée Lauder Advanced Night Repair Concentrated Recovery PowerFoil Mask**, £64 for 4, esteelauder.co.uk. A foil-backed sheet mask soused in this much loved ANR serum, with extra hyaluronic acid. Give it time to work its magic.
- **Maskologist Lavender Youth Miracle Hydrogel Mask**, £84.50 for four, maskologist.com. Yes, wildly expensive, and it's also fiddly and slippery. But it's a very pretty, super-hydrating gel mask which, after you've used it on your face, will dissolve in water, so you could use it for a hydrating rub-down on your body in the bath or shower.

Here are three great gel sheet masks from specialist brands:

- **Viscoderm Hydrogel Patch**, £36, thetweakmentsguide.com. A home-use product from the company that makes the popular 'injectable moisture' injections Profhilo and Viscoderm Hydrobooster, this mask contains top-grade hyaluronic acid, bisabolol, and aloe vera. It's a three-piece mask, which includes a piece for your neck, in a solid gel which sticks the mask onto your face and slowly releases its contents into the skin.

- **Medik8 Ultimate Recovery Biocellulose Masks**, £57 for 6, thetweakmentsguide.com. Hydrating and calming, these masks can be used after cosmetic procedures, as well as just to soothe dry skin. They cling onto the face really well.

- **MZ Skin Vitamin-infused Facial Treatment Mask x 5**, £90, mzskin.com. Distinctively glamorous, these two-part masks are red and shiny and drenched in so much hydrating serum (with hyaluronic acid, vitamin C, brightening liquorice) that while they are on your face, you can amuse yourself massaging the excess into your neck, your hands, your arms...

CREATE YOURSELF A BEAUTY RITUAL

One way to look after your skin is to create a beauty ritual that suits your goals and your schedule.

The ritual doesn't have to be complicated, unless you want it to be. It could be as simple as running a bath with a dash of fragrant oil in it, lighting a candle, and climbing in, maybe with a face mask on, to simply relax for 10 minutes. And locking the door, if you have children or a partner who will just wander in and take up your me-time.

Have a Facial

Better still than a beauty ritual, get someone else to do the massage and the masks for you, and throw in some superior cleansing along with extraction, a skin peel, perhaps a quick once-over with a laser to brighten the skin, or whatever else takes your fancy.

Traditional facials might not go much further than a bit of light pampering and the chance for a lie-down, but newer facials have the potential to be extremely effective. These newer facials incorporate high-tech machinery – such as laser or IPL machines to reduce redness and age spots, or radiofrequency to tighten the skin – along with the hot towels, lymphatic drainage, and aromatherapy massage.

There are so many facials that it's hard to know where to start. I like the sort I call 'facials plus' – because they offer some extra, skin-boosting benefits, such as skin-tightening radiofrequency, or mechanical deep-cleansing, or a gentle skin peel, or a touch of microneedling, on top of the more normal cleansing and massaging. There's a lot more about all of these on my website, thetweakmentsguide.com.

Home-Use Beauty Gadgets

There is a huge range of beauty devices that you can use at home. Whenever I mention these types of products, people always ask me, 'Are they worth it?' I usually answer with another question: 'How much are you going to use it?' If a device becomes a regular part of your home routine, and you use it several times a week, then you are bound to see the benefits of it, and of course it's worthwhile. But if you just use the device a few times, don't really get the point of it, and leave it to gather dust under the bed… then no, spending money on the device won't be worthwhile.

This section tells you about three devices I really like (and use).

> You can find most of these beauty devices at currentbody.com.

LED DEVICES

LED light therapy devices offer red and near–infra-red light, which has proven benefits for the skin, and they're easy and relaxing to use.

If the mention of infra-red light is ringing a bell as a danger signal, don't worry – it's all about the dose. The small dose of infra-red these devices deliver has measurable benefits, as it reaches deeper into the skin, to stimulate its lower levels, and can stimulate bone repair, too. The infra-red also has a calming effect on the mind. Red LED light, meanwhile, encourages the skin to remodel itself from the inside, which means better hydration, firmer skin from increased collagen production, and a softening of pigmentation.

A programme of LED treatment at a clinic with a professional-grade machine involves treatments twice a week for a month. The effects are cumulative, so you just need to put in the sessions. I have had measurable improvements in skin wrinkling, pigmentation and skin redness with the Dermalux Flex MD, after using it five times a week for three months. The Flex is a medical-grade LED light therapy device designed for smaller clinics, but you can also buy it for home use (£1,914, thetweakmentsguide.com). There are many lower-powered home-use LED devices available, though the lights in these are rarely powerful or precise enough to achieve genuine improvements in the skin.

MICROCURRENT DEVICES

Microcurrent gadgets use low-level electrical currents to tone the muscles in the face. Do they work? Yes, particularly if you use them consistently – like going to the gym for the rest of your body, these gadgets work best if you develop a routine and keep it up, rather than popping in every 10 days or so. I love the NuFace devices (also available at thetweakmentsguide.com); friends swear by the FaceGym Pro (facegym.com), which delivers similar treatment in a slightly different way.

MASSAGE DEVICES FROM CLARISONIC

Clarisonic is famous for its cleansing brushes. The latest one, the Mia Smart (£185, thetweakmentsguide.com), can be used with a number of different click-to-fit treatment heads. One of these is a face-massaging attachment with three rubbery bumps on it, which claims that it will tighten and lift the skin at the same time as softening wrinkles.

The rubbery bumps vibrate and deliver 'micro-massage motions' into your skin, 27,000 of them per minute, and these in turn stimulate collagen production in the skin. You can use the device with any skincare serum, cream, or oil that you like, for three minutes at a time, morning and evening. The device helps products sink deeper into the skin, too.

Using the Mia Smart sounds like a chore, but it's surprisingly addictive. Results from trials look encouraging – users report tighter, smoother skin and less visible pores.

The Bottom Line: Indulging Your Skin

Giving your skin some extra love and attention is really good for it. Whether it's a once-a-week home facial routine involving exfoliation and a face mask, or a once-a-month trip to a beauty salon or skin clinic for a professional treatment, see if you can make time for it. Your skin will thank you for it.

PART THREE

HOW TO BUILD A SKINCARE ROUTINE, AND THE 12 BIGGEST QUESTIONS ABOUT SKINCARE

Now you have all this information, here's the part where you have to do the work – deciding what is right for you and your skin. I can't promise to tell you precisely what your skin needs. But I hope that by walking you through the various choices, I can help you make the right decision for yourself.

HOW TO BUILD A SKINCARE ROUTINE

All these products! All these ideas! Where should you start?

The idea of embarking on a whole 'skincare routine' may seem daunting – but here's the thing: You could start very simply.

In order to work out a routine that will work for you and your skin, think about what you're hoping to achieve. Are you wanting to improve patchy pigmentation, or make your skin look fresher? Also, be honest with yourself: how bothered are you about skincare? Are you prepared to buy lots of products, and use them every day, or would you prefer a minimal routine?

You don't have to do a huge amount to make your skin happier and healthier, but if you want to make a change in your skin, you need to be doing something different to whatever it is you're doing now.

The Minimalist Approach to Skincare: If You Do Just One Thing…

Whether it's because you don't have the inclination to be that bothered about skincare, or you're lacking the time – or the cash – to fuss around with multiple products, that's fine. Do the minimum, with the right products, and you can make a huge difference to your skin.

When people come to see me for a consultation – usually about tweakments, though we always cover skincare too – and I find they're not using effective skincare, this is the step-by-step way that I try to persuade them into it.

- If you do one thing – wear a moisturising sunscreen during the day.
- If you do two things – wear a moisturising sunscreen during the day and cleanse thoroughly at night.
- If you do three things – use a sunscreen in the morning, cleanse your face in the evening, and use a retinoid product in the evening.
- If you do those three things, you may find you need a moisturiser as the retinoid may make your face dry. So that's a fourth thing.
- Want a fifth? Add in some antioxidant protection before your sunscreen in the morning. Oh, and maybe you could cleanse your face first.

And that's it. Five products, max.

This is the basis of what I do by way of skincare. I've put down more detail about my own skincare routine in the section 'Question 12: What's Your Own Skincare Routine?' on page 242.

But to get back to the point, if you aren't in the habit of using skincare, and aren't planning to take much time out of your day for it, you could definitely make improvements in your skin just by cleansing and using a retinoid at night, and wearing moisturising sunscreen during the day. Truly.

The Maximalist Approach: If You Want to Try Everything…

Take it easy! You may feel more secure if you have a cupboardful of products to play with, but more isn't necessarily better. There is only so much your skin can handle at any one time. If you tend to hop around between products, it might be time to settle down and get strategic.

- Read through Rules 1–5, and decide what you actually need.

- Pick a cleanser. Actually, I'll allow you two cleansers, as you're bound to be a person who wants to double-cleanse.

- Add in a toner or an essence.

- Consider an exfoliant, and keep it for occasional use rather than everyday use.

- Choose a hydrating serum, for everyday use; and a moisturiser for back-up hydration; and an eye serum or cream; and maybe a neck cream,

- Select a treatment serum or two – maybe a vitamin C serum for the morning, and a retinoid for the evening. And ok, you could have a peptide serum, too – why not, they're good.

- Don't forget a sunscreen.

- Maybe have a pampering face-mask or two, as a treat for weekends.

Introduce each of these into your skincare routine one at a time, just in case your skin takes exception to one of them. If you start them all at once, and your skin kicks off, flares up, or breaks out, you won't know which product caused the problem.

Once you're settled in your new routine, clear out the old products that you're not using. They don't last forever. There will be a small symbol on the label showing an open jar, which says how long the product is good for – 12M means 12 months.

The Targeted Approach: Building a Regime to Treat a Specific Skin Concern

You might have one pressing issue you want to work on, such as rosacea, or pigmentation, or crepey skin. These and other skincare concerns are covered in the section 'The 12 Big Questions – and Their Answers' (see page 186), along with suggested daily regimes.

WHAT ARE THE 12 BIG QUESTIONS ABOUT SKINCARE?

So, what are the questions that I get asked most often about skincare? They cover all the most pressing concerns, from pigmentation, via wrinkles, to crepey necks.

Here goes:

- Question 1: Can skincare soften my wrinkles?
- Question 2: How do I reduce pigmentation marks, age spots, and melasma?
- Question 3: My skin is so sensitive. What can I do?
- Question 4: What can I do about rosacea?
- Question 5: Help, I've got spots! What can I do about adult acne?
- Question 6: I've got large pores. Can skincare help?
- Question 7: My skin is so dry. Do I need a richer cream?
- Question 8: My skin feels rough. How can I make it smoother?
- Question 9: Why does my skin look dull?
- Question 10: The menopause is wrecking my skin. What can I do?
- Question 11: Can skincare help my crepey neck?
- Question 12: What's your own skincare routine?

WHICH PRODUCTS SHOULD YOU USE?

The best products for you are the ones that suit your skin and your budget. I have listed my favourite products in all these categories earlier in the book; but I have to stress, just because I like them and they suit my skin doesn't automatically mean that they are right for you. You may have to experiment a bit to find your own favourites (but that's the fun part, isn't it?).

To find the lists of products I've recommended in each of these categories, you'll need to flick back to the relevant page.

- **Cleansers.** See the section 'What to Use for Cleansing Your Skin' on page 40.

WHY ISN'T THERE A QUESTION ON ISSUES WITH EYES?

Actually, there's one huge question I've left out, but there's a reason for that. So many of us have issues with our eyes – dark circles, hollow under-eyes, hooded upper-eyes, eye bags, puffiness -- but here's the thing. No skincare product or regime is going to magic away any of those complaints.

Some of these things – like dark pigmentation below the eyes – may be genetic. Others, like eye bags or hollowing, creep up with age. Pretending a cream will fix them is not helpful.

So – what to do about eyes?

First, keep the skin in the eye area hydrated. Use moisturisers and sunscreens that you are using elsewhere on your face around the eyes (you'll want fragrance-free products around the eyes).

What about treatment products? I put these all around my eyes, too, though I know skin specialists would not recommend this as a general rule. Instead, they would recommend you invest in a specialist eye cream, with a light texture and the treatment ingredients you are looking for, such as hyaluronic acid for hydration, peptides or retinol to strengthen the skin, make it more resilient, and soften wrinkles; or vitamin C to brighten the skin and reduce the appearance of pigmentation. See the section 'Great Eye Creams to Try' on page 129 for a list of great eye products, some of the few which are really worth trying.

- **Toners and essences.** See the section 'A Few Words About Toner' on page 53.
- **Exfoliants.** See the section 'So What Are the Different Ways of Exfoliating?' on page 60.
- **Hydrating serums.** See the section 'Great Hydrating Serums' on page 73.
- **Antioxidant serums.** See the section 'Great Antioxidant Serums' on page 79
- **Vitamin C serums.** See the section 'Great Vitamin C Products' on page 82.

- **Peptide serums.** See the section 'Great Peptide-Based Serums for Wrinkle-Busting' on page 91.

- **Retinoids.** See the section 'Great Retinol Products to Try' on page 103.

- **Anti-pigmentation serums.** See the section 'Great Pigmentation-Reducing Serums to Try' on page 107.

- **Anti-acne serums.** See the section 'Great Anti-Acne Serums to Try' on page 110.

- **Anti-inflammatory serums.** See the section 'Great Calming Anti-Inflammatory Serums to Try' on page 114.

- **Moisturisers.** See the section 'Which Moisturiser Should I Use?' on page 121.

- **Sunscreens.** See the section 'Which Sunscreen Should I Use?' on page 149.

THE 12 BIG QUESTIONS – AND THEIR ANSWERS

If there is something in particular that's bothering you about your skin, you may well find it covered in this section.

Question 1: Can Skincare Soften My Wrinkles?

Here's the good news: skincare can genuinely help improve the appearance of wrinkles. These are the types of products that will really help you with this.

FLASHCARD: SOFTENING WRINKLES

- Nourish your skin with an antioxidant serum, such as vitamin C.

- Keep your skin hydrated, with a hyaluronic-acid based serum.

- Include a peptide serum for collagen boosting.

- Wear sunscreen daily.

- Use a retinoid at night to regenerate your skin.

- Add a moisturiser when you need it.

NOURISH YOUR SKIN WITH VITAMIN C OR OTHER ANTIOXIDANTS

Vitamin C serum will help your skin defend itself against the environment (though not to the extent that you can skip wearing sunscreen). It will also help produce new, skin-strengthening collagen, which will soften the look of wrinkles, and tone down pigmentation into the bargain. So a well-formulated vitamin C serum, like one of those in the following lists, is a good investment. You can read in more detail about vitamin C in the section 'To Strengthen and Brighten the Skin: Vitamin C Serum' on page 80, and you'll find a list of some of my favourite vitamin C products in the section 'Great Vitamin C Products' on page 82.

ADD HYALURONIC ACID FOR HYDRATION

Dry skin wrinkles more swiftly that well-hydrated skin, so if your skin is on the dry side, and you are not already using a moisturising serum containing hyaluronic acid (HA), add one of these into your skincare routine. This can go on either before or after your vitamin C serum.

I so wish this ingredient wasn't termed 'acid', just because that word alone makes people suspicious of it. It's the gentlest thing in the skincare-ingredient book, a naturally occurring substance that has a near-miraculous ability to hold onto water – each hyaluronic acid molecule can hold up to a thousand times its own weight in water. We have hyaluronic acid in our connective tissue, in our nerve tissue, and in our eyes; and it's a major component of the skin and it helps the skin to both make and maintain collagen and elastin. So the skin knows it and likes it.

Hyaluronic acid works best when sealed into place with a product – such as moisturiser, or a moisturising sunscreen – on top of it. You can read more detail about hyaluronic acid in the section 'To Soften Dry Skin: Hydrating Serums' on page 71, and there's a list of some of my favourite hyaluronic acid serums in the section 'Great Hydrating Serums' on page 73.

If you're the sort of person who reads ingredient labels, hyaluronic acid may be listed as Sodium Hyaluronate, which is the salt form of hyaluronic acid, and does the same job.

INCLUDE PEPTIDES, FOR COLLAGEN BOOSTING

Peptides are ingredients which act like chemical messengers to turn on particular biochemical processes in the skin. Find the right key, or peptide, to switch on a process – such as collagen production – which is slowing down with age, and you could be looking at a great result. Peptides work well with other wrinkle-fixing skincare like vitamin C and retinoids. The best-known peptide for wrinkles is Matrixyl 3000, which is old-fashioned, but reliable.

You can read more about peptides and how they work in the section 'To Build Collagen and Reduce Wrinkling: Peptide Serums' on page 90, and there's a list of great peptide serums in the section 'Great Peptide-Based Serums for Wrinkle-Busting' on page 91.

USE SUNSCREEN, EVERY DAY

The most vital skincare product you can own is a moisturising sunscreen, which you must wear every day – because what really hastens ageing in the skin is daily exposure to ultraviolet light. Wearing sunscreen reduces the effects of UV light on the skin, and that means fewer wrinkles over time.

I know I seem to be harping on about sunscreen, but it is absolutely vital. If you want to know why I feel so strongly about sunscreen, there's more detail in Question 2, the one about managing pigmentation, on page 191. You can find a list of some of my favourite sunscreens on page 149. I don't mind which sort you use, as long as you wear the stuff.

AT NIGHT, ADD A RETINOID, FOR SKIN REGENERATION

The next step is to start using a cream containing some form of vitamin A, such as retinol. This ingredient is part of the retinoid family and is chemically related to vitamin A. It can be transformative for the skin because it kick-starts collagen production and at the same time reduces the rate of collagen breakdown in the skin, so your existing collagen lasts longer, and new collagen is made faster.

Retinoids also speed up the rate at which older, slow-moving skin cells renew themselves, which has an exfoliating effect on the skin; reduce oiliness, which in turn reduces the chances of blocked pores and acne; and quieten down the production of excess pigment in the skin. Put together, all these effects make the skin look clearer and less wrinkled, so products containing retinol are a great addition to any skincare regime, whatever your age (they're also very helpful for younger skin suffering from acne).

You need to start slowly with retinoids, just twice a week at first, and gradually build up a tolerance for them.

How often should you be aiming to use a retinoid? Some skin specialists will encourage you to work towards using a retinoid every night; others will say this is too much for most skin, and will advise using them every other night, or for an occasional month-long course of skin-boosting.

What's right for you? Be guided by how your skin responds. You want to be stimulating your skin to repair itself, but not pushing it to the point that it becomes irritated and sore. If retinoids are making your skin red, flaky and dry, back off and give your skin a break.

See the section 'To Combat Ageing and Boost Skin Renewal: Retinol and Other Retinoids' on page 97 for more detail about retinol, retinoids, and other ingredients derived from vitamin A. See the section 'Great Retinol Products to Try' on page 103 for a list of products containing retinol and other retinoids.

The idea that retinol 'speeds up' skin cell turnover may sound like a bad idea – after all, isn't too much cell-proliferation associated with cancer? But what retinol and other retinoids do, more accurately, is normalise skin cell turnover. So in older skin, where skin cell turnover has slowed down, retinol will speed up turnover. But in skin that's shedding cells too fast (a process called hyperkeratosis, which is a big contributor to acne), retinol can slow this down.

WRINKLES: THE REGIME

Here's what a daily regime for improving the appearance of wrinkles might look like.

Morning Routine

Cleanse

Start by cleansing with whichever cleanser you prefer.

Exfoliate

I'd skip the exfoliation. If you are using a retinoid at night, that will have an exfoliating effect on your skin, and that may well be enough. If you want to, add in an acid toner after cleansing, a couple of times a week.

Treat

Treat your skin with a vitamin C serum. Use this after cleansing, on dry skin. Just use a few drops, and pat it around your face, your neck, and your décolletage with your fingertips. Let it sink it.

Once your skin has absorbed the vitamin C serum, apply your hydrating serum. You could apply the hydrating serum first if you prefer; it really depends on the texture of your chosen products. It makes sense to apply the lighter serum first. If the vitamin C serum feels as if it has a heavier or oilier texture, put the hydrating serum on first.

If you're using a peptide serum, you could add it on top of these two. If that feels like too much product, you could use the peptide serum alternately with the vitamin C. Or you could wait and use the peptide serum at night.

Moisturise

If your skin still feels a bit dry after all that, add a little moisturiser. Again, take this from your hairline down to your breastbone.

Protect

Top this all off with sunscreen. Any sort of sunscreen that you like, and cover all the skin that will be exposed during the day.

Evening Routine

Cleanse

Cleanse your face thoroughly, so that you can get rid of all the dirt, sweat, bacteria, and make-up that may have piled up on your face during the day. Then, you'll have a fresh, clean surface for your treatment products. Ideally, do a double-cleanse (see the section 'Try Double-Cleansing' on page 51 for more on double-cleansing). I like to use an oil, cream, or balm for the first cleanse, then a rinse-off gel wash for the second.

Treat

If you're new to retinol, start slowly by using it, sparingly, twice a week, and give your skin time to acclimatise to it before you try to use it more frequently. Piling on too much too soon is a recipe for redness and irritation. See the section 'To Combat Ageing and Boost Skin Renewal: Retinol and Other Retinoids' on page 97 for more advice on using retinoids.

What to use on the other nights when you're not using a retinoid? This is where your peptide serum comes in. Apply it – again, hairline to breastbone – and let it sink in.

If your skin can't cope with retinol, just use vitamin C serum again. Once the serum has been absorbed, you could follow it with peptides.

Moisturise

Give the retinoid plenty of time to be absorbed – purists will say half an hour; but it it's already bedtime, 10 minutes is better than nothing – then add the peptides, if you're using them, and then pop some moisturiser over the top. Why? Because that retinoid is very likely to make your skin feel a bit dry, and using moisturiser will help counteract this. Use any moisturiser you like; the only job it is doing here is holding moisture in the skin.

Question 2: How Do I Reduce Pigmentation Marks, Age Spots, and Melasma?

Pigmentation marks – from ever-expanding freckles, via age spots, to patchy skin tone – are one of the biggest skin-related complaints, particularly for anyone with darker skin.

WHAT CAUSES PIGMENTATION PROBLEMS?

Before we get on to how to treat pigmentation problems, here's a quick recap of what we are talking about. 'Pigmentation' is just the colouring of the skin, which is determined by the amount of the brown or black pigment melanin that it contains. The problems come in the form of 'hyperpigmentation', when the skin produces excess melanin, and this clusters together in a way that makes the skin tone look spotted or patchy.

The pigment in our skin is there to protect us from UV light – both from UVB, which you can think of as the 'burning' rays that you get in hot summer sun, and from UVA, the longer-wavelength 'ageing' rays. UVA and UVB rays work together to produce a tan in the skin. UVA darkens the pigment that we already have in the skin, and UVB encourages the pigment-producing cells, the melanocytes, to produce more pigment. Why? In order to try to protect the skin's DNA from damage.

Even when we're not getting UVB from summer sunshine, UVA reaches our skin every day. UVA rays also pass through glass, such as car windscreens. This slow, everyday exposure adds up over time and shows up in the skin as spots or patches of pigmentation, where the melanin produced by those melanocytes has clustered.

WHAT ARE THE TYPES OF HYPERPIGMENTATION?

If you ask a consultant dermatologist like Dr Natalia Spierings, who has a private practice in London, she will point out that she needs to know the cause of hyperpigmentation before thinking about how to treat it.

These are the three main sorts of pigmentation concerns:

- **Everyday sun-related pigmentation.** The most common sort of pigmentation, this could be from lifelong exposure to ultraviolet light, which results in speckled pigment across the skin or clusters of pigment known as age spots. 'Ultraviolet light' means boring old everyday daylight, not just strong summer sunlight. There's more detail on this in 'Rule Five: Protect Your Skin' on page 140.

- **Post-inflammatory hyperpigmentation (PIH).** The next most likely sort of inflammation, post-inflammatory hyperpigmentation results from acne, from eczema, or from lasers being incorrectly used on the skin. The inflammation makes the melanocytes, the pigment-producing cells in the skin, produce more pigment.

- **Melasma.** This is a particularly troublesome type of pigmentation possibly caused by hormonal fluctuations as well as genetics and UV light, though the exact cause of melasma is not known. Melasma often shows itself as a butterfly-shaped mask of darker skin across the middle of the face.

HOW SKINCARE CAN HELP WITH EVERYDAY PIGMENTATION AND POST-INFLAMMATORY HYPERPIGMENTATION

Tackling pigmentation with skincare doesn't have to be a long, slow journey – not if you are carefully diagnosed by a professional, get medical-grade treatment products, and stick with them. 'Most of my pigmentation patients get virtual clearance within four weeks of consistent treatment,' says Dr Spierings. 'The issue is really about maintaining the clear skin or keeping pigmentation away.'

I'll start with the best products and protocols for treating everyday pigmentation and post-inflammatory hyperpigmentation, then will come back to melasma in the section 'How Skincare Can Help with Melasma' on page 198.

FLASHCARD: REDUCING PIGMENTATION

- Avoid the sun.

- Use sunscreen, every single day.

- Slow down pigment formation with an anti-pigmentation serum.

- Add a retinoid to encourage skin renewal and reduce pigmentation.

    or

- Try prescription skincare.

- If you don't see improvements, get professional help.

Start with Sun Protection

Protecting your skin from UVA and UVB is fundamental to managing pigmentation.

'The first and most important thing is staying out of the sun, because that will make pigmentation darker,' says Dr Spierings. 'It is a much easier message to send to people ("wear sunscreen every day, always") than to explain the nuisance of the reality [of sun avoidance]. In addition, no one makes any money from people covering up and avoiding sun exposure entirely – it doesn't lend itself to the sale of expensive skincare products to help people rationalise their purchase for "health" reasons.' Wear sunglasses and a hat when you're outside.

Wearing sunscreen will not only prevent future damage but will also stop the damage that has already been done from getting worse. That means using high-factor sunscreen, every day: SPF30 in winter, SPF50 in summer, and reapplying it at lunchtime if you can, whatever your skin colour. Sunscreen is even more vital during and after any course of treatment for pigmentation, because you need to protect the newly cleared skin. So yes, it's a continuous process – once you start to notice pigmentation and do something about it, it becomes a long-term commitment, as you can't give up on protecting your skin, or the pigmentation will come racing back.

'Generally, I will start treatment for pigmentation with skincare,' says consultant dermatologist and dermatological surgeon Dr Nis Sheth, from the St John's Institute of Dermatology in London. 'The first thing to use is sunscreen – and the right type. If you have melasma, for instance, it is important not just to protect against UVA and UVB rays, but to use some kind of physical protection, too, like a hat.'

Don't think you can skip sunscreen if your skin tone is darker. Aesthetician Dija Ayodele, who specialises in treating skin of colour, points out that pigmentation is the main bugbear for many of her patients.

'For most of my clients, this pigmentation is post-inflammatory hyperpigmentation and general discolouration resulting from sunscreen not being rigorously applied in our culture,' she says. 'But once I explain, especially to older ladies, that if they're complaining of pigmentation and won't wear sunscreen, we're on a hiding to nothing, then people of colour become much more accepting of wearing SPF every day.'

Use Pigment-Fading Treatment Products

The right skincare can help to fade existing brown marks, but you need to use it consistently, every day, and with care. As I mentioned above, you must also commit to using sunscreen every day.

The key ingredients for fading pigment markings in the skin fall into different categories. First, there are the ingredients that stop the skin making so much pigment in the first place. These include vitamin C, arbutin (aka bearberry extract), liquorice, kojic acid, and azelaic acid. These all belong to a group of substances called tyrosinase inhibitors, and they work by blocking the action of tyrosinase, an enzyme used in the pigment-making process. (In a skin cell, tyrosinase oxidises an amino acid, tyrosine, to create the melanin pigment, if you want the detail.) You can read in more detail about vitamin C in the section 'To Strengthen and Brighten the Skin: Vitamin C Serum' on page 80, and there's a list of some of my favourite vitamin C products in the section 'Great Vitamin C Products' on page 82.

Then there's niacinamide, a version of vitamin B3 (niacin) which helps reduce pigmentation by blocking the transfer of melanin from the melanocytes that make it to the keratinocytes, the skin cells where it sits and shows up.

> Along with these ingredients, there are many specific anti-pigmentation serums containing one or more of these ingredients. For more about these products, take a look at the section 'To Reduce Pigmentation: Anti-Pigmentation Serums' on page 105. There's a list of my favourites among these products in the section 'Great Pigmentation-Reducing Serums to Try' on page 107.

Alpha hydroxy acids can help reduce pigmentation marks in the skin, too. These exfoliating acids, which include glycolic acid and the gentler lactic acid, have a peeling action on the skin, encouraging the shedding of outer, pigmented layers so that fresher, clearer skin grows through from underneath.

Add a Retinoid to Reduce Pigmentation and Improve Skin

'Retinol creams can help with pigmentation, too,' says Dr Sheth. 'They're not as good as prescription lightening agents, but they have less risk of irritation.'

See the section 'To Combat Ageing and Boost Skin Renewal: Retinol and Other Retinoids' on page 97 for more detail about retinol, retinoids, and other ingredients derived from vitamin A. See the section 'Great Retinol Products to Try' on page 103 for a list of products containing retinol and other retinoids.

All these products offer some evidence that they give results. I'm phrasing that with caution, because when I asked Dr Spierings if there were any widely available products she could recommend, she simply compressed her lips and shook her head; as a consultant dermatologist, she would encourage you straight onto prescription skincare.

With all these pigment-blockers and skin brighteners, you will have to keep using them continuously for some time in order to see results.

The Prescription-Only Pigment Buster

Prescription skincare is more effective for treating pigmentation than any over-the-counter skincare.

The gold-standard treatment that a dermatologist can prescribe for tackling pigmentation is a cream containing 4 per cent hydroquinone, a well-proven pigment-buster. This cream should be applied as directed, only on the actual pigmentation patches, morning and night; it will take at least eight weeks to work.

'The best treatment for pigmentation,' says Dr Spierings, 'is to use a topical retinoid [eg the prescription-only tretinoin] combined with hydroquinone. I would prescribe hydroquinone in a strength of between four and eight per cent for two or three months to clear the pigmentation, then I would reduce the concentration of hydroquinone, and reduce its use to three times a week, for maintenance of the results.'

It can be difficult to get access to dermatologists, because there just aren't so many of them per person in the UK as there are in countries like the USA or France. But there are new online dermatology services that are really worth known about, such as Dermatica (dermatica.co.uk) and Skin+Me (skinandme.com). You can upload photographs of your skin, fill in an online consultation form, and have a dermatologist prescribe an appropriate product for your skin's condition. The product is sent to you in the post, and the company keeps tabs on your progress. These services cost from £19.99 per month, which is an absolute bargain compared to the cost of an appointment with, and prescription products from, a private dermatologist.

PIGMENTATION: THE REGIME

Here's what a daily regime for managing pigmentation might look like.

Morning Routine

Cleanse

Start by cleansing with whatever kind of cleanser you prefer.

Exfoliate

If you want to exfoliate – you don't have to, but it can help with brightening the skin – use an acid toner based on alpha hydroxy acid such as lactic acid (gentler) or glycolic acid to wipe over your skin after cleansing. When you're new to this, try it twice a week before using it more often.

Treat

Pick a treatment serum. That could be a vitamin C serum, or one with azelaic acid or niacinamide, any of which will limit the amount of new pigmentation that your skin is creating, and use it every morning. If you like to use a hydrating serum, apply it next.

Moisturise

If your skin feels dry after the serum, pat some moisturiser over the top.

Protect

Finish off with sunscreen. UV rays are what provoke your skin into creating more pigment in the first place, so protect yourself from them!

Evening Routine

Cleanse

As in the morning, cleanse with whichever product you prefer. I'd go for a balm or oil cleanser to shift everything including the sunscreen from your face, then follow up with a wash-off gel cleanser, to remove the oil left by the first round of cleansing.

Treat

Apply your treatment product. This could be the same serum that you used in the morning – maybe a vitamin C serum – or it could be a product containing retinol or a stronger type of retinoid, or a prescription product. When you are starting with any kind of retinoid, only use it twice a week, then increase the use if your skin is ok with it. On the other nights, use the treatment serum that you are using in the morning.

If you have been given a prescription product for treating pigmentation, use it as directed.

Moisturise

Give your treatment product time to be absorbed (up to half an hour for a retinoid), then moisturise, to keep your skin from dehydrating overnight.

HOW SKINCARE CAN HELP WITH MELASMA

The other form of hyperpigmentation is melasma, the butterfly-shaped 'mask' of dark pigment which is often triggered by hormonal changes in the body. Melasma can show up during pregnancy, or when using birth control pills or hormone replacement therapy. It which gets worse with exposure to UV light. Melasma usually affects women, but a small number of men develop the condition, too.

Melasma is dreaded by sufferers, skin experts, and dermatologists alike because, even after treatment, it is likely to recur. So rather than 'fixing' melasma, treatment is more a question of managing it, and managing it carefully and consistently can be a slow and frustrating business, though there is a lot you can do with the right skincare.

FLASHCARD: MANAGING MELASMA

- Protect your skin scrupulously with sunscreen.

- Slow down pigment-creation with a treatment serum.

- Add a retinoid to encourage skin renewal and reduce pigmentation.

  or

- Try prescription skincare.

- Consider adding tranexamic acid to your routine.

- If you don't see improvements, get professional help.

You'll see from the Flashcard that the advice for treating melasma is very much the same as for other types of pigmentation – so refer back to the section 'How Skincare Can Help with Everyday Pigmentation and Post-Inflammatory Hyperpigmentation' on page 193 if you skipped that bit. But here are a few extra thoughts about managing melasma that you might find useful.

So how should you treat melasma? It depends who you ask, but experts who spend a lot of time treating it all prefer highly specialised skincare. Here are two examples:

- Dr Natalia Spierings will put patients straight onto a prescription blend of hydroquinone and tretinoin, as she would when treating patients with other forms of pigmentation. She finds this treatment is very effective.

- Dr Nick Lowe, one of the UK's best-known dermatologists, prefers using a course of in-clinic skin peels, backed up by vitamin C serum, sunscreen, and oral tranexamic acid (see the next section for details about this) at home, to get a handle on melasma.

- Dija Ayodele finds that a specialist pigment-reducing cream called Cyspera gives great results. She will often use chemical peels for her patients at Westroom Aesthetics, and will encourage them to use vitamin C serums and Cyspera at home, insisting that if they want to see results, daily sunscreen is non-negotiable.

THE NEW MELASMA-FIXER: TRANEXAMIC ACID

One extra option that Dr Spierings, Dr Lowe, and Dr Sheth both agree on and recommend is that it is well worth trying oral tranexamic acid if you are struggling with melasma.

Tranexamic acid is a medicine that is used to treat heavy bleeding during menstrual periods. The mechanism by which tranexamic acid works to reduce pigmentation is not entirely clear, but it can be helpful. Here's the science.

'It is likely that tranexamic acid helps melasma by working to reduce levels of the enzyme plasmin levels in keratinocytes [skin cells],' says Dr Spierings. 'Plasmin in keratinocytes increases alpha-melanocyte-stimulating-hormone and may induce synthesis of arachidonic acid, which both stimulate the production of melanin. Tranexamic acid inhibits the activation of plasminogen activator.'

Tranexamic acid is available as tablets without prescription from UK pharmacies, though it is strongly recommended that you take it under expert supervision.

IS PHYSICAL SUNSCREEN OR CHEMICAL SUNSCREEN BETTER FOR MELASMA?

While all skincare experts are very clear that anyone with melasma needs to protect their skin from UV light – after that, there's a good deal of disagreement as to the best way to do this.

I've been told by some experts that anyone with melasma should only use physical sunscreens, and by others that they shouldn't just use physical sunscreens, because chemical sun filters are more effective and less easy to dislodge from the skin.

Another area of disagreement is over the issue of whether heat makes melasma worse. This is the standard line among many skin experts, so they advise that patients with melasma should only use chemical sunscreen filters – which work by absorbing light energy in the skin and converting it into heat – if these are combined with physical protection. That means using a sunscreen that combines both types of filters (many do) or layering a physical sunscreen on top of a chemical one.

And Dr Natalia Spierings, who has reviewed the scientific evidence on melasma treatments over the past 10 years, has pointed out to me that there is no connection between melasma and heat.

Where does that leave you when you're trying to work out how to protect your skin? Using sunscreen is crucial. As to the type of sunscreen? If you are getting professional treatment, follow the advice of whoever is treating you. Maybe choose a combination sunscreen. I don't mind which type you use, as long as you use it.

It's also going to be far more difficult to improve the melasma of anyone who is taking an oral contraceptive or who has a hormone IUD, because either of these will prompt ongoing pigmentation in the skin if your melasma is hormonal.

Dr Spierings finds that tranexamic acid is 'extraordinarily effective over a three-month course, when combined with topical hydroquinone and a retinoid. It is able virtually to clear melasma.'

As a topical ingredient, tranexamic acid is starting to be used in skincare products such as these:

- **The Inkey List Tranexamic Acid Night Treatment**, £14.99, cultbeauty.co.uk. An overnight brightening mask, this contains 2% tranexamic acid to help reduce pigmentation and improve skin texture.

- **Murad Replenishing Multi-Acid Peel**, £48, murad.co.uk. There's glycolic acid, lactic acid, malic acid, and salicylic acid in here as well as tranexamic acid, to brighten, exfoliate, and improve moisture levels in the skin.

- **SkinCeuticals Discoloration Defence Serum**, £85, skinceuticals.co.uk. A new, daily-use dark-spot corrector with niacinamide. I haven't tried it, but the brand's clinical trials show impressive results.

MELASMA: THE REGIME

Here's how you might treat melasma on a daily basis. If you're trying tranexamic acid tablets, take them as advised by your practitioner.

Morning Routine

Cleanse

Start by cleansing with your favourite cleanser.

Exfoliate

If you want to exfoliate – you don't have to, but it can help with brightening the skin – use an acid toner based on alpha hydroxy acid such as lactic acid (gentler) or glycolic acid to wipe over your skin after cleansing. When you're new to this, try it twice a week before using it more often. I'd prefer you didn't use an acid toner more than three times a week.

Treat

Next comes a treatment product. This could be a vitamin C serum or a specific anti-pigmentation product. Add a hydrating serum if your skin feels dry after this.

Moisturise

Moisturise, if your skin still feels dry.

Protect

Top this off with sunscreen for daily protection. After reading the advice above, you may want to use a sunscreen that combines both chemical and physical filters, or to layer a physical sunscreen over the top of a chemical one.

Evening Routine

Cleanse

Cleanse thoroughly. I'd go for a balm or oil cleanser to shift everything including the sunscreen from your face, then follow up with a wash-off gel cleanser, to remove the oil left by the first round of cleansing.

Treat

For overnight treatment, you could use one of the following:

- A vitamin C serum.
- A product with retinol or a stronger type of retinoid – if you are not using this every night, use the serum that you're using in the morning on retinoid-free nights.
- An anti-pigmentation product – use this as directed on the packaging, which will probably tell you to use it twice a day, every day.
- A prescription product – if you have a specific prescription product, use that as directed.

Moisturise

Once your serum or retinoid or prescription product has been absorbed, moisturise with anything you like, to keep your skin feeling comfortable overnight.

Question 3: My Skin Is So Sensitive. What Can I Do?

Sensitive skin is tricky, because when you know what might happen when you use products it doesn't like, and you don't want to risk the redness, soreness, itching, and flare-ups that might result, it can make you reluctant to put anything on your skin at all.

WHY IS MY SKIN SO SENSITIVE?

Your skin's sensitivity might be genetic; it might be a reaction to your lifestyle, or to your stress levels; but what it comes down to is that your skin barrier is in a bad way, or 'compromised', as a dermatologist would put it. 'Skin barrier'? Well, the job of the outer layers of your skin is to provide a waterproof barrier between you and the outside world, to keep moisture in your skin and your body, so that you don't shrivel up and dry out; and to keep out bacteria and viruses, rain and bathwater, and external aggressors like pollution, as best it can.

```
┌─────────────────────────────────────────────────────────┐
│              FLASHCARD: CALMING SENSITIVE SKIN            │
│                                                           │
│   •   Cleanse your skin gently.                           │
│                                                           │
│   •   Hydrate your skin lavishly.                         │
│                                                           │
│   •   Pile on the barrier-repairing lipids.               │
│                                                           │
│   •   Protect your skin with sunscreen.                   │
│                                                           │
│   •   Choose fragrance-free products.                     │
└─────────────────────────────────────────────────────────┘
```

WHAT'S IN THE SKIN BARRIER?

You can think of the skin cells in this outer layer of your skin (the stratum corneum) as a densely packed layer of tiles (lower down in the skin, the cells are more like bricks in a wall, but they get flattened once they reach the surface). What keeps them happy is being sandwiched together by a mixture of fatty substances or lipids, which include cholesterol, ceramides, and essential fatty acids and which provide a kind of inter-cellular mortar which makes the whole layer into a waterproof barrier that keeps the world at bay.

When this barrier is in good shape, all is fine. But when this barrier is not in good shape and becomes tattered, then water escapes more easily from the lower layers of the skin, making it feel dry and rough on the surface. Also, bacteria and skincare ingredients which wouldn't bother a more resilient complexion can get in and irritate the skin. Your skin then suffers an unpleasant cycle of soreness and dryness.

WHAT SKINCARE CAN IMPROVE THE SKIN BARRIER?

Two things that will really help build the strength of the skin barrier are loading it up with moisture in the form of a hyaluronic acid serum (see the section 'To Soften Dry Skin: Hydrating Serums' on page 71), and then reinforcing the lipid layer with moisturisers that contain ceramides, cholesterol, and essential fatty acids (see the sections 'To Calm Irritated and Reactive Skin: Anti-Inflammatory Serums' on page 111 and 'Moisturisers for Sensitive Skin' on page 125). The hyaluronic acid will help retain extra water in the outer layers of the skin, and the lipids will seal this into place and fill in the gaps in the 'mortar' among the 'bricks' of the skin cells. Then top these off during the daytime with sunscreen. Make sure that your products are fragrance free – fragrance is a well-known irritant.

IS SENSITIVE SKIN THE SAME AS REACTIVE SKIN?

Yes, more or less: sensitive skin reacts far more easily to things – to the weather, to skincare, to medication – than it ought to do; so from that point of view, sensitive skin *is* reactive skin. The sort of sensitive-skin reaction that most people get is not the sort of reaction that you'd get with an allergy – the latter is usually much more severe, immediate, and obvious – and it can vary according to the state your skin is in on a particular week.

WHAT SKINCARE IS BEST FOR SENSITIVE SKIN?

How to soothe and strengthen sensitive skin without setting off a reaction can seem an alarming prospect, but it can be done. You just need to choose the right products – calming products, hydrating products, and lipid-rich barrier-repair products.

Gentle cleansing and using a moisturising sunscreen daily are vital. It is very well worth trying the sort of products that are called 'anti-redness' and 'calming', particularly ones from 'doctor' or cosmeceutical ranges such as Epionce (try the Lytic range), NeoStrata, SkinMedica, SkinCeuticals, PCA Skincare, iS Clinical, Medik8 (the Calmwise range), ZO Skincare, Paula's Choice (the Calm products), and Jan Marini.

When skin is feeling really sensitive, it may find some of the chemical filters used in the chemical, or absorbing, type of sunscreens harder to tolerate, so mineral sunscreens may be a better choice. You can find a list of suggested sunscreens in the section 'Which Sunscreen Should I Use?' on page 149.

CAN I USE VITAMIN C OR RETINOL ON SENSITIVE SKIN?

Maybe in a while you can, and they will benefit your skin – but please, not now. While your skin is sensitive, give it some time and concentrate on calming any irritation, cramming more moisture into the skin, strengthening the skin barrier, and protecting it from UV light. Then when it's stronger, you can try whatever you like.

SENSITIVE SKIN: THE REGIME

The key focus here is calming irritation, hydrating the skin, and rebuilding the skin barrier, to allow your skin to get back to its main job of protecting you from the outside world.

Morning Routine

Cleanse

Cleanse your skin with something gentle and creamy.

Treat

Try a calming serum with anti-inflammatory ingredients. Add a hydrating serum, to improve moisture levels.

Moisturise

Use a lipid-packed cream to hold in the hydration and improve the skin barrier.

Protect

Protect your skin with a fragrance-free sunscreen.

Evening Routine

Cleanse

Use a gentle cleanser.

Treat

Hydrate your skin with your hyaluronic acid serum.

Moisturise

Finish with a lipid-rich moisturiser.

Question 4: What Can I Do About Rosacea?

When there is a little bit of redness across your nose and cheeks, maybe not always, but more often than not… how do you know whether it is a normal, healthy colour or whether it's a bit of a problem? It can be hard to tell, given that we have all grown up being told that 'getting a bit of colour in our cheeks' is a good thing.

And skin just does go red when it's provoked. Exercise, sunshine, and heat will do the trick, as will stress and embarrassment.

That sort of redness is normal. But if a flushed colour persists, or you get ruddy patches that flare up occasionally, or you get flare-ups accompanied by a rash of spots, here's the news: you might have rosacea.

FLASHCARD: CALMING ROSACEA

- Exfoliate lightly to clear dead skin cells.

- Use anti-inflammatory products to calm the redness.

- Pack in moisture with hydrating serums, and hold it there with ceramide-rich moisturiser, to strengthen the skin barrier.

- Protect with sunscreen.

- Consider seeing a dermatologist for professional guidance.

WHAT IS ROSACEA?

Rosacea is an unfortunate skin condition known as 'the curse of the Celts' because it is most obvious on pale skin. A dermatologist will tell you that rosacea is a chronic condition that mainly affects the convex surfaces of the face – the cheeks, chin, nose, and forehead. Chronic? Yes, that means it's not something you can get rid of, so you need to find ways to manage it. Derms will also tell you that rather than being some kind of sensitivity in the skin, rosacea is a disease of the oil glands, so it's similar to acne. The excess oil causes inflammation in the skin which leads to redness and spots.

Although the precise nature of rosacea is still a matter of scientific debate, the latest research points up that it is an inflammatory response by the body's immune system, in reaction to 'neuro-vascular dysfunction' – which translates as 'something going wrong with the messages between nerves and blood vessels'.

To complicate matters, rosacea may be made worse if your skin happens to host an unusually high number of the microscopic skin mites called demodex on your skin. (We all have these mites. They scoff dead skin, which helps get rid of it. That sounds revolting but is perfectly normal.)

WHAT DOES ROSACEA LOOK LIKE?

One of the odd things about rosacea is that it can make the skin feel rough and dry rather than oily. Rosacea is also widely under-diagnosed. Then there's the way that not all rosacea looks the same, which means that part of the difficulty in identifying rosacea is that it shows up in many different forms. Apart from making the face look flushed, rosacea can show up as tiny raised red bumps or acne-type pustules, or as an increased number of thread veins on the face. Add to that the way rosacea tends to come and go, and you can see why it is tricky to spot, and why it isn't diagnosed as quickly or as often as it should be.

Rosacea can be very mild, where your skin just has the odd tendency to flush – or it can be very obvious and persistent. It tends not to be obvious before the age of 30, and it tends to get worse the older you get. Rosacea might be most common in fair, Celtic types, but it affects people of all skin colours. It often goes undetected in darker skin, just because it's not so obvious, and harder to identify.

WHAT MAKES ROSACEA WORSE?

If this is starting to sound familiar, you will already know that it doesn't take much to make rosacea kick off. Common triggers include many of the normal things that make life fun, such as coffee, alcohol, spicy food, hot baths, and particularly sunshine – another reason for wearing an SPF every day.

WHAT CAN BE DONE ABOUT ROSACEA?

Anyone who struggles with rosacea will know, it's not just maddening to have a red flush across your face, but those flushed capillaries can settle in and become persistently obvious thread veins, and the weathered look that those veins give to a face does make it look older. If the redness settles around the nose, it's a look that's – unfairly – associated with hardened drinkers; in fact, drinking too much alcohol doesn't cause the redness, but it does dilate the blood vessels that are there, so it makes an existing problem more obvious.

But using the right skincare can help you manage rosacea. So can redness-reducing light treatments – you'll find that information on my website (thetweakmentsguide.com) and in my other book, *The Tweakments Guide: Fresher Face.*

Key Skincare Steps for Rosacea

If your skin is prone to flushing, you may be hesitant to use new products, or any products on it, in case they make it flare up. But with rosacea, you need to take action rather than leaving it be, otherwise it will just get worse.

You can start with the types of products I've mentioned here and see what they can do for you. Not everyone with rosacea responds to the same products in the same way, so if you're finding it slow to make improvements, consider seeing a skin specialist or a dermatologist who can provide prescription products that may help.

If you're wondering about sticking with your existing products while you introduce new ones, make sure that the ones you are using don't contain fragrance, because fragrance, or 'parfum' as it may be listed in the small print of the ingredients, is irritating to skin that isn't in great condition.

Exfoliate, Carefully

You may be wary of exfoliating, but a quick wipe-over with a salicylic acid toner can be very helpful. Salicylic acid – beta hydroxy acid – will help to keep pores clear, reduce oiliness in the skin, provide a gentle exfoliation, and improve skin hydration. Also, it's anti-inflammatory, which helps bring down the redness in the skin. Start by using it twice a week, to see how your skin takes to it. You can read more about beta hydroxy acid in the section 'What Is Beta Hydroxy Acid and What Can It Do for My Skin?' on page 88. For product suggestions, see the section 'Great Beta Hydroxy Acid Products' on page 89.

Reduce the Inflammation

Bringing down the inflammation in the skin is key to getting rosacea-prone skin into a happier state. Ingredients to look for include niacinamide, which has an anti-inflammatory action and which also helps strengthen the skin barrier, and azelaic acid, which is anti-inflammatory and also anti-bacterial (useful if you have the type of rosacea that is throwing up spots).

It is well worth trying the sort of products that are called 'anti-redness' and 'calming'. You can read more about these in the section 'To Calm Irritated and Reactive Skin: Anti-Inflammatory Serums' on page 111, and there is a list of suggested products in the section 'Great Calming Anti-Inflammatory Serums to Try' on page 114. On the high street, skincare ranges like Rosaliac from La Roche-Posay are a good place to start. Even more effective are calming products from specialist cosmeceutical ranges such as Epionce (try the Lytic range), NeoStrata, SkinMedica, PCA Skincare, SkinCeuticals, iS Clinical, Medik8 (the Calmwise range), ZO Skincare, Paula's Choice (the Calm products) and Jan Marini.

Rebuild the Skin Barrier

If you are suffering with rosacea, it's a fair bet that your skin barrier is not in good shape. The skin barrier is the outer layer of the epidermis, and it is there to hold moisture in the skin (there's more about this in the section 'Question 3: My Skin Is So Sensitive. What Can I Do?' on page 202, if you haven't just read it). When this barrier isn't working properly, the skin becomes dry and irritable.

So, to help repair the barrier, use a hydrating serum with hyaluronic acid, to supply molecules of moisture that will sink into the skin, then seal this into place with a moisturiser containing the sort of vital skin lipids – ceramides, cholesterol, and essential fatty acids – that can help your skin barrier regain its equilibrium. You can read more detail about hydrating serums in the section 'To Soften Dry Skin: Hydrating Serums' on page 71, and there's a list of some of my favourite hydrating serums in the section 'Great Hydrating Serums' on page 73. There are relevant moisturiser suggestions in the section 'Moisturisers for Dry Skin' on page 121.

Don't Forget the Sunscreen!

Of all the factors that can make your rosacea kick off – from certain foods to hot showers – the one that always makes it worse for 85 per cent of people with the condition is ultraviolet light. That means you really, really need your sunscreen, every day. There's a list of suggested sunscreens in the section 'Which Sunscreen Should I Use?' on page 149.

How Can a Dermatologist Help My Rosacea?

The expert advice that you will get from a qualified dermatologist will certainly help you to get your rosacea under control. A dermatologist will analyse the type of rosacea that you have and prescribe specialised skincare products and treatments that should help you to manage the condition. Also, they will monitor your progress, so that if particular treatments or products aren't doing the trick for you, they can adapt your regime to find something more effective.

> I say 'qualified' dermatologist because 'dermatologist' isn't a protected medical term, so quite a few skin practitioners call themselves dermatologists when they're not. If you want to check whether someone is a qualified dermatologist, look them up on the specialist register of the General Medical Council (www.gmc-uk.org).

Prescription creams that a dermatologist might suggest for you include Rosex and Mirvaso. Another, Soolantra, can help if your rosacea is being made worse by the demodex mite – but if that's not your particular problem, it won't do the trick. Then there's Finacea, where the active ingredient is azelaic acid. You may have heard of Finacea as a possible acne treatment; it works on rosacea in a similar way, by reducing the skin cells' over-production of keratin (which blocks up the pores and provokes acne), thus keeping the pores clearer. Azelaic acid also knocks back the bacteria that drive inflammation in rosacea as well as acne.

Dermatologists may also prescribe antibiotics to reduce the inflammation that goes along with rosacea, or beta-blockers to reduce the flushing.

Untreated rosacea can develop into rhinophyma, where the nose becomes swollen and bulbous. If you have this problem, a dermatological surgeon can treat it (surgically) by shaving down the excess skin to restore the nose to its normal shape.

ROSACEA: THE REGIME

Here is what a skincare routine for rosacea might look like.

Morning Routine

Cleanse

Start by cleansing with a gentle, creamy cleanser that won't aggravate your skin.

Exfoliate

A quick wipe-over with a salicylic acid tonic will help clear clogged pores, provide gentle exfoliation, and bring down inflammation. Use this just twice a week to start with.

Treat

By way of treatment, you could pick a specific anti-redness serum from one of the brands above, and follow this with a hydrating serum. If you have a prescription treatment product, use it as per the instructions.

Moisturise

Moisturise your skin to hold that hydration in place.

Protect

Then add sunscreen, to protect your skin from UV light.

Evening Routine

Cleanse

Preferably, do a double-cleanse, with gentle, fragrance-free products, to shift the sunscreen and whatever else has accumulated on your face during the day.

Treat

If you're using a specific anti-redness treatment serum, apply that once your skin is clean and dry. After this, or instead of this, layer on a hydrating serum. If you're using a prescription treatment product, apply it as directed.

Moisturise

Finish off with a ceramide-rich moisturiser. If you have a moisturiser that also includes cholesterol and essential fatty acids, so much the better.

Question 5: Help, I've Still Got Spots! What Can I Do About Adult Acne?

I feel for you! If you're finding that spots are still a problem as you move through your thirties, forties, and fifties, and wonder how you can still suffer with acne-type blemishes when you are so far past puberty – well, it's not much comfort, but you are not alone.

Adult acne – doctors class it all as acne, whether it's a few occasional spots or a mass of inflamed pustules – is on the increase, and doctors and dermatologists tend to point the finger at many contributing factors in our modern lifestyles.

Spots are at root a hormonal problem. For women, this means spots are most likely to emerge when hormone levels fluctuate, as they do every month; or when starting or stopping contraceptive pills; or in the run-up to menopause; or when starting on hormone replacement therapy (HRT) or bioidentical hormones (BHRT).

Stress also throws our hormones out of balance, as does going short on sleep. These both raise levels of cortisol (the stress hormone) and androgens (male hormones).

Having too many androgens on the rampage encourages the skin to produce more oil in each of its many hair follicles, and at the same time makes those follicles shed the skin cells that line them faster than usual.

Oily follicles full of dead skin cells block up quickly. We all have a certain amount of acne bacteria (*Propionibacterium acnes*, if you want its proper name) on our skin, which isn't a problem until it gets stuck in a blocked, oily pore. That is a recipe for inflammation and swelling – and the spots start breaking out.

Eating too much sugar will make a tendency for spottiness worse, too, since digesting sugar leads to spikes in insulin levels, which in turn prompts the release of more androgens. Drinking too much sugar, either as fizzy drinks or in the form of alcohol, has much the same effect. Eating oily food, on the other hand, won't give you spots or make them worse, whatever you heard when you were growing up (and the omega-3 essential fatty acids in oily fish are great for reducing inflammation, which may help acne).

For women, there are some hormone-management options which may help. Some types of the contraceptive pill, such as Yasmin (which combines drospirenone, a synthetic form of progesterone, and ethinyl estradiol, a synthetic form of oestrogen) can help reduce acne. For older women, hormone replacement therapy can moderate the hormonal fluctuations in the run up to and during the menopause. Talk to your doctor if either of these sound like options for you.

Meanwhile, here are the more direct, topical ways you can tackle blemishes with skincare.

REDUCE ADULT ACNE WITH SKINCARE

There's a great deal you can do to reduce spots with skincare. The aim is to reduce levels of skin oiliness, keep pores clear and not clog them up with the wrong sort of products, and reduce inflammation.

FLASHCARD: TREATING SPOTS

- Keep pores clear with salicylic acid.

- Treat acne with anti-inflammatory serums containing ingredients such as niacinamide or azelaic acid, or specific anti-acne serums.

- Use a hydrating serum to counteract dryness.

- Protect your skin with sunscreen to reduce inflammation in the skin and prevent hyperpigmentation of blemishes.

- Use a treatment product with a retinoid such as retinol at night to reduce skin oiliness and help repair damaged skin.

- Consider getting professional help and prescription products if over-the-counter skincare isn't doing the job for you.

Exfoliate to Keep Pores Clear

Every spot that ever existed started off as a blocked pore, so doing what you can to keep the pores clear is crucial for reducing spottiness. I wouldn't recommend using a physical, scrub-type exfoliant, as this will just aggravate the inflammation in any acne which you already have or which is developing.

What's easier and kinder to your skin is to use a salicylic acid toner or serum which you wipe over your skin after cleansing. You can build up to using this every day, but I recommend using it every three days, then every other day, to begin with.

You could use an alpha hydroxy acid toner based on lactic or glycolic acid to exfoliate the surface, but I'm really keen on salicylic acid (which is beta hydroxy acid) because it is 'lipophilic' – in other words, it dissolves in oil. That makes it the only skincare ingredient that reaches into pores and cleans them out, by exfoliating both the surface of the skin and the inside of the pore, so it is hugely helpful for managing blemishes and skin oiliness and stopping pores from becoming clogged.

Also, salicylic acid (like the alpha hydroxy acids) will improve skin hydration, which is good for acne-prone skin, and it is anti-inflammatory, so it will help to calm breakouts that way, too.

Pick a Treatment Product (or Two) to Bring Down Inflammation

Using a treatment product containing one of the following ingredients will help calm the inflammation that is part and parcel of acne, reduce skin oiliness, and help keep pores clear. You can find a list of suggested products containing some of these ingredients in the section 'To Clear Breakouts: Anti-Acne Serums' on page 109.

- Salicylic acid, in addition to its exfoliating and hydrating abilities, has an anti-inflammatory effect on the skin.

- Niacinamide, a type of vitamin B3, is also anti-inflammatory and can reduce oil production in the skin. It helps improve skin texture and tone, so it's really helpful for anyone who suffers with oily skin and breakouts.

- Azelaic acid is anti-bacterial as well as anti-inflammatory and slows down the overproduction of skin cells which contributes to clogging up the pores, so it's a terrific ingredient for tackling acne.

- Benzoyl peroxide kills bacteria that are driving the flare-up of spots, and takes down inflammation that way. It is really effective, though it tends to make the skin very dry, and can stain your bedclothes. It works by oxidising the acne bacteria – which is effective, but creates free radicals, so it's not something to use long-term, as it will have an ageing effect on the skin. If you're going to use it, use it at night, then pile on an antioxidant serum in the morning, to make up for it.

- Using a vitamin-A derivative such as retinol at night can really help skin that is prone to spots. Retinol and other retinoids help by reducing the oiliness of the skin and preventing pores from becoming clogged, as well as stimulating the growth of new collagen that will help heal blemishes. See the section 'To Combat Ageing and Boost Skin Renewal: Retinol and Other Retinoids' on page 97 for more detail about retinol, retinoids, and other ingredients derived from vitamin A. See the section 'Great Retinol Products to Try' on page 103 for a list of products containing retinol and other retinoids.

Don't pile these ingredients one on top of another. If you're using salicylic acid in the morning after cleansing, then, ok, you could use a serum with niacinamide or azelaic acid or both after that. You could use that same serum in the evening, or a product with benzoyl peroxide, or a retinoid, but just one at a time.

Keep Your Skin Hydrated

You might be tempted to want to 'dry out' your skin if it is oily; but even if your skin is producing too much oil, it still needs moisture, because oil and water are two very different things. It might sound unlikely, but it is quite possible to have skin that is both oily and dehydrated at the same time, because skin that is short on moisture and feels dry will start producing more oil to try to hold onto what little water there is within it.

Any light serum based on hyaluronic acid (HA), which is super-hydrating and adds no oil to skin, will do the trick. A hydrating serum will sink into your skin and go to work there, and if your skin is feeling dry, you might want to use a moisturiser on top of it, to seal it into place. Choose an oil-free moisturiser, rather than a creamy one, as acne-prone skin can do without the extra oil you get in creamy or richer moisturisers. You can read more about hydrating serums in the section 'To Soften Dry Skin: Hydrating Serums' on page 71. You'll find a list of some of my favourite hydrating serums in the section 'Great Hydrating Serums' on page 73.

Don't Forget the Sunscreen

I know I say this all the time, but you really need a sunscreen, because acne is an inflammatory skin condition and, guess what, all inflammatory skin conditions are made worse by exposing them to ultraviolet light. Also, UV light on damaged skin is a recipe for post-inflammatory pigmentation, where the tail ends of breakouts remain as pigment marks on the skin.

TRY NOT TO SQUEEZE, PICK, OR POP SPOTS

I know that for many of us it feels irresistible, but picking or squeezing spots is a terrible idea. Why? Because it will spread the infection under the skin, tear the skin, take longer to heal, and possibly leave a scar.

But If You Have To...

But if you really can't leave it alone… approach the process like a surgical procedure, and bear in mind that you can only pop spots that have already come to a white head.

Dip a clean flannel in hot water then put it on the spot for a couple of minutes, to soften the skin.

Clean the area with surgical spirit. Wrap your fingers in tissue. Get a needle and wipe this with surgical spirit. Use this like a lance, across the white head of the spot, going in one side and coming out the other. Then very gently squeeze at the base of the spot to push the pus out.

If this doesn't work, leave the spot be; it is not ready to pop, and prodding at it will just make it worse. Either way, wipe over the area again with surgical spirit, then put on a spot treatment or a pimple patch. (A pimple patch? Yes, they're a great idea. They're like small sticking plasters with antibacterial ingredients on the inside, which stick over spots, cover them up so your wandering fingers can't rub or scratch them, and bring down the inflammation).

When you have skin with a tendency to break out, you need to find a sunscreen that is light enough not to clog pores and make things worse. Look for a sunscreen that is oil-free. There's a list of these in the section 'Which Sunscreen Should I Use?' on page 149.

HOW CAN A DERMATOLOGIST HELP WITH ACNE?

A dermatologist will get you onto a regime of a basic cleanser plus prescription products. You might be given Finacea (azelaic acid) for the morning, to reduce redness and the over-growth of keratin that makes pores more likely to block up; or Duac, which combines an antibiotic (clindamycin) with benzoyl peroxide, which dries up oily skin. In the evening, you might use a retinoid, perhaps Differin (which contains a retinoid called adapalene) or a gel or cream containing tretinoin, which is retinoic acid.

Retinoids, particularly at prescription strength, are very effective at making the skin less oily, clearing blocked pores, and stimulating skin repair and renewal from the inside; but they need to be used with respect and carefully monitored. Overusing retinoids will quickly make your skin dry, red, and irritated. Even if you're using retinoids cautiously, you will need a plain moisturiser to load over the top, to keep your skin comfortable, and sunscreen for daily protection.

A dermatologist may also prescribe you antibiotics, to reduce the inflammation of acne, which will take several months to show any effect. If all else fails, there is always Roaccutane, which is vitamin A in tablet form. Roaccutane is very effective at shrinking oil glands, which will reduce spottiness and also make the rest of the skin very dry.

Roaccutane (isotretinoin) also has a real image problem, as it is widely thought to provoke low mood and depression, though this isn't borne out by wider studies. As well as drying up oil in the skin, and leaving lips dry and cracked, it can dry out the eyes and mucous membranes, too. Side effects include increased sensitivity to UV light, and for women, it is vital not to become pregnant while taking isotretinoin as it can cause birth defects; your doctor may insist you use two forms of contraception. Many dermatologists now prescribe Roaccutane in much lower doses than they used to, which take longer to work but make the drug easier to tolerate. One six-month course may be enough to clear the skin for good.

ACNE: THE REGIME

Here's what a daily regime for dealing with acne might look like.

Morning Routine

Cleanse

Remove excess oil from your face without stripping the skin with a wash-off gel cleanser. You might like one that contains salicylic acid or glycolic acid for a mini-dose of exfoliation as you cleanse.

Exfoliate

You could wipe your skin over with salicylic acid for its pore-clearing and anti-inflammatory effects, though if you are using a retinoid at night, bear in mind that that will already be having an exfoliating effect on your skin. Start by using salicylic acid twice a week, then step up to three times a week if your skin is ok with it.

Treat

Try an anti-acne serum (there's a list of suggested products in the section 'Great Anti-Acne Serums to Try' on page 110), or an anti-inflammatory serum with niacinamide or azelaic acid. Add a hydrating serum if you like, or just go for an oil-free moisturiser.

Moisturise

Using an oil-free moisturiser will help keep your skin hydrated, and counteract the drying effects of retinoid-based treatments or prescription acne-busting products. You can find my suggestions for oil-free moisturisers in the section 'Moisturisers for Oily Skin' on page 124.

Protect

Sunscreen. Always sunscreen. Choose one that you like the texture of, and use it diligently.

Evening Routine

Cleanse

Cleanse carefully to clear everything off your skin. I'd suggest a cream-based cleanser to start with, followed with a wash-off gel to remove the film of oil that creamier cleansers tend to leave. Though if your skin is getting dry from anti-acne treatments, that film of oil may be something you don't want to remove. You decide.

Treat

If you're using a retinoid, whether it's a prescription product or an over-the-counter cream with retinol in it, night time is the time for it. With any retinoid, start slowly, using it just twice a week. See the section 'Strong, Stronger, Strongest: Meet the Retinoids' on page 97 for details of the various types of retinoids, and the section 'How to Use Retinoids' on page 100 for information on how to acclimatise your skin to them.

If you're not using a retinoid, you could use the anti-acne serum that you used in the morning, as long as it's one that says you can use it twice a day. Or you could use a peptide serum or a vitamin C serum. Or – radical thought – you could just give your skin a break, use a hydrating serum, then leave it be.

Moisturise

Moisturise with anything you like. Seriously. If you're using moisturiser to counteract the drying effect of retinoids, then use any product which suits your skin and which feels comforting, and which will stop your skin drying out overnight. If you're not using a retinoid, an oil-free moisturiser may suit you better.

Question 6: I've Got Large Pores. Can Skincare Help?

Some of us just do have large pores. Or pores that are much more visible than we'd like them to be. This isn't a health hazard; although if your pores, like mine, are bigger than average – big enough for facialists always to comment on them and set about cleaning them out – you're probably well aware of them and wish they were less obvious. So here's what you can do – though honestly, large pores are not something to stress about. They might seem huge to you, but I bet no one else has even noticed them.

WHY DO WE GET LARGE PORES?

The size of your pores is determined by your genes. If your pores are on the larger side, particularly over your nose and chin and forehead, it is usually because you have oilier skin. If the sebum, the oil that your skin produces to help keep itself lubricated, flows freely out of your pores, all is fine. But when pores become blocked with a combination of old dead skin cells and oil, which oxidises into a black plug known as a blackhead, you really start to notice them.

As so often with skin issues, things tend to get worse as you get older. The skin becomes less good at making collagen, the supportive protein that gives skin its structure, and that slight slackening means that pores dilate a fraction and appear bigger. So if you're getting older and you've been wondering whether your pores are larger than they used to be or whether you're imagining it – I'm afraid you're not. Your pores really are growing, just a tiny bit but inexorably, by the year.

The good news? Skincare can definitely improve the appearance of large pores. And while we're talking in detail about pores, it's worth mentioning that pores don't open and close like flower petals, whatever you may have heard. They just don't.

FLASHCARD: LARGE PORES

- Keep pores clear by exfoliating with salicylic acid or alpha hydroxy acids.

- Use retinol to strengthen the skin and reduce oiliness.

- Use sunscreen for general protection and to slow down the rate of skin ageing.

MANAGING LARGE PORES WITH SKINCARE

The key to managing large pores with skincare is to keep them clean, because when plugs of sebum build up in a pore, they tend to stretch the pore – which, unsurprisingly, makes that pore more obvious. To help here, use products that reduce oiliness, and then strengthen the skin with retinoids that build up the collagen, which will not only firm up your face but will make pores appear smaller, too. Then, of course, wear sunscreen, to preserve the skin quality.

First, Exfoliate

Gentle exfoliation is vital, to get rid of the dead skin cells that clutter up the skin's surface and to begin to wear away the surface of the blackheads. There are two ways to exfoliate, either physically or chemically.

As I said in Rule Two (see page 60), I'm not keen on physical exfoliants, because it's too easy to irritate the skin by scrubbing away at it and upsetting the skin barrier. I prefer the 'gommage' type exfoliants, and the Dr Levy's 3 Deep Cell Renewal Micro-Resurfacing Cleanser (£39, cultbeauty.co.uk). The Dr Levy product has smooth scrubby bits of organic rice in it, but it also contains glycolic acid, the benefits of which I'll explain in a sec; and if you leave the product on for five minutes, like a mask, it gives a deeper glycolic exfoliation.

What I generally prefer to physical scrubs is a chemical exfoliation of the face with a product based on glycolic or salicylic acid, partly because it avoids all the scrubbing or polishing. These acids aren't as harsh as they might sound. Glycolic acid is an alpha hydroxy acid (AHA), a water-soluble acid that gently dissolves the bonds that hold old dead skin cells onto the skin's surface, so wiping your face over with a glycolic product exfoliates it without scrubbing. If you have sensitive skin, look for products with lactic acid or mandelic acid, which have a less pronounced effect on the skin than glycolic acid (they have larger molecules, which don't penetrate so far into the skin). But if these products sting rather than just tingling, just stop using them.

You can find a list of great chemical exfoliation products in the section 'Chemical Exfoliants That Do a Brilliant Job' on page 64. Using any of these twice a week will do the trick.

Clean Out Your Pores with Salicylic Acid

Face scrubs or alpha hydroxy acids will sweep away dead cells on the skin's surface. That may be enough for you, but if you have an issue with oily skin, what you really need to do is to clean out the pores themselves. The best home-use product for this is salicylic acid.

Salicylic acid is a beta hydroxy acid (in fact, it's the only beta hydroxy acid) and it is 'lipophilic', which means that it can dissolve in oil, so it can actually weasel its way into clogged, oily pores and clean them out while also exfoliating the surface of the skin. I love salicylic acid, because I still have combination skin and it's really useful on the oily bits. There's a list of suggested beta hydroxy acids in the section 'Great Beta Hydroxy Acid Products' on page 89.

Use Products That Reduce Skin Oiliness

One effective way to reduce oil-production at source is to use a retinol-based product. As well as slowing down the oil output, retinol-based products (I've mentioned some of these in the section 'Great Retinol Products to Try', starting on page 103) will also speed up the sluggish cell turnover in older skin, improve collagen production, and bring newer, stronger skin cells up to the surface. Stimulating collagen production is good for pores, too, because when the skin is firmer, the pores are less obvious.

LARGE PORES: THE REGIME

These are the steps that can help you towards clearer pores.

Morning Routine

Cleanse

Choose a wash-off cleanser, perhaps one with a bit of glycolic acid or salicylic acid in it, to begin the process of chemical exfoliation.

Exfoliate

Wipe over your face with salicylic acid, to exfoliate both the surface and the inside of the pores. Start by doing this twice a week, and increase to every other day if your skin is ok with it.

Treat

Use any treatment serum that you have on the go; an antioxidant such as vitamin C is always a good choice. Follow with a hydrating serum.

Moisturise

If your skin feels dry, pick an oil-free moisturiser that won't block your pores.

Protect

Finish off with sunscreen – again, a lightweight one.

Evening Routine

Cleanse

Do a thorough cleanse, finishing with a wash-off cleanser.

Treat

Once your skin is dry, apply your retinoid (or vitamin C serum, if you're not using a retinoid) and let it sink in. When it has been absorbed, follow with a hydrating serum.

Moisturise

Finish with any moisturiser that you like, though if your pores are prone to blocking up, it makes sense to choose an oil-free one.

Protect Your Pores with Sunscreen

Ultraviolet light speeds up the ageing processes in the skin, and when skin sags, pores look more obvious. That's another reason why it's worth wearing sunscreen. Choose a lightweight formula, maybe one that is oil-free, so that it doesn't block up those pores. You can find a list of sunscreen suggestions in the section 'Which Sunscreen Should I Use?' on page 149.

Question 7: My Skin Is So Dry! How Can I Soften It?

Dry, tight-feeling skin is no fun to live with. The simple answer would seem to be: moisturise. Up to a point, that works, but it's not the whole answer. Here's how to transform dry skin into a happier, hydrated version of its former self.

FLASHCARD: SOFTENING DRY SKIN

- Build moisture levels with hydrating serums.
- Improve the skin barrier with vital skin lipids.
- Try acid exfoliation to smooth the surface and boost hydration.
- Use a retinoid at night to improve skin function.
- Remember the sunscreen – every day.

WHY IS MY SKIN SO DRY?

There's usually more than one thing contributing towards your skin feeling dry. For a start, your genes may mean you just have skin that doesn't produce so much sebum, or oil, which keeps the skin barrier feeling comfortable and enables the skin to hold onto moisture. (Yes, it's a skin barrier issue, again). Washing the skin dries it out, particularly if you use hot water, and even more so if you use a face wash that strips oil out of the skin.

Ageing doesn't help, either, as our skin makes less of its own hyaluronic acid, the naturally occurring substance that holds many times its own weight in water and so helps the skin hang onto moisture. And once the skin barrier is in trouble, or 'compromised', then water escapes from the skin into the air faster than it should, which dries the skin out further.

WHY DOESN'T A RICHER MOISTURISER DO THE TRICK?

Part of the problem is that we often think – certainly if you're my age, ie 55-plus – that the way to tackle dry skin is to use a heavier, richer moisturiser, because the richer the moisturiser, the more of an effect it will give, right? Well, no. A rich, creamy moisturiser will feel comforting on the skin, but it will just sit on the surface of the skin and not actually do that much to replace missing moisture within the skin or to restore the skin barrier to better health.

WHAT DOES DRY SKIN NEED?

The simple answer is that dry skin needs more hydration – as in moisture, right down in and around the skin cells. Hydration makes skin feel more comfortable and function better. As a knock-on benefit, hydrated skin looks smoother because it is plumped up, which means that fine lines and wrinkles become slightly less obvious.

The other thing dry skin needs is a better barrier, to stop that moisture from escaping, and I'll get onto that in just a moment.

HOW TO MAKE THE SKIN BETTER HYDRATED – PART 1

You can start by using a hydrating serum. Choose one that contains 'humectant' ingredients such as hyaluronic acid and glycerin, which will sink into the top layers of the skin, hold onto moisture, and make the skin feel more comfortable. You can read more about these in the section 'To Soften Dry Skin: Hydrating Serums' on page 71 and find a list of suggested products in the section 'Great Hydrating Serums' on page 73; but in a nutshell, they will make the skin feel more comfortable.

You can also improve skin hydration by using products that stimulate lazier, older skin cells into producing more of their own hyaluronic acid. But before you do that, get your skin barrier in better shape.

STRENGTHEN YOUR SKIN BARRIER

The other crucial part of improving dry skin is to nudge your skin barrier into better health. For this, you need to use a moisturiser that can deliver all the key lipids, or fats, that help to sandwich together the outer cells of the skin into a flexible, waterproof layer. Those lipids are ceramides, cholesterol, and essential fatty acids, and if your moisturiser has some natural moisturising factors – NMFs – too, even better. Filling the gaps in the barrier will help seal in the moisture and keep the skin feeling less dry and much happier. See the section 'Moisturisers for Dry Skin' on page 121 for suggestions of moisturisers for dry skin.

HOW TO MAKE THE SKIN BETTER HYDRATED – PART 2

Once your skin barrier is stronger, you can experiment with alpha hydroxy acids (AHAs). If you have dry skin, you might be wary of using these, but they can be really helpful.

AHAs are best known as a way of giving the skin a chemical exfoliation. That might not sound like a good idea if your skin is dry, but an acid toner clears the skin's surface, allowing for better absorption of any other products that you're using. Acid toners with AHAs are also great for boosting hydration within the skin. You could start with an acid toner in the morning a couple of times a week, or try an overnight product.

DRY SKIN: THE REGIME

Here's how you can work on improving dry skin.

Morning Routine

Cleanse

Pick a creamy, wipe-off, or wash-off cleanser.

Exfoliate

Skip exfoliation at first until you have spent a few weeks coaxing your skin barrier into better shape, then start gently with an acid toner after cleansing, a couple of times a week.

Treat

Treat your skin with hyaluronic acid serum to pack in moisture.

Moisturise

Choose a moisturiser with essential skin lipids – ceramides, essential fatty acids, and cholesterol – to restore the skin barrier

Protect

Top off the serum and moisturiser with a sunscreen. You know you need it.

Evening Routine

Cleanse

Use your cleanser thoroughly to shift grime and sunscreen from your face.

Treat

As with the acid toner in the mornings, wait a couple of weeks until your skin barrier is improving and your skin is starting to feel less dry, then begin using a product with retinol, or a stronger retinoid in it, at night. Go slowly, and if your skin objects, back off, and try again in a few weeks' time. If your skin really doesn't agree with retinol, opt for a vitamin C serum, and/or a peptide serum, instead.

Moisturise

Once your treatment product has been absorbed, finish off for the night with a layer of moisturiser.

Question 8: My Skin Feels Rough. How Can I Make It Smoother?

Skincare can be a big help in improving skin texture, and softening any roughness in the skin obviously makes it smoother. Hydrating the skin cells with moisture plumps them out and helps disguise fine lines. Encouraging the skin cells to turn over faster and boost the production of collagen and elastin strengthens the skin and makes it look fresher and smoother, too.

FLASHCARD: SMOOTHING ROUGH SKIN

- Hydrate and strengthen your skin barrier.
- Exfoliate with an alpha hydroxy acid.
- Strengthen the skin with vitamin C serum and retinol.
- Protect your smoother skin with sunscreen.

WHY DOES SKIN BECOME ROUGH?

If your skin is feeling rough to the touch, it means your skin barrier isn't working as well as it should do. The skin barrier, the water-proof outer layers of your skin, is meant to hold moisture inside your body and keep the world out, but if life, the weather, too much washing, or even over-enthusiastic use of too many skincare products has roughed it up, it won't be able to do its job properly.

IS THIS REPEATING WHAT YOU SAID IN THE PREVIOUS ANSWERS?

Yes, it is. Dry skin, rough skin, and sensitive skin tend to be overlapping concerns. Once your skin barrier is in trouble, the skin will start to dry out; its texture will feel rough, rather than smooth; and because the barrier isn't in good shape, your skin will begin to feel more sensitive to the environment and to the products you put on it.

WHERE DO I START TO MAKE MY SKIN SMOOTHER?

Here are the steps for making your skin smoother. They may be starting to sound familiar.

Nourish Your Skin Barrier To Better Health

First, you want to strengthen the skin barrier, by packing more moisture into the skin with a hydrating serum based on ingredients like hyaluronic acid and glycerin. You can read more about hydrating serums in the section 'To Soften Dry Skin: Hydrating Serums' on page 71.

The second part of strengthening the skin barrier is to reinforce the lipid layer at the top of it with ceramides, cholesterol, and essential fatty acids. You can read more about these ingredients in the section 'Which Moisturiser Should I Use? (see page 121).

Exfoliate for a Smoother Feel

Try an acid toner containing an alpha hydroxy acid, perhaps lactic acid or glycolic acid or a mixture of the two. This will help to unstick dead skin cells that are cluttering up the surface of the skin and leave your complexion looking fresher and more radiant and feeling smoother, too. A clear skin surface means that other products you use on the skin will be better and more evenly absorbed, too. You can read more about acid exfoliation in the section 'Chemical Exfoliation with Acids and Enzymes' on page 62.

Strengthen Your Skin from Within

Once the skin barrier is more comfortable, you can start to work on stimulating regeneration in the skin.

In the mornings, you could use a vitamin C serum or an antioxidant serum after cleansing, to help your skin defend itself against the environment, and to assist with collagen production. You can read more about antioxidant serums in the section 'To Protect Against Environmental Damage: Antioxidant Serums' (see page 74) and about vitamin C serums in the section 'To Strengthen and Brighten the Skin: Vitamin C Serum' (see page 80).

The best-known ingredients for all-round skin improvement are retinoids, so think about adding in a night-time product that includes retinol or another type of retinoid. This will help your skin to create more collagen, which will keep it firm; and will improve the turnover of skin cells on the skin's surface, which will make the skin smoother and also reduce pigmentation. You can read more about retinol and retinoids in the section 'To Combat Ageing and Boost Skin Renewal: Retinol and Other Retinoids' (see page 97).

ROUGH SKIN: THE REGIME

This section lays out a full regime involving all the elements I mentioned above. I'd suggest starting with a barrier-boosting phase 1, before moving on to phase 2.

Phase 1: Morning Routine

Cleanse

Pick a gentle cleanser, for the sake of your skin barrier.

Treat

Use a hydrating serum to sink extra moisture into the skin.

Moisturise

Seal this in with a moisturiser full of skin-friendly lipids such as ceramides.

Protect

Add a sunscreen, for general protection.

Phase 1: Evening Routine

Cleanse

Gently cleanse as you did in the morning.

Treat

Use the same hydrating serum, to keep adding more moisture back into your skin.

Moisturise

As in the morning, you want to use a lipid-rich moisturiser to nurture your skin barrier back to good health.

Phase 2: Morning Routine

Cleanse

As above, stick with a gentle cleanser.

Exfoliate

Add in an acid toner twice a week and assess how it affects your skin before using it more often.

Treat

Boost skin health with a vitamin C serum, followed by a hydrating serum.

Moisturise

Seal the serums in place with a ceramide-rich moisturiser.

Protect

Finish your morning routine with a sunscreen.

Phase 2: Evening Routine

Cleanse

Use your gentle cleanser to remove sunscreen and everything else from your face.

Treat

Add in a product with retinol or another retinoid – starting slowly (twice a week at first) and monitoring your skin carefully for any signs of distress. Redness or peeling means you need to go slower with it, and moisturise more. When it has sunk in, apply a hydrating serum.

Moisturise

Finish off with a lipid-rich moisturiser to keep your skin comfortable overnight.

Question 9: Why Does My Skin Look Dull?

If your skin is looking dull, several factors could be conspiring to cause this. Here's the lowdown on how to give your skin back its radiance and put together a skincare regime to get your skin glowing.

FLASHCARD: BRIGHTEN DULL SKIN

- Exfoliate to clear the skin's surface.

- Boost skin radiance with vitamin C.

- Hydrate for healthier skin.

- Protect your fresher skin from UV damage.

WHAT CAUSES DULLNESS?

The main things that make skin look dull are:

- Dry skin
- A rough texture with an uneven surface
- Patches of old dead skin cells cluttering up the skin's surface
- Change-of-season weather
- Hormonal ups and downs

If your skin has lost its glow, it may be suffering from more than one of these factors at once.

DULLNESS FROM HORMONAL CHANGES

Stress affects hormone levels in the skin, which can upset the skin in all manner of ways, including making it look dull. For women, taking a contraceptive pill can have a knock-on effect on the skin. After pregnancy, as levels of both progesterone and oestrogen fall back towards normal, skin can look dull – it's partly not having that glowing radiance that pregnancy can often bring, but the sheer exhaustion and stress of looking after a new baby doesn't help, either.

Using radiance-boosting acids will help. Products with glycolic, lactic, and salicylic acid are fine to use when you're breastfeeding.

A more challenging issue for women is managing the effects of dwindling hormone levels around the menopause. This is such a big issue, I've split it off into a separate question of its own (Question 10, page 234).

If you're wondering about men's hormone levels – those fall with age, too, but in a slow and steady way, and without the same savage effects on the skin.

Here's what you can try to brighten up your skin.

SEASONAL SKIN DULLNESS

What do I mean by change-of-season weather causing dull skin? It's that general sulky sallowness that our skin often gets at the end of the winter after too long indoors with central heating, but also at the end of the summer, when any remnants of a tan that we may have picked up over the summer have faded. These are both good times to bring a skin-brightening acid into your skincare regime. You don't have to keep on using the acid the whole time; you can just use it for a boost when you need it.

EXFOLIATE WITH SKIN-SMOOTHING ACIDS

Regular exfoliation will smooth, clear, and soften the skin's surface, and allow better penetration of any other products you are using. I'd prefer that you do your exfoliating not with a harsh, physical scrub, but with an acid-based chemical exfoliant, which will dissolve the bonds that are holding old dead skin cells onto your face so that they are quietly shed, revealing smoother, brighter skin beneath. Alpha hydroxy acids, beta hydroxy acid, or polyhydroxy acids can all do this, and will help improve your skin's hydration into the bargain. See the section 'Chemical Exfoliation' on page 62 in Rule Two for more on acid exfoliation and for product suggestions.

TRY A GLOW-BOOSTING SERUM

Another key product that will help brighten your skin is a vitamin C serum, which helps the skin defend itself against the environment, supports collagen production, and helps reduce pigmentation. You can read more about antioxidant serums in the section 'To Protect Against Environmental Damage: Antioxidant Serums' on page 74 and about vitamin C serums in the section 'To Strengthen and Brighten the Skin: Vitamin C Serum' on page 80.

Just so you know – an alpha hydroxy acid, particularly glycolic acid, will tingle a bit when you put it on the skin. If the tingling goes on, you can mute it with a moisturiser, as above, but if it is really stinging, just rinse it off, and leave it for a while. It may be that your skin barrier isn't in great shape, and that you need to spend a few weeks coaxing that into better shape before you try again with the acid. If you're unsure of how your skin will react to any new product, and particularly to an exfoliating acid, patch-test it on a small area of skin and keep an eye on it for a day or two, before going for broke and wiping it over your whole face.

MORE MOISTURE MEANS SMOOTHER SKIN

Hydrate like a mad thing with serums that pack moisture back into the surface layers of the skin. These will make your skin feel more comfortable – and smoother, too. Smoother skin reflects the light more evenly than dull, rough skin, so smoother skin always looks that bit brighter.

You can read more about hydrating serums in the section 'To Soften Dry Skin: Hydrating Serums' on page 71, and there's a list of some of my favourite hydrating serums in the section 'Great Hydrating Serums' on page 73.

Then seal in this extra moisture with a cream containing ceramides, essential fatty acids, and cholesterol. Doing this will improve the health of the skin barrier and allow your skin to function more normally, hold onto moisture like it should, and develop a healthy radiance. You can read more about these ingredients in the section 'Which Moisturiser Should I Use?' (see page 121).

DON'T FORGET THE SUNSCREEN

At the risk of repeating myself, again…. you need sunscreen. You particularly need sunscreen when using alpha hydroxy acids, as these may make your skin more sensitive to UV light. You'll also want to protect your newly radiant skin from damaging UV rays. There's a list of suggested sunscreens in the section 'Which Sunscreen Should I Use?' on page 149.

DULL SKIN: THE REGIME

Here's what a radiance-boosting regime might look like:

Morning Routine

Cleanse

Use whichever cleanser you prefer – though if you already know you're ok with glycolic acid, you might like a wash-off product based on an alpha hydroxy acid or a beta hydroxy acid, to make a start on the exfoliating process.

Exfoliate

Wipe your skin down with a lightweight hydroxy acid–based product. Start by using this just twice a week, especially if your skin is sensitive. If you prefer, you can use an acid toner at night.

Treat

Follow with a vitamin C serum (see the section 'Great Vitamin C Products' on page 82 for suggestions) and then with a hydrating serum (see the section 'Great Hydrating Serums' on page 73 for my suggestions).

Moisturise

If your skin feels it needs more moisturiser, use a ceramide-rich serum or cream. See the section 'Which Moisturiser Should I Use?' on page 121 for suggestions.

Protect

Protect your skin by applying sunscreen – any sunscreen. Alpha hydroxy acids make skin more sensitive to UV light, so sunscreen is vital.

Evening Routine

Cleanse

Use a cream or lotion cleanser to shift the sunscreen and everything else from your face.

Treat

Instead of using an acid toner in the mornings, you could use a glycolic acid product in the evening, twice a week. What's the difference? If you simply use a glycolic acid product on its own, and don't put anything on afterwards, it gives a stronger effect, which means more overnight radiance-boosting (if you go and put moisturiser on afterwards, the water in the moisturiser neutralises the acid). You might think it would leave your skin dry, but it won't, because alpha hydroxy acids improve skin hydration. Strange but true.

If this all goes fine and you want to ramp up the acid, increase your morning acid toner to three or four times a week, mornings only. Or you could go for a stronger acid in the evenings, as above. But please be sensible. You're looking to stimulate your skin into producing fresher, better hydrated skin, not to provoke it into redness and peeling – so don't overdo it.

On nights when you're not using a glycolic product, you could use a vitamin C serum, or any skin brightening serum you liked. Or a retinoid. Or just some peptides. It's up to you.

Moisturise

Choose a product that suits your skin type. A cream with ceramides, cholesterol, and essential fatty acids will help keep your skin barrier happy. As above, don't moisturise if you're using a glycolic acid product, and want it to have a more pronounced effect.

Question 10: The Menopause Is Wrecking My Skin. What Can I Do?

Hormone levels have a big impact on the skin. During the menopause, the supply of oestrogen plummets. Actually, the trouble starts years before that, in the 'peri-menopause' phase, the run-up to the menopause itself. There's no easy way to tell whereabouts you are on this journey, but you're bound to feel it.

Along with the havoc the falling hormone levels cause to our moods and self-esteem and thermo-regulatory systems, our skin suffers. Collagen production is affected, as is the skin's ability to retain moisture, so post-menopause, skin swiftly becomes thinner, drier, and more fragile. Menopausal skin also tends to look dull, as drier, thinner skin doesn't reflect the light in the way that plumped up, firmer skin does. So that's the bad news. It's all very normal, all very natural, but it's not great to live with.

Hormone replacement therapy can work miracles here by restoring the oestrogen supply. Well, when I say miracles, it won't make you look like Jennifer Aniston – but it will prevent the drop-off in collagen levels, so your skin stays firmer; maintain sebum levels, so your skin doesn't get so dry; and improve skin hydration and the skin barrier. All of these will do more than any cream or serum to keep your skin in good nick.

DO I NEED TO CHANGE MY SKINCARE WITH THE SEASONS?

No and yes. You don't need to change your products with the season so much as you need to pay attention to how your skin is behaving differently depending on the season, and adjust the way you're treating it accordingly. Here are examples:

- **Spring.** Our skin tends to look a bit lacklustre after a long winter. A great time to freshen it up by adding an acid toner to your regime. The toner will improve skin radiance through gentle exfoliation and give it back its glow.

- **Summer.** The weather is warmer – if we're lucky – and without the drying effects of cold wind and central heating, you may find you need a more lightweight, gel-based hydrating moisturiser. And if you're not already using sunscreen every day, now is the time to make sure that you are.

- **Autumn.** Our skin tends to look a bit dull as any tan we picked up over the summer starts to fade, perhaps leaving pigmentation patches in its wake. Again, it's time for the exfoliating acids if those aren't something you're using on a regular basis, and maybe a specific anti-pigmentation product, to even up your skin tone.

- **Winter.** A combination of colder weather and drier air in our homes, thanks to central heating, frequently upsets our skin. Counteract this by keeping up your skin's hydration levels with plenty of hyaluronic acid–based serums, tamped down with a moisturiser containing ceramides or cholesterol to help keep your skin barrier in good repair.

In the UK, hormone replacement therapy (HRT) is available on the NHS, via your GP; or you can go for the more personalised form, bioidentical hormone replacement therapy (BHRT), which is usually only available privately. But not everyone wants to use hormone replacement therapy; and it's also a no-go for anyone who has had an oestrogen-related cancer.

If hormone supplementation is a non-starter for you, you're back to skincare. You could try one of the newer product ranges formulated specially for menopausal and post-menopausal skin, or you could stick with a classic cosmeceutical approach to reviving ageing skin.

```
┌─────────────────────────────────────────────────────────────┐
│            FLASHCARD: SUPPORTING MENOPAUSAL SKIN              │
│                                                               │
│  •  Tackle dull skin (and boost hydration) with alpha hydroxy acids. │
│                                                               │
│  •  Try antioxidant serums like vitamin C to support skin health. │
│                                                               │
│  •  Hydrate like a mad thing, with hyaluronic acid serums.    │
│                                                               │
│  •  Use moisturisers with essential skin lipids to hold the hydration │
│     in place.                                                 │
│                                                               │
│  •  Add retinoids at night to reboot collagen production.     │
│                                                               │
│  •  Have peptides to hand, for further skin-firming.          │
│                                                               │
│  •  Consider hormone replacement therapy (HRT or BHRT).       │
│                                                               │
│  •  Apply sunscreen, every day.                               │
└─────────────────────────────────────────────────────────────┘
```

EXFOLIATE WITH GLOW-BOOSTING ACIDS

Light and regular exfoliation will also help to keep your pores from blocking up, which is useful if the hormonal swings and round-abouts that come with the menopause start giving you the sort of spots and breakouts you haven't had since you were a teenager. Acid toners based on alpha hydroxy acids can help you here. If you find your skin is becoming actively oily, it's worth trying an acid toner based on salicylic acid (the beta hydroxy acid) rather than an alpha hydroxy acid. Whichever you choose, start by using it just twice a week, to see how your skin gets on with it, before using it more often. You can read more about exfoliating acids in the section 'To Exfoliate and Brighten Dull Skin: Hydroxy Acid Serums' on page 84.

TRY VITAMIN C SERUMS TO BRIGHTEN THE SKIN

Vitamin C serums support collagen production in the skin, help your skin to defend itself against the environment, and reduce pigmentation, which makes the skin brighter, too. They're a great daily addition to your skincare routine.

You can read more about antioxidant serums in the section 'To Protect Against Environmental Damage: Antioxidant Serums' (see page 74) and about vitamin C serums in the section 'To Strengthen and Brighten the Skin: Vitamin C Serum' (see page 80).

HYDRATION IS VITAL

Because the menopause is making your skin thinner and drier, you really need to major on hydrating serums, to feed more moisture back into the skin. You can read more about hydrating serums in the section 'To Soften Dry Skin: Hydrating Serums' on page 71.

ADD RETINOIDS TO STIMULATE COLLAGEN PRODUCTION

Adding retinol, or another form of retinoid, into your skincare regime will encourage your skin to renew itself, to counteract the slowing down of the process by which the skin makes new, fresh skin cells, and to generate more collagen which helps keep the skin firm.

Start slowly with any retinoid. You can read more about retinol and other retinoids and how to use them in the section 'To Combat Ageing and Boost Skin Renewal: Retinol and Other Retinoids' on page 97.

THROW IN SOME PEPTIDES, FOR FURTHER SKIN STRENGTHENING

There are a lot of suggestions here already, but if you fancy something else, a peptide-based serum can help firm and strengthen the skin. There's more about peptide serums in the section 'To Build Collagen and Reduce Wrinkling: Peptide Serums' on page 90, along with product suggestions.

DON'T FORGET THE SUNSCREEN

You're going to all this trouble to revive and regenerate your skin. Ultraviolet rays are not your friend. You know it makes sense to wear sunscreen. You can see a list of sunscreen suggestions in the section 'Which Sunscreen Should I Use?' on page 149.

LATEST SKINCARE OPTIONS FOR MENOPAUSAL SKIN

Here are three skincare ranges formulated specially for menopausal and post-menopausal skin. You might think they're just clever marketing, but these brands appear to offer genuine benefits.

- **Phytomone Pause Hydra Creme**, £138, phytomone.com. A luxurious cream based on phytoestrogens (plant-based bioidentical hormones, derived from soya) which bind to oestrogen receptors in the skin, to kid it into thinking that there's still oestrogen around, so that it will go ahead and go on making collagen.

- **VENeffect Anti-Ageing Intensive Moisturiser**, £148, cultbeauty.co.uk. Key moisturiser from this range based on plant oestrogens, aka phytoestrogens, which mimic the effects of oestrogen on the skin to boost its fading glow.

- **Emepelle Serum**, £135, and **Night Cream**, £175, emepelle.co.uk. Impressive new range of cosmeceutical skincare which combines all the key actives – antioxidants, peptides, niacinamide, and retinol – with a branded ingredient they call 'MEP technology' which makes the skin behave as if the skin still had pre-menopausal levels of oestrogen. The clinical results – achieved on properly aged skin – show brighter, clearer, better hydrated skin within eight weeks.

COSMECEUTICAL OPTIONS FOR MENOPAUSAL SKIN

Another way to deal with menopausal skin is to stick with a classic cosmeceutical regime.

MENOPAUSAL SKIN: THE REGIME

Here's what a daily regime might look like.

Morning Routine

Cleanse

Choose a creamy cleanser that will be gentle on your skin.

Exfoliate

Try acid toners based on alpha hydroxy acids to exfoliate your skin and improve skin radiance.

Treat

Apply a Vitamin C serum, then a hydrating serum.

Moisturise

Make sure the added hydration is trapped in your skin with a layer of moisturiser.

Protect

Don't forget the sunscreen.

Evening Routine

Cleanse

Use the same product as in the morning, and cleanse thoroughly.

Treat

If you're using a retinoid, use it on clean dry skin, and allow it to absorb. On nights that you're not using a retinoid, or if retinoids don't agree with your skin, use a vitamin C serum for a night-time treatment. If you like, follow either of these with a peptide serum, for further skin support.

Moisturise

Once everything else has sunk properly into your skin, add a layer of any moisturiser you like.

Question 11: Can Skincare Help My Crepey Neck?

The best thing you can do for your neck and décolletage is to use the same skincare on it that you use on your face, and to give it the same amount of UV protection.

Ideally, we would all have started doing this in our late teens. But until my late thirties, I had never thought to wear sunscreen every day, let alone to use the sunscreen on my neck and on any skin exposed by a scoop-neck t-shirt, not until a helpful dermatologist (Dr Nick Lowe) pointed it out to me about 20 years ago. Dr Lowe added that the trouble with the décolletage is that it is slightly tip-tilted at the perfect angle to catch the sun, like our very own solar panel, which means that it is all the more in need of protection.

But somehow most of us manage to forget about all that, and if we do invest in expensive serums and sunscreens, we rarely take them further south than the jaw. Which is fine until you hit your forties, but the older you get, the more annoying it becomes as your neck seems to age faster than your face, and your décolletage gives the game away about every single time it saw too much sun. So, whatever age you are, start looking after your neck right now, and your future self will thank you.

FLASHCARD: SKINCARE FOR A CREPEY NECK

- Nourish your skin with an antioxidant serum, such as vitamin C.
- Keep your skin hydrated, with a hyaluronic-acid based serum.
- Include a peptide serum for collagen boosting.
- Wear sunscreen daily.
- Use a retinoid at night to regenerate your skin.
- Add a moisturiser where you need it.

If you would like to use a specific neck cream, there are a great many available. I've mentioned a handful that I like in the section 'Great Neck Creams' on page 135.

WHY DOES THE NECK AGE SO FAST?

Necks just are different. The skin here is thinner than on your face, which means that it collapses more easily into wrinkles and folds, particularly given the way we twist and turn and stretch and compress our necks the whole time. Then there's the fact that there are precious few oil glands in neck skin to keep the skin supple. It all gets much worse when you hit the menopause and, thanks to the reduction in oestrogen, your skin gets drier and loses elasticity.

Does our new fondness for technology make the problem worse? Some skincare companies – ones with neck creams to promote – have claimed that constantly dropping your head forward to look at your phone ages the neck ('Beware of Tech Neck!' they warn) but I don't really buy that argument. I can see bending your head forward is dire for your posture and exaggerates the folds in the skin, but it's not actually doing anything bad to the skin.

HOW CAN SKINCARE HELP MY NECK?

Even though the skin on the neck is different to the face, I'd really encourage you to use on your neck the same skincare that you are using on your face, to help it look fresher and less crepey. If you've read this question section through from the start, you may have noticed that the Flashcard for treating the neck is the same as the one for treating wrinkles. If you turned straight here, you can flick back to the section 'Question 1: Can Skincare Soften My

Wrinkles?' on page 186 to see why I've recommended the various different treatment steps.

NECK CARE: THE REGIME

Here's what a daily regime for smoothing a crepey neck might look like.

Morning Routine

Cleanse

It seems almost too obvious to say, but you should cleanse your neck in the same way that you cleanse your face.

Exfoliate

You could use an acid toner to help with exfoliating your neck, but go gently. My neck is usually happy to be wiped down with an acid toner as long as I don't do it more than twice a week. Any more than that, and it starts to go red and prickly. Your neck might feel the same.

Treat

A vitamin C serum – or a different sort of antioxidant serum, if you prefer – will help nourish and strengthen your skin, so add that next. If you're using a hydrating serum, layer that on once the first serum has been absorbed.

Moisturise

Seal those serums in with a moisturiser.

Protect

Add a sunscreen, to fend off the UV rays. I prefer not to use a tinted sunscreen or a mineral one on my neck, just because of the way sunscreen inevitably rubs off on the neckline of whatever I'm wearing. A mineral sunscreen will leave whitish smudges, while the tinted sunscreen leaves a beige trail.

Evening Routine

Cleanse

As in the morning, give your neck a gentle, thorough cleansing.

Treat

I'd suggest using an active, skin-stimulating serum in the evening – like a retinoid – but I'd also suggest you use if with even more caution than on your face. Why? Because the skin on our necks is that bit thinner and has fewer oil glands than the face, so a retinoid will make it feel dry and irritable more quickly than the face. So be really strict, when you start, about only using your retinoid twice a week, and only increasing its use gradually, in line with what your skin can tolerate.

If retinoids really don't agree with your skin (I'm in a permanent state of negotiation with my neck about how much I can use a retinoid on it without it kicking off and becoming irritable), try a peptide serum in the evenings, or stick with vitamin C.

Moisturise

Seal the serum in with whichever moisturiser you like.

Question 12: What's Your Own Skincare Routine?

It's tricky to answer this precisely, as I'm always trying out new skincare products to see what they're like. But while the detail of what I'm using varies from month to month, the general gist of it is fairly consistent.

As I've mentioned before, my regime is pretty straightforward: In the mornings, after cleansing, I use a vitamin C serum, followed by a moisturising sunscreen.

In the evening, after cleansing, I use a retinoid, followed by a moisturiser.

And that's it.

You think I'm fibbing? You think that's a bit minimal for a beauty-editor type? Well, ok, sometimes I use a hydrating hyaluronic acid serum, or a peptide serum, before the sunscreen. Once or twice a week I'll use a glycolic acid product instead of the retinoid at night. Sometimes I'll slap on a facemask, too.

But the antioxidant–SPF–nightly retinoid model is the basis of my regime I come back to.

MY SKINCARE ROUTINE

To break it down a bit further...

My Morning Routine

Cleanse

I like a wash-off cleanser. I don't mind whether that's a cleansing oil, or a gel, but usually I'll go for something that rinses off very cleanly, like a glycolic-acid face-wash. I'd rather not have a film of oily cleanser left on the skin because it will get in the way of the serums that I use.

I don't usually bother with toners and essences.

Exfoliate

Rather than using an acid toner in the mornings, I prefer to use a glycolic acid product in the evening, twice a week. Also, I'm usually using a retinoid of some sort, which also has an exfoliating effect, so I reckon that's enough.

Treat

Vitamin C serum, or another antioxidant serum, is my morning go-to. Once that has been absorbed, I'll assess whether I need a layer of hydrating serum on top of it.

Moisturise

I don't usually use a moisturiser in the mornings. If I do, it will be a lightweight one, as my skin is still oily down its central panel.

Protect

I will happily use any sunscreen that comes my way, and have favourites at all price points.

My Evening Routine

Cleanse

I'll double-cleanse, in order to get rid of all sunscreen, make-up, grime, bacteria, and oil that has stacked up on my face during the day. I'll use a cleansing oil, or a cleansing cream, for the first cleanse, then go again with a wash-off gel cleanser to remove any oil left on my skin.

Treat

Most evenings, I will use a retinoid of some sort, perhaps a prescription cream with tretinoin/retinoic acid (around 0.025%), or a cream with retinaldehyde or r-retinoate, or a straightforward 1% retinol from a medical brand.

I'll wait until this has sunk in properly, then follow it with moisturiser, any moisturiser.

A couple of times a week, I'll use a glycolic acid product in the evening. This involves wiping my face with a glycolic acid solution, letting it dry, and that's it. I don't apply moisturiser afterwards, because the water in the moisturiser neutralises the acid, so it is a stronger treatment if just left on its own. It doesn't leave my skin dry, because alpha hydroxy acids like glycolic acid improve skin hydration.

HOW DO YOU DECIDE WHICH TYPES OF PRODUCTS TO USE?

For cleansers, I'll try anything. I usually settle on a creamy cleanser for a first cleanse, followed by a wash-off cleanser for the second cleanse. In terms of price points, I'm mostly happy with high-street cleansers – the product is, after all, going straight down the drain – but there are a few, mainly glycolic acid–based cleansers, that I'm happy to pay more for because I can see and feel the difference they make.

When it comes to treatment serums, I want products that are genuinely effective, preferably those which have been put through sufficient testing to be able to prove they can give the results they claim. These are the products that make most of the changes in the skin, and they do it with pricey, high-tech ingredients and sophisticated formulations, which makes them expensive.

Moisturisers have a basic job to do: to hold moisture in the skin. I'm happy using cheap moisturisers, though expensive ones, with a luxurious texture and a complicated formula, feel lovely. The key question for me is, can they do their job without going oily and slippery within a couple of hours, and making my skin break out in pimples, which it will still do overnight, given half a chance?

With sunscreens, it depends. I want a 'broad-spectrum' product that has a high SPF and good UVA protection, too. A lovely formula that sinks into the skin well and doesn't leave my skin looking chalky, or shiny, or dull is a bonus.

You can find many of my favourite products over on my website, thetweakmentsguide.com.

GLOSSARY

aesthetician: A skincare expert who does hands-on work at a skin clinic or salon.

acetyl hexapeptide-8: A neuropeptide that can inhibit muscle contractions in the skin. When applied in a serum, it is meant to relax wrinkles.

acid mantle: A very fine (and slightly acidic) layer on top of the skin, made of sebum mixed with sweat, which serves to stop bacteria, viruses, and other potential attackers or contaminants from getting into the skin.

acid toner: A strong form of toner designed to chemically exfoliate the skin using alpha hydroxy acids or beta hydroxy acid.

active ingredients: In a skincare product, the ingredients that do the work. They should be scientifically proved to have a particular effect on the skin.

adapalene: A prescription retinoid used to treat mild to moderate acne. Products such as Differin contain adapalene.

age spots: Brown spots on aged skin resulting from UV damage that creates these clusters of melanin.

alpha hydroxy acids (AHAs): A group of acids containing lactic, malic, and glycolic acids. They work wonders on the skin by loosening the bonds holding dead skin cells onto the surface of the skin, to give a gentle chemical exfoliation that brightens the skin. They also improve skin hydration and soften pigmentation.

alpha-linolenic acid (ALA): An omega-3 essential fatty acid which the body can't make itself, and has to be consumed (in foods including walnuts, chia seeds, and flaxseed oil). This acid is vital for the health of the skin, making it softer and better hydrated.

amino acids: The molecular building blocks that peptides and proteins are made up of.

androgens: Sex hormones that, among many other things, make the skin produce more oil.

anthocyanins: Purple antioxidants found in blueberries, black beans, and red cabbage.

antioxidant: Molecular compounds that protect the skin from damage by free radicals, unstable molecules that accelerate ageing in the skin.

arbutin (barberry extract): An ingredient that can help to reduce pigmentation by inhibiting tyrosinase (the enzyme that makes pigment in the skin) from making more melanin.

Argireline: Acetyl hexapeptide-8, a topical neuropeptide wrinkle-relaxer.

ascorbyl palmitate: A form of vitamin C – although this seems to be one of its least effective forms.

avobenzone: An ingredient in UV-absorbing sunscreen that absorbs UVA light and converts it to heat energy.

azelaic acid: A tyrosinase inhibitor – a product that helps to reduce pigmentation by preventing this enzyme from making more melanin. Also reduces redness and inflammation in the skin, and helps to reduce acne by killing the bacteria that can cause it, and reducing keratin build up that would normally promote acne too.

bakuchiol: A plant-derived ingredient with antioxidant, anti-inflammatory, and anti-bacterial properties. Useful for skin resurfacing. Bakuchiol is popularly thought of as a 'retinol alternative'; it is an antioxidant rather than a retinoid, but it appears to give some of the same effects of softening wrinkles and improving skin tone and texture that you can get with retinol.

benzoyl peroxide: A blemish-buster that dries up oily skin. It moves through the oil into the pores to clear them out by exfoliation, kills the bacteria causing the spots to flare up, and reduces inflammation at the same time.

beta-glucan: A soothing, moisturising ingredient. A humectant.

beta hydroxy acid (BHA): Also known as salicylic acid, an exfoliating ingredient that is great for decongesting acne-prone skin, as it can dissolve through oil in blocked pores to where it is most effective. BHA is also anti-inflammatory.

bioidentical hormone replacement therapy (BHRT)): The treatment of menopause symptoms with hormones that are identical on a molecular level to the hormones that the body makes naturally.

blood plasma: The liquid part of the blood that the red and white blood cells, and all the proteins and other molecules, are suspended in.

carcinogenic: Cancer-causing.

carotene: An orangey-red antioxidant found in carrots, mango, and pumpkin.

ceramide: A type of lipid (fat molecule) found in the skin that forms part of the skin's lipid layer, which makes it waterproof. Ceramides are vital to the proper functioning of the skin barrier and to keeping the skin smooth and hydrated.

cholesterol: A type of skin lipid (fat molecule) that is essential to the proper functioning of the skin and its barrier. Cholesterol helps keep the skin soft and smooth.

cleanser: A product which removes dirt, oil, and dead skin cells from the face.

clinical trial: A series of experiments done by scientists to determine the safety and effectiveness of new products, devices, or treatment regimes.

collagen: A protein that gives structure to the skin, keeping it firm and youthful-looking.

contact allergy: Inflammation of the skin where it has been in contact with something to which it is allergic.

copper peptide: A peptide (a chain of amino acids) which helps to smooth and improve the skin.

cortisol: A stress hormone.

crow's feet: The wrinkles that form in the skin at the outer edges of the eyes when we smile.

dermal matrix: The gel-like substance in the space between cells in the skin, including collagen and elastin fibres.

dermis: The lower layers of the skin, below the epidermis.

detergents: De-greasing agents, used as skincare ingredients that dissolve oil.

docosahexaenoic acid (DHA): An omega-3 fatty acid found in oily fish. Helps to keep the skin soft and well-hydrated by improving the integrity of the cell membranes.

double-cleansing: Cleansing twice in a row, usually in different ways.

efficacy: Effectiveness.

eicosapentaenoic acid (EPA): An omega-3 essential fatty acid found in oily fish, vital for the good health and functioning of the skin.

elastin: A protein found in the skin that helps to keep it springy. It breaks down with age and UVA exposure, as does collagen, creating wrinkles.

emollient: A type of moisturiser which works by smoothing over the skin's surface, filling in tiny cracks in the skin barrier.

enzyme: A protein which accelerates biological reactions and processes in the body, like breaking down or building up other molecules.

Epidermal Growth Factor (EGF): A molecule that occurs naturally in the skin, whose main role is to repair whatever needs repairing in the skin.

epidermis: The outermost layer of the skin (the stratum corneum is the outermost layer of the epidermis). It sits on top of the dermis and works as a barrier to viruses and bacteria as well as sealing water into the skin. Most products need to penetrate through the epidermis to be able to get to the living cells below where they can have the biggest impact.

essences: Lightweight lotions which deliver beneficial ingredients into the skin.

essential fatty acids: Fatty acids which are necessary for good health, but which the body can't make itself, so we have to eat them as part of our diet.

essential oil: An oil containing concentrated extracts from plants. Essential oils are a 'natural' way of giving products a scent. They are often irritating to sensitive skin.

exfoliation: A process that removes dead skin cells from the surface of the skin, revealing the brighter, fresher skin below. Exfoliation can be physical or chemical.

face peel: Also known as a 'chemical peel', a process that removes the outermost layers of the skin by wounding it in a controlled way, after which a 'wound-healing response' occurs, regenerating the skin underneath, after which the dead surface skin is shed. The skin below is fresher and smoother than the old skin. Few modern face peels are so extreme that old skin literally peels off, but they are still called face peels.

fatty acids: Molecules that perform various functions, such as forming part of cell membranes, and forming part of the skin's lipid layer which surrounds the cells in the epidermis and helps to keep the skin waterproof.

ferulic acid: A skin-friendly antioxidant which is often combined with vitamin C.

fibroblasts: Cells in the skin that make collagen.

formulation: The recipe of ingredients in a product.

free radicals: Unstable molecules lacking an electron that damage other molecules by stealing one of their electrons. Free radicals can accelerate ageing in the skin.

gene expression: The process by which certain genes are 'switched on' (or off) to influence activity – for example, within the skin.

gluconolactone: A polyhydroxy acid (PHA). It is a chemical exfoliant, has an anti-acne effect, and is a good choice for sensitive skin.

glutathione: A powerful antioxidant that is good for lightening pigmentation.

glycation: A process by which sugar (from food) 'crystallises' and hardens the collagen fibres in the skin and makes them more brittle.

glycerin: A natural moisturising factor that occurs in skin, helping to keep it hydrated and protected. Also widely used as an ingredient in skincare as a humectant (moisturiser).

glycolic acid: An alpha hydroxy acid which chemically exfoliates the skin by weakening the bonds holding dead skin cells onto the surface of the skin. Glycolic acid helps the skin to be better hydrated, more radiant, and more even in tone.

glycolipids: Fatty molecules present in cell membranes.

growth factors: 'Signalling proteins' made from short chains of amino acids, that stimulate particular processes, such as creating collagen, within the skin. Growth factors are controversial, because some used in skincare are derived from human sources.

high energy visible (HEV) light: Light within the spectrum of daylight, and also the blue light that emanates from screens. Skincare science is starting to show that HEV light is damaging to the skin, but the extent to which this is the case is debated.

homosalate: An ingredient in UV-absorbing sunscreens which absorbs UVB light and converts it to heat energy.

hormone replacement therapy (HRT): A form of hormone therapy in which hormones are given to a menopausal woman to effectively replace the hormones lost in the menopause, treating its symptoms.

humectant: An ingredient that draws water to itself. A humectant is normally moisturising, because when applied to the skin, it draws water out of the air and into the skin.

hyaluronic acid: A skin-hydration–boosting molecule which occurs naturally in the human body. A humectant.

hydration (of skin): The extent to which water is absorbed and retained in the skin tissue.

hydrolysed: Split up into smaller molecular parts by a chemical process called hydrolysis.

hydroquinone: The gold-standard, prescription-only pigment-buster – great for hyperpigmentation such as age spots and post-inflammatory hyperpigmentation.

hydroxypinacolone retinoate (HPR): A strong, effective retinoid which is also gentle on the skin.

hyperkeratosis: A condition in which skin cells (keratinocytes) are produced too quickly. Hyperkeratosis in hair follicles in the skin is a major contributing factor to acne. Retinol can normalise the skin cell production rate.

idebenone: A very powerful antioxidant.

inflammation: The body's response to irritants and harmful substances or damage. It involves increasing blood flow to the irritated or damaged area to deliver more white blood cells and healing molecules there, which is why the surrounding skin goes red (and warm).

infra-red light therapy: Invisible light which can reach down into the dermis and stimulate repair in the skin. Near–infra-red light is helpful when delivered at the right intensity, and at a wavelength of 830nm, in measured doses. Too much infra-red light can cause inflammation and pigmentation in the skin.

intense pulsed light (IPL): A tweakment in which broad-spectrum light (a collection of lots of different wavelengths) is pulsed into the skin. IPL is really effective at reducing pigmentation and redness. IPL can also be used for hair removal.

keratin: A structural protein in the skin.

keratinocytes: Skin cells. Keratinocytes form 90% of the epidermis. Their main function is as a barrier to the outside world.

kojic acid: A pigmentation-reducing ingredient which works by inhibiting the enzyme tyrosinase, preventing it from making more melanin (pigment).

lactic acid: A gentle alpha hydroxy acid which chemically exfoliates the skin.

lactobionic acid: A polyhydroxy acid, which gently chemically exfoliates the skin.

lanolin: An occlusive moisturiser which works by creating a film on the skin to stop moisture from escaping. Lanolin also works as an emollient, smoothing over the surface of the skin and filling in any cracks in the skin barrier.

L-ascorbic acid: A form of Vitamin C, so it is an antioxidant. L-ascorbic acid is useful for fading pigmentation, stimulating the skin to produce more collagen, and boosting the skin's protection against UV light.

laser treatment: A treatment in which light of specific wavelengths is beamed into the skin to break up clusters of pigmentation (such as age spots, post-inflammatory hyperpigmentation, or thread veins). Laser can also be used for hair removal, but this uses different wavelengths of light.

LED face mask: Physical masks with LED lights on the inside that shine red and/or infra-red light into the skin to stimulate remodelling of the skin from the inside out, meaning increased collagen production, better hydration, and reduction in pigmentation. Blue LED light is used to denature acne bacteria.

lipid layer: A layer of fat molecules surrounding the skin cells in the outer layers of the epidermis that helps to make the skin waterproof.

liposomes: Little bubbles of fat molecules called phospholipids which are an excellent delivery system for nutrients such as vitamin C, or active ingredients in face creams.

liquorice: A tyrosinase inhibitor, which works to reduce pigmentation by preventing more melanin from being made.

lycopene: An antioxidant found in tomatoes, watermelon, and grapefruits.

lymph: Plasma-like fluid that flows from the spaces between the cells in tissues to the bloodstream, carrying with it the waste products from those cells.

malic acid: A gentle alpha hydroxy acid which chemically exfoliates the skin.

mandelic acid: An alpha hydroxy acid which chemically exfoliates the skin. Unlike other alpha hydroxy acids, mandelic acid is oil-soluble (like beta hydroxy acid) so it can help clear blocked pores. Also has antibacterial properties.

Matrixyl 3000: A peptide which has been shown to boost collagen production in the skin.

mask: A product applied to the face and left on it for a short period of time. Masks give the skin a big, blanket coating of a treatment, delivering a bigger dose of active ingredients. Masks come in different forms: there are sheet masks for draping over the face, and there are products for painting or smearing directly onto the face and then washing off.

melanin: The pigment that gives skin its colour and protects us from radiation damage by UVB light by absorbing this energy.

melanocytes: The specialised cells in the skin which produce melanin.

melanosomes: Subcellular bubbles that store melanin within melanocytes once it has been produced, and then transport that pigment to nearby keratinocytes (skin cells).

melasma: A condition triggered by hormones where pigmentation, often in a butterfly-shaped 'mask' shape, shows up on the face. A tricky condition that needs careful management as it cannot be 'cured'.

micellar cleansing water: A cleanser which can grab the oil and dirt off the face in tiny bubbles called 'micelles' and carry them away. These are effective, but it is a good idea to follow micellar cleansing by rinsing the face with water, just because these cleansers leave behind a thin layer of surfactants – cleansing agents – that may irritate sensitive skin.

microcurrent devices: Devices which use low-level electrical currents to stimulate and tone muscles in the face. They do work, but they need to be used often and consistently to be effective.

microneedling: A tweakment in which thousands of tiny, controlled wounds are created in the skin by short needles (typically 0.1–3mm long). Microneedling helps skincare products to percolate deeper into the skin and be more effective and, if the needles are long enough, the pricking creates a 'wound-healing response', flooding the skin with growth factors which increase collagen production. This helps with wrinkling, stretch marks, pigmentation, and scarring.

mineral oils: Occlusive, moisturising ingredients derived from the process that makes petrol.

natural moisturising factors (NMFs): A mixture of salts and amino acids that help the skin cells to hold on to water. Natural moisturising factors are soluble in water, which is why washing the face and hands too much can dry the skin, as these NMFs can leach out of the skin.

niacin: Vitamin B3. An anti-inflammatory antioxidant which improves the texture and tone of skin.

niacinamide: A version of vitamin B3. Niacinamide is good for reducing pigmentation, reducing inflammation (so it is great for breakouts), and strengthening the skin barrier.

neuropeptide: A type of peptide (protein-like molecule) that nerve cells use to communicate with each other.

octisalate: An ingredient in chemical sunscreens which absorbs UVB light.

oestrogenic (effect): Mimicking the biochemical action of oestrogens.

oleic acid: One of the key components of olive oil.

omega-3 fatty acids: Fats which are part of the lipid layer. They are vital for the good functioning and hydration of the skin.

oxidation: A chemical process in which electrons move from one substance to another. Oxidation occurs everywhere in the body. In the skin, the process creates harmful free radical molecules, which accelerate ageing processes. Antioxidants can scavenge up and neutralise free radicals.

oxybenzone: An ingredient in chemical sunscreens which absorbs UVB (and some UVA) light.

palmitoyl pentapeptide-4: A peptide which boosts collagen production in the skin; better known by its trade name, Matrixyl.

panthenol: A chemical precursor to vitamin B5. An ingredient which, as a humectant with anti-inflammatory properties, is soothing and healing to the skin.

pantothenic acid: Vitamin B5. Helps to bind moisture into the skin.

parabens: Preservatives which are widely misunderstood as being carcinogenic and harmful; in fact, they are neither carcinogenic nor harmful.

parfum: The catch-all term for fragrance ingredients. Parfum can be irritating to sensitive skin.

peel: A treatment which encourages the shedding of outer layers of skin, revealing the fresher, clearer skin growing through from underneath.

peptides: A molecule which, like a protein, is composed of chains of amino acids. A peptide is a shorter chain than a protein. Peptides act as chemical messengers within and between cells.

pH: A measure of the acidity (or basicity) or a substance. pH values range between 1 (extremely acidic) and 14 (extremely basic). Skin's normal pH is slightly acidic, at around 4.5–5.5.

photo-ageing: Skin ageing caused by UV (and other light) damage – that is to say, most skin ageing.

phytic acid: The gentlest alpha hydroxy acid, which is used more as an antioxidant than as an exfoliant.

phytoestrogens: Plant oestrogens. These are used in some menopausal skincare to mimic the effects of lost oestrogen on the skin, boosting its radiance.

pigmentation: The colouring of the skin, which is determined by the amount of the pigment melanin it contains. Often used as shorthand to mean *hyper*pigmentation – clusters of melanin under the skin showing up as age spots or post-inflammatory hyperpigmentation.

placebo: An inert substance or treatment which is used as the control substance or treatment in a clinical trial – something you compare the substance or treatment you're looking at to, to see how much difference there is between the results of the two tests.

plasma: The liquid component of blood, which gets pushed through the walls of the blood vessels into the spaces between cells in the rest of the body, and then drains back into the bloodstream as lymph.

polyhydroxy acids (PHAs/PHBAs): Ingredients which are similar to alpha hydroxy acids (AHAs), but gentler – these are chemical exfoliants which are good for sensitive skin. Polyhydroxy acids also do not make the skin more sensitive to the sun in the same way that AHAs do.

polyphenols: Plant-based vitamins found in apples, berries, and tea. Polyphenols help the skin to defend itself against its environment.

post-inflammatory hyperpigmentation: A type of pigmentation in which dark marks arise where the skin has been damaged by, most typically, acne scarring.

radiofrequency: A tweakment which tightens the skin by heating up the skin with radiofrequency energy, causing the collagen to contract. This tightens and firms sagging skin.

resveratrol: An antioxidant which boosts the energy of the mitochondria. It is found in red wine, but at such low doses that drinking red wine doesn't deliver resveratrol's protection effectively.

retinoate: A salt or ester (different chemical forms) of retinoic acid.

retinoic acid: Also known as tretinoin, the strongest and most effective form of retinoid. Retinoic acid is so potent that it is only available on prescription, as its use needs to be overseen by a doctor or dermatologist. Retinoic acid can cause irritation in the skin, so it needs to be used with caution.

retinoids: A family of skin-improving ingredients which are all derived from vitamin A and work to make the skin look fresher and smoother by increasing (or, in the case of hyperkeratosis, normalising) the rate of skin cell turnover, exfoliating it. Retinoids also increase the amount of collagen in the skin, reduce skin oiliness, and soften pigmentation.

retinol: A retinoid used in over-the-counter skincare. Retinol is considerably easier to tolerate than retinoic acid.

retinyl ascorbate: An antioxidant, an ester of vitamin A and vitamin C.

retinyl palmitate: The weakest of the retinoids.

retinyl retinoate: A new form of hybrid retinoid that is much stronger than retinol, yet is much more gentle on the skin. It is also stable under light, so can be used during the daytime.

rhinophyma: A skin disorder which can develop when rosacea goes unchecked, where the skin swells and thickens. One characteristic sign of rhinophyma is a swollen and bulbous red nose.

Roaccutane: Isotretinoin, aka vitamin A in tablet form – the wonder treatment for acne. Taking Roaccutane can make the skin incredibly dry.

rosacea: A chronic skin condition where the convex surfaces of the face (cheeks, forehead, nose, chin) are red and spotty due to a problem with the oil glands causing inflammation in the skin. There also seems to be miscommunication between the nerves and the blood vessels, which contributes to it.

salicylic acid: Beta hydroxy acid. This is a chemically exfoliating ingredient which is also great for acne-prone skin as it is able to move through oil, and get down into the pores where it is really needed, to exfoliate accumulated oil and skin cells.

sebum: A thin oil made by the skin's sebaceous glands, which helps to keep the skin supple and waterproof. It can contribute to acne when it stays, stagnant, in pores along with dead skin cells and bacteria, and blocks them up.

sensitive skin: Skin where the barrier function is damaged, so that it becomes overly reactive to the environment and to skincare products, and will become hot, red, itchy or flaky and uncomfortable.

serum: A runny, liquid product with a high concentration of active ingredients designed to be fully absorbed into the skin and bring about a change in it. Serums act as concentrated booster treatments for the skin.

skin barrier: The outer layer of the skin, which separates and shields us from the outside world (including things like bacteria). A good skin barrier seals moisture into the skin and keeps the texture of the skin smooth.

sodium ascorbate: A mineral salt form of ascorbic acid, aka vitamin C.

sodium ascorbyl phosphate: A form of vitamin C which is an antioxidant and may help to boost collagen production and reduce acne.

sodium hyaluronate: The salt form of hyaluronic acid which, like HA, is great at binding moisture into the skin, but is slightly more stable.

stratum corneum: The outer layers of the skin, composed of dead skin cells sandwiched together with the skin lipids (fats) cholesterol, ceramides, and essential fatty acids.

sulphates: Foaming detergent ingredients which have a bad reputation as they can irritate the skin. However, since sulphates are used in wash-off products, they are usually only a problem for sensitive skin.

sun protection factor (SPF): The rating for a product which tells you how much UVB light it can protect you from, either by blocking or absorbing the light. In general, products with a higher SPF also offer higher UVA protection, as the ingredients are usually used in proportion to one another, to offer what is called 'broad-spectrum protection'.

surfactant: A foaming ingredient that acts like a detergent to remove oil from the surface of the skin.

tetrahexyldecyl ascorbate: A stable form of vitamin C which is also soluble in oil.

thread veins: Capillaries (the smallest of the blood vessels) which have become broken or enlarged, and therefore visible as miniscule red lines on the face.

titanium dioxide: An ingredient in 'physical' sunscreens, which works by reflecting back the light. It gives broad-spectrum coverage and protection.

toner: A liquid designed to remove any last scraps of cleanser from the skin, and deliver beneficial ingredients that may exfoliate or hydrate the skin.

toxicologist: Someone who studies the adverse effects of chemical substances on living organisms.

tranexamic acid: An oestrogen receptor blocker which, when taken as tablets, can be helpful for managing melasma as it can prevent extra pigmentation from occurring. Some dermatologists have found that tranexamic acid combined with topical hydroquinone and a retinoid is able to almost clear melasma completely.

tretinoin: Retinoic acid, a form of vitamin A. The strongest and most effective form of retinoid.

tyrosinase: An enzyme involved in the production of melanin (pigment), which is therefore a great target for ingredients trying to reduce hyperpigmentation.

ubiquinone: An antioxidant also known as coenzyme Q10, which can have ageing-preventative effects,

ultraviolet light (UV): An invisible form of light present in daylight (i.e. all year round, not just on sunny days). It is composed of UVA and UVB rays, and has a multitude of ageing effects on the skin. These effects are known as 'photo-ageing', from the Greek work (*photos*) meaning light.

UVA: A subtype of ultraviolet light, popularly known as 'the ageing rays', which is present in daylight (i.e. all year round, through cloud cover and through windows), and which reaches deep into the skin to break down collagen and elastin. UVA darkens existing pigment in the skin.

UVB: A subtype of ultraviolet light which is only present in significant doses in the UK in summer sunshine, and which causes melanocytes (pigment cells) to make more pigment. UVB, known as 'the burning rays', is also the type of ultraviolet light responsible for sunburns and for helping the human body produce its own vitamin D.

urea: A humectant (moisturising) ingredient which helps the skin hold onto water.

vitamin A: An antioxidant which also improves many aspects of skin repair, including boosting levels of collagen in the skin, and is very effective at reducing acne. Retinoids are derived from vitamin A.

vitamin B3 (niacin): An anti-inflammatory antioxidant which improves the texture and tone of skin. Great for acne-prone skin.

vitamin B5 (pantothenic acid): An ingredient which helps to bind moisture into the skin.

vitamin C: An antioxidant vitamin which, used in skincare, can reduce pigmentation in the skin, improve skin texture, boost skin collagen and elastin levels, and help the skin defend itself against the environment.

vitamin D: A hormone with roles in regulating the immune system and keeping the bones strong through its actions on calcium levels in the bloodstream. Humans can consume vitamin D and also synthesise vitamin D when exposed to sufficient levels of UVB light.

vitamin E: A hydrating, anti-inflammatory antioxidant which helps to heal the skin.

whitehead: A pore clogged by skin debris and sebum, enclosed by skin.

zinc oxide: An ingredient in physical sunscreens which reflects back the light.

zinc sulphate: An ingredient which can soothe inflamed acne.

INDEX

Page numbers in **boldface** indicate glossary entries.

ALSO AVAILABLE BY THIS AUTHOR

The Tweakments Guide:
Fresher Face
by Alice Hart-Davis

£14.95

thetweakmentsguide.com

Everything you've ever wanted to know about non-surgical cosmetic procedures, by the woman who has tried them all.

If you are curious about tweakments and you want independent, unbiased advice on which ones do what, and how, this is the book you need. Would facial fillers, wrinkle-relaxing injections, or ultrasound treatment work for you? What does a treatment feel like? How much would it cost? And how do you find a good, safe practitioner and avoid the cowboys?

Alice Hart-Davis is an award-winning journalist and aesthetics industry expert who has spent many years investigating the fast-moving and confusing world of tweakments.

REVIEW

The Tweakments Guide: Fresher Face

Reviewed by Sarah Stacey, co-founder of BeautyBible.com

To celebrate **World Book Day**, we want to tell you a little bit about this 'Encyclopedia Beautannica', written by our long-time colleague **Alice Hart-Davis**.

'Tweakments' cover all those aesthetic cosmetic procedures that do not involve surgery. So, for instance, chemical peels, souped-up facials, face-plumping fillers, skin-smoothing lasers, IPL treatment for pigmentation, and a myriad others in this fast-moving world – not forgetting Botox, the first one in the field.

If you're in your teens or twenties, with a face as smooth as a baby's bottom, this probably isn't for you. (Though you might be concerned with acne scars, facial redness, etc. – so actually don't dismiss it.) But as the years go by, many women we know – and yes, us too – really want a comprehensive guide to what's available. And you simply could never get a better one than this.

Alice has been intrepidly researching and writing about these tweakments for nearly 20 years – the good, the bad, and the might-almost-make-you-ugly (we have dreadful flashbacks to the 'trout pout' era…). Her teams of testers have also been trialling rafts of treatments for possible inclusion and writing up their reports for the book. (We always say: 'Alice goes out and tries these treatments so WE don't have to!')

The impetus to write **The Tweakments Guide** came when a 50-year-old friend (Ellie) emailed her just after 'a horror moment in the mirror'. Alice dedicated her book to Ellie 'and everyone else who has looked in the mirror and wondered whether a tweakment might help – and if so, what are these things anyway, and where should you start…'

We're gripped, riveted, and totally in awe of the colossal amount of work that has gone into creating this guide – key to add that it's transparently honest. Also, given the deplorable lack of regulation in this arena, Alice has included an essential chapter on choosing the best practitioner and keeping safe.

There's a website of the same name, with practitioners nationwide and masses of other information, which is about to be launched. Do look it up and subscribe for regular updates, thetweakmentsguide.com. (It has a comprehensive section on Staying Safe – which really is the most important thing of all.) You can buy the book on the site, too.

VISIT MY WEBSITE FOR MORE

To find out more about skincare and tweakments, visit my website:
www.thetweakmentsguide.com

Explore Your Options for Skincare and Tweakments

Using the website's interactive online resource, you can:

- Explore all the skincare, tweakments, and home-use devices that can help with specific concerns about your face.
- Filter tweakment options based on your budget and on how you feel about treatments that involve needles.
- Find great tweakment practitioners all around the UK – the ones I would trust with my own face.

Decide Whether You Need Skincare, Tweakments, or Both

Skincare and tweakments should complement each other: some issues are best addressed with skincare, some with tweakments, and some with both. What is best for you will vary depending not only on the issues that you want to address but also on your skin type and how much you are looking to spend.

Visit the Online Shop

Visit my website's online shop to browse the selection of my favourite specialist cosmeceutical skincare products, most of which are mentioned in this book.

Get in Touch with Me

Let me know what you think of this book and the website. I'm @alicehartdavis on Instagram, Twitter, LinkedIn, and Facebook.

TOP 10 SKINCARE MYTHS

Myth: The skin needs to breathe.
Truth: Skin does not respire. See page 26 for more on this.

Myth: Your pores open and close.
Truth: Your pores do not open and close like flower petals. See 'Question 6: I've Got Large Pores. Can Skincare Help?' on page 219 for more about large pores.

Myth: Drinking water will hydrate your skin.
Truth: Drinking water will hydrate your body, but not your skin. See 'How Drinking Water Affects Skin Moisture Levels' on page 75.

Myth: You need to keep changing your skincare because your skin will 'get used to it'.
Truth: If your skincare is working, that's great; don't change your skincare just for the sake of it. You need to adapt your skincare when something about your skin changes. See 'Do I Need to Change My Skincare with the Seasons?' on page 235.

Myth: Eating oily foods gives you acne.
Truth: Oily foods don't cause acne. See 'Question 5: Help, I've Still Got Spots! What Can I Do About Adult Acne?' on page 212.

Myth: Parabens are evil.
Truth: Parabens are safe and commonly used preservatives, but they've been unfairly demonised by bad science and popular hysteria. See 'What's Wrong with Parabens?' on page 21.

Myth: Tanning is good for you.
Truth: Sunshine on your skin feels great, but tanning is a sign of damage in the skin. See 'Skin Cancer – What Are the Risks?' on page 143.

Myth: If it's not sunny, you don't need sunscreen.
Truth: You need sunscreen as much to protect against the UVA rays, which come through clouds and windows all year round, as against the 'burning' UVB rays: see 'Does My Skin Need Protection?' on page 140.

Myth: Oily skin needs to be 'dried out'.
Truth: Oily skin needs water as much as any other skin type: see 'Why Oily Skin Needs Hydration Too' on page 127.

Myth: 'Natural' products are better than 'chemical' ones.
Truth: All substances have a chemical formula, even water and beeswax, so all products, even if they're called 'natural', contain chemicals. See the section 'Making Sense of the 'Natural' vs 'Chemical' Debate' on page 18.

Printed in Great Britain
by Amazon